# REMINISCENCES

# REMINISCENCES

## FRANZ LEICHTER

# REMINISCENCES

*iUniverse books may be ordered through booksellers or by contacting:*

*iUniverse*
*1663 Liberty Drive*
*Bloomington, IN 47403*
*www.iuniverse.com*
*844-349-9409*

*Because of the dynamic nature of the Internet, any web addresses or links contained in this book may have changed since publication and may no longer be valid. The views expressed in this work are solely those of the author and do not necessarily reflect the views of the publisher, and the publisher hereby disclaims any responsibility for them.*

*Any people depicted in stock imagery provided by Getty Images are models, and such images are being used for illustrative purposes only.*
*Certain stock imagery © Getty Images.*

*ISBN: 978-1-6632-1328-0 (sc)*
*ISBN: 978-1-6632-1327-3 (e)*

*Library of Congress Control Number: 2021920861*

*Print information available on the last page.*

*iUniverse rev. date: 03/20/2023*

# CONTENTS

# PREFACE

In these reminiscences, I seek to recount my life not just for my children and grandchildren, who know me and lived through some of the events I describe, but also for descendants I will never know and for friends and acquaintances. I have not covered every aspect of my life but focused on those events that I consider significant. As I went along, I added episodes just because I got pleasure remembering them or felt for honesty's sake they should be disclosed. I went off on some tangents as one memory led to another.

One of my reasons for setting down my reminiscences is that as I became older, I so regretted not having asked my father about his life, particularly with my mother, of whom I know so little. Once he was gone and as I became older, there were so many questions I wished I had asked. I was too involved in my life and the future to look back and ask these questions while he was still alive. I hope this stab at an autobiography will answer questions about my life.

# CHAPTER 1

# 1938–1943: EARLY CHILDHOOD, SMUGGLED OUT OF AUSTRIA AND TO THE US

## EARLY YEARS TO THE ANSCHLUSS IN 1938

It pains me that I have so few memories before I reached seven and a half years old. Of course, one remembers little of one's baby and toddler years, but I think many people have more remembrances of when they were five, six, and seven than I possess. I clearly have repressed many childhood recollections. What I do remember is sort of episodic—my mother singing my favorite song (Brahms's "Lullaby") as I fell asleep, being in the large garden behind our apartment in Mauer, on the outskirts of Vienna, where we moved in 1935.

My earliest years were in an apartment in the heart of Vienna. It was near the Donaukanal, which traverses Vienna and near the apartment of my grandparents, where my mother grew up. Theirs was a large apartment looking onto a park and playground, where I surely went to play. My family's life then was what may be considered upper-middle class. My father, Otto, was an editor of the socialist daily, the *Arbeiter-Zeitung*, and my mother, Käthe, founded and led the women's division of the Arbeiterkammer, an official agency that represented the interests of workers. It had features of an unemployment office and government labor department. My brother, Henry, was six and a half years older and rounded out the family. Both my parents were very active in the social-democratic political party, the Social Democratic Workers' Party of Austria (after 1945, it was called the Socialist Party of Austria. Today it is called the Social Democratic Party of Austria). During the 1920s and early 30s, the socialists ran Vienna and created a social program of housing, day care, parks, and more, which gave this period the name Rotes Wien (Red Vienna). It was an exciting time.

Our lives were upended when in February 1934 there was a fascist coup that took over the Austrian government and Vienna. My parents had to flee to Zürich. In 1935, they returned to Vienna and, to be less visible, moved to Mauer. Both being out a job, I don't know how they supported themselves. Many meetings of the underground opposition were held there. My father was then a member of the executive committee of the Revolutionary Socialists, one of the main opposition groups.

One of my earliest recollections is being kept out of a room (there were only two in our Mauer apartment, which was on the first floor of a two-story building) where my mother, father, and Henry played chamber music. I very much resented being kept out and in the supervision of my grandfather, Samuel Leichter, (Papa's father—my mother's father, Josef Pick, died years before I was born and shortly after Henry's birth in 1924). Even then, it showed my aim to be in the center of the action.

Once my grandfather took me shopping for a suit (in Vienna at this time, it meant short pants), and my grandmother, Regine Leichter (Müller) ended up berating him for not using family connections to get a lower price. Whether I realized it at the time or not, my grandmother ran the family. Her devotion to my father and ambition for him are what I believe gave him his drive to succeed as well as great self-confidence. Tragically, both my father's parents perished in the Holocaust. Like many Viennese Jews, they were sent to Theresienstadt Ghetto, a concentration camp outside of Prague. Records show my grandfather died there, maybe in 1940 or 1941. My grandmother, who was far stronger, survived only to be shipped to Auschwitz in 1943 and murdered there.

The memory of my other grandmother (Mama's mother), Lotte Pick (Rubinstein), is even less specific. If I remember her at all, it is as a grandmother who was indulgent and provided me with lots of sweets. Actually, as my mother's memoir shows, she was an accomplished linguist and led an active life. She also met a tragic end. Unable to carry on with my mother in jail and the Nazis having forced her out of her apartment, she committed suicide, I believe in 1939.

I have only two memories of my father from when I was five or six—neither happy. In one, he chased me around the dining room table in anger over something I had done (he had the Leichters' anger). The other is some argument with him when I said, "I wish you were back in the hospital." Actually, my father had not been hospitalized. The fascist government had jailed him for his underground activities and opposition. This was kept from me by telling me he was in a hospital. Of course, I learned the truth. By referring to the hospital, I was either going along with the myth or using it to annoy him. In view of the loving and close relationship we built later, it is disconcerting that I have only these two distinct memories of him from my early childhood. This may also be due to my father's work as an editor of the *Arbeiter-Zeitung*. He must have worked into the night. Also, his political activities required many meetings away from home.

I don't know what I knew about my parents' political activities. Although I have no specific memories and to avoid building "recollections" out of later acquired information, I believe I was aware then and remember feeling that they were important people who had many friends and acquaintances since there were many meetings in our apartment.

I have some remembrances of being in Zürich, where my parents had fled in 1934 after a fascist coup took over all of Austria. The Social Democratic Workers' Party was banned. I believe I was taken there after my parents had fled. My only actual remembrance there is chasing girls about my age on the street, not for romance but in male animosity, calling them *blöde mädchen* (dumb girls).

When the family returned to Vienna in 1935, we moved to Mauer on the city's outskirts. I started school there in what was the first grade.

I do have some recollections of the Anschluss in March 1938. Shortly afterward, there was a prominent Nazi parade in the neighborhood. It may have had to do with the burial of a Nazi leader. The back of the garden of our house was across from a cemetery, and I seem to remember watching the cortege and marchers arriving at the cemetery. My most vivid memory is going back to school, probably a couple of days after the Anschluss. We used to start each school day with some national song or maybe a pledge of allegiance to Austria. Now, on the first day back, the school started with a "Heil, Hitler" and some pledge to the German nation, of which we were now a part. This struck me as hypocritical. I smiled but not outwardly. It was maybe the first time I became conscious of how malleable the public can be. I didn't stay in school for more than a few days. Either my mother took me out or I was kicked out as a Jew.

Not long afterward, we left Mauer. Henry says it was May 29, 1938. But it seems strange that my mother lingered in Mauer so long when the Gestapo had already gone to our home there looking for my father. Fortunately, he got out and quickly fled to Paris using a false passport, which the socialist government of Czechoslovakia provided to leading Austrian socialists, including my mother. After my father left, there was a harrowing event one night when Nazi hoodlums came to our house and painted "JUDE" on the windows. My mother, exhibiting her courage and control, got them to leave by telling them that they were waking up her children. I was asleep and have no direct recollection. But this is not a family myth. We do have a photograph of the windows with "JUDE" painted on them. I do remember we abandoned our house by sneaking out of the back and going into hiding.

The next few months are a blur. I believe I was with my grandmother at first and then with our housekeeper, Frau Weninger. She was a local, non-Jewish domestic who, like others who worked in our house, was treated as a colleague and a family friend by my mother. As a result, they were helpful when the need arose in these awful days. She was loyal to my mother and one of the decent Austrians. Throughout the Nazi era, she hid some of our family heirlooms. While I know she faced deprivation, she never sold any items and returned them to my father when he came to Vienna in 1947.

On May 30, my mother was arrested. She and Henry, using false passports, were to leave Austria that day. She had been betrayed to the Gestapo by a close family friend, Hans Pav, who had become an informer. Before leaving with Henry on a train to Zürich, she called her mother. The phone was answered by a man who identified himself as being from the Gestapo. She was told that if she did not immediately come to her mother's apartment and give herself up, her mother would be arrested. My mother went to the apartment and was immediately arrested. I never saw her again. I was very close to and dependent upon my mother. To be torn away from her was a shock that left psychological scars.

(Pav was arrested after the war and sentenced to a jail term. The court found that it was not proven that his betrayal of my mother and others led to their death. Strange. It certainly led to my mother's death.)

My mother had made arrangements for Irma Turnsek to smuggle me out of Vienna as her son. Irma had been my nursemaid. Because my mother befriended her, as she did with all our domestic help, Irma became a friend and fellow socialist. She had a son my age, Helmut, who was my close friend. It was probably in July 1938 that the plan to smuggle me out of Austria was carried out. Irma was not Jewish and had passports for her and Helmut to leave Austria, and then visas to go to England. The plan was for her to take me to Belgium as her son. She would then go on to England and, after settling in, return to Vienna to get Helmut. All I remember is a train ride with Irma, where she told me to call her *Mutti* (Mom). I continued to call her Irma, which may have raised some suspicion in our fellow compartment passengers. Suppose one had pointed this out to the officials who checked our papers? I had no idea of the danger we faced traveling through Germany. Looking back, it seems a perilous and questionable plan. But these were desperate times, and options were very limited.

We made it to Belgium, where I was deposited with Fritz and Katia Adler, two very close family and political friends. Fritz was the son of Victor Adler, the founder of the Austrian Republic after World War I. During that war, as an antiwar act, Fritz assassinated the Austrian foreign minister in a café. He did not seek to flee but gave himself up. He was sentenced to death but was pardoned at the war's end. He later became the secretary-general of the International Socialist Party.

The Adlers were on their vacation on a beach. It was there I learned to ride a bike. After a few days, my father came from Paris to fetch me. After we arrived at the Paris train station, my father went to look for a taxi. It took him some time. I thought he had abandoned me. This reflected the fears I had acquired from the trauma of being separated from my mother. Abandonment has been a factor in the Leichter psyche. Elsa, my father's second wife, noted that for the Leichters, there was always the confusion of who abandoned whom? As a child, I must have had the feeling that my mother was responsible for not being in my life. Did she abandon me, or did we abandon her in Vienna? Was my father not sufficiently forceful in convincing her to leave Vienna instead of lingering there too long after the Anschluss? But how could she leave without arranging for her children to get out? And what about her widowed mother? These were desperate times, and the decisions were painfully hard.

I don't know how long I was in Paris with my father before we went to a summer resort at a beach, probably in Normandy. I wonder now where my father got the money. He had very limited financial resources, and as his letters (to my mother, which he wrote as a diary because he was unable to send it to her at Ravensbrück, the German concentration camp she was sent to) made clear, he had to scrounge around by writing for a socialist archive in Holland. We did stay in what I am sure was an inexpensive pension at the beach. Maybe we left Paris when the city effectively closed down in what was, and still is, Known as fermeture annuelle (summer vacations). While we were there, my father was anxiously awaiting news about whether Henry was able to get out of Vienna. We would regularly go to the local post office to see if there was a telegram. One day, returning from the beach, as we passed the post office, my father, discouraged that we had no news about Henry, said he would not bother going in. Either he asked me or I volunteered to go in. I came out with a telegram that announced that Henry was safe in Zürich. What relief and joy.

## PARIS 1938–1940

In spite of all the fears and confusion I felt as I came to Paris to be with a parent whom I did not know well, our stay there for me was so positive. I bonded with my father and came to love Paris—a feeling I still have. This speaks to how well my father took on the role of parent.

I don't remember when Henry came to Paris and the one-room pensions we shared. For this, I rely on Henry's autobiography of his early years, *Eine Kinderheit.* He dates it to early August 1938. Eventually, we moved into a very comfortable apartment in the southwest of Paris, which was situated on a little hill. From our apartment, we had a magnificent view of Paris—the Eiffel Tower, the Arc de Triomphe, and across to Sacré-Cœur. The city lay at our feet. I would look out and be excited at the thought that I would show this to my mother. At no time did I believe that she would not join us. My father's letters to my mother, which he could not send (really a diary; more about these later), certainly convey that hope. If he had doubts, he kept these to himself.

Henry and I were both enrolled in a nearby school, the Lycée Michelet. I was back in the first grade. I remember how miserable my first day in school was. I of course spoke no French. My classmates treated me with curiosity. But I soon learned the language and adjusted quite well. It helped that Henry was in the same school. Children do have an easier time adjusting to new conditions. I think I was able to quickly adapt to my new environment. This reflected a need to fit in and be accepted. Anyhow, I did so well in school that I won the class's first prize for academic achievement. I quickly learned to speak fluent French, which sadly is the second language I have forgotten.

My father was just marvelous in creating a home for Henry and me. He took on parenting with real dedication. He became a good cook even though in Vienna I doubt he ever went into the kitchen. He took us through Paris. On weekends, we often went for long walks in the woods. I recollect him entertaining us by mimicking people, which he did very well. And he never allowed the difficulty of his life to darken Henry's and my lives. He did, I am sure, share some of his worries with Henry, but my age shielded me from being told about and understanding the hardship he had to deal with. He was now a refugee, deprived of and terribly worried for his wife, whom he deeply loved. At the same time, he had the sole care of his children for the first time. He was seeing Europe come apart under Adolf Hitler's aggression, and his belief in socialist progress shattered. He was disgusted with the sterile and unrealistic discussions among the Austrian socialist refugees in Paris, with whom he was not getting on well. He was uncertain about his employment and about how he could support us. Nevertheless, he created a loving and supportive home for Henry and me. It says something about him that he chose an apartment far from the ghetto, which most Austrian refugees created for themselves in Paris.

In Paris, Henry and I both forged a strong, loving attachment with our father, which lasted until his death in 1973. So, strange as it may seem, I have good memories of our stay in Paris, and my love for the city dates to these difficult times.

In the summer of 1939, I was sent to a children's camp in southern France. I have two recollections. One day with my friends, we went into the woods and ate many nonedible berries off some bush. A few of my friends got sick, and a doctor was called. I felt fine but was examined by him. He asked how many berries I ate. I gave some figure of less than ten, although I probably ate five times as many. I was told that it was fortunate I had eaten so few, or else I too would be sick. This is when I first learned to be skeptical of doctors.

Just as we were to return to Paris from camp, war broke out when Hitler attacked Poland in September 1939. My father was then interned in a camp. (The French put all German and Austrian refugees into camps even though most were Jews who had fled Hitler.) Some of the other children's parents were also refugees and interned. As a result—and maybe travel arrangements were difficult to make—the camp kept us for a few more weeks. I am not sure when we returned to Paris. But on the trip back, I was considered one of the poorly behaved kids who had to travel in the compartment of the camp's director. And as there were not enough seats, I was put in the luggage rack above the seats.

My father was let out of internment, and Henry also returned from the camp he attended. We were back together. It turned out the elementary school in the Lycée had become a hospital for wounded soldiers. My father, who strongly believed in education, was determined that I attend school. The only one within walking distance from our home was a Catholic parochial school, where he enrolled me. There was no problem in accepting a Jew, but as a new student, I was seated way in the back of what I remember as a very large class. After my first test, the teacher moved me to the front because I had done so well.

I had what at the time I considered a fearful experience. Coming to school one day, I saw that all my classmates' little backpacks had been left in neat rows in the schoolyard. It then occurred to me that we had been told to get to school early to be marched to church to celebrate some saint's day. I put my school bag down and, in great fright, ran to the church. It was a big edifice. I went in among many worshippers. No one noticed me. When the service was over, I joined my class in marching back to the school. My earlier absence had not been detected. I had avoided the frightful consequences I expected from my teachers. I was not worried about the saint's reaction. Not so long ago when visiting our old neighborhood in Issy-les-Moulineaux, I went to that church. It may be apocryphal, but I heard that my parochial school was bombed shortly after we left Paris and that there were casualties among the students.

I attended the parochial school throughout what was called the phony war with little fighting. But we were caught up in life during war. We had ration cards and had to stand in long lines for our allotted food. Gas masks were issued, but based on some inane bureaucratic reasoning or shortages, children under ten were not provided with gas masks. This bothered me, not so much for fear I might be gassed but for not having this symbol of war readiness. I also envied my brother for having one. I do remember air raids—or at least alarms—which had us scrambling into our building's cellar until the all-clear sounded. I don't know whether there were any real air raids at that time. Our building was not far from a military airport. Maybe these were false alarms or authorities sounding the alarm to make people feel that the nation was at war.

In April, the German Army moved into France after overrunning Belgium and Holland. It easily broke through the French defenses and went around the supposedly impregnable Maginot Line. It quickly moved toward Paris. We had to flee, leaving our apartment with all our possessions except some clothes. I did manage to pack my collection of Doctor Dolittle books, which I loved and are still with me, and my stamp collection. We went by train to the city of Montauban, in southern France, together with many of the Austrian socialist refugees. As one of the leaders, my father was involved in the group settling in this city about seventy-five miles north of Marseille. Again, my father, deeming it important for Henry and me to attend school, enrolled us in a local public school. He continued to try to make our lives as normal as possible. Obviously, this was not easy. We shared a room in a local hotel and, I assume, hung out with our fellow refugees, trying to figure out what to do next. I don't remember much of our stay there, which may have lasted two or three months. It was while we were there that the French capitulated to the Germans, and the new French regime under Marshal Pétain came into power. He had been a French hero in World War I but now headed the despised Vichy regime, which collaborated with the Germans.

# TO THE US

I wish I knew how my father managed to get us a visa to the US. Sadly, the United States Department of State (State Department) was hostile to Jewish immigrants, and getting a visa was difficult. There did exist Jewish and refugee organizations; mainly helpful to us was the Jewish Labor Committee (JLC), which helped refugees to get visas to the US. In her book about Franklin D. Roosevelt (FDR) and Eleanor Roosevelt during the war, *No Ordinary Times*, Doris Kearns Goodwin tells of a dinner at Joseph Lash's (Eleanor's close young friend) in or about July 1940, where Eleanor met with Joseph Buttinger, who had been a former leader of the Austrian underground with my father (more about him later). Also present was a prominent German socialist refugee. They told her about the many political refugees in southern France who were at great risk of being turned over to the Gestapo. As Goodwin describes it, Eleanor picked up the phone and called FDR and told him something needed to be done. This may have initiated the State Department issuing a certain number of visas, in my understanding, to professionals who faced persecution. This story is also told in Blanche Wiesen Cook's biography of Eleanor.

Only a few years ago, I met with the director of the JLC to see what records existed. I checked archives in the FDR Library at Hyde Park and the archives of the JLC at the Wagner Labor Archives at New York University. There I found some lists that had my father's name as someone the JLC was seeking a visa for and saying that it paid for our voyage to the US. I also learned that before visas were approved, top leaders of the American Federation of Labor and Congress of Industrial Organizations met with the State Department to confirm that no communists were included. Sadly, the failure of the FDR administration to admit all but a few Jewish immigrants condemned many to death. I admire FDR, but this was his biggest failure.

We did get the precious visas. My father, Henry, and I went to Marseilles to get the visas from the US consulate. I remember my father promising that I might see Americans do strange things like sitting on top of a desk. This showed how even at tense moments, he could ease the situation. I was probably more interested in seeing a strange American than what would happen to our visas. I believe we met with Hiram Bingham, the deputy counsel. Bingham became a hero working with Varian Fry—who headed an American mission to help refugees—in issuing visas and helping thousands of refugees to the US.

In 2006, I was invited to speak at a ceremony honoring Bingham on the issuance of a stamp in his honor. I was the only one there who had received a visa from him. Bingham was badly treated by the State Department, who objected to his giving out these visas. He was given a minor diplomatic post in South America. I think only in the early 2000s did the State Department apologize and the post office issue a stamp in his honor.

Probably toward the end of August 1940, with our visas in hand, together with most of the Austrian group, who also received visas, we went to the French/Spanish border. To leave, we needed a French exit visa, which we did not possess. We purposely went to a smaller crossing in the French town of Cerbère. This was the route developed by Fry in his effort to save Jewish/political refugees. I don't believe Fry was involved in our escape. He did save many prominent persons. I believe we spent one night in Cerbère. I shared a bed with my father, in which I unfortunately peed. It probably was the result of anxiety I must have felt, though I have no specific recollection of being concerned about our situation. My father took it in stride.

The next morning, we went to the station to take the train to cross the border to Barcelona. We waited until the last moment to go through immigration, knowing we did not have the exit document to let us leave

France. The official took our papers, looked through them, and, knowing we did not have the exit visa but apparently having sympathy for escaping Jews, waved us through with a "Passe." In *Eine Kinderheit,* Henry says this occurred at night and that the official wanted to go home so as not to make out a report and waved us on. I am quite sure my recollection is the right one because we never stayed overnight in Barcelona before continuing through Spain.

We were not safe yet. After crossing the border, we had to go through Spanish immigration. Our suitcases were checked. Mine had my stamp collection, which included some envelopes with canceled stamps on them and names of the sender. My father got quite agitated and angry because some of the envelopes were from prominent socialists, and he was afraid this might catch the attention of the Spanish police. However, the officials did not bother with the envelopes and probably did not know the names on them. But my father's passport was taken to a back room. We suspected that names were checked against lists from the Gestapo. We held our breath. The official came back with my father's passport and waved us back onto the train to Barcelona. Throughout it all, I remember being equally concerned about getting through and getting a window seat on the train. Both were achieved. I certainly was somewhat aware of the dangers we faced, but my understanding was quite hazy, and it partly had the feel of an adventure rather than a life-threatening situation.

We were the first of the Austrian group to try this exit from France. When we succeeded, my father must have called back to let the rest of the group know it was safe. However, there was another immigration official on duty the following day and on other days who refused to let them through. A number had to get out of Spain by crossing the Pyrenees on foot with a guide. As some were in their seventies, this was quite an ordeal. In books about Fry (one called *A Hero of Our Own* by Sheila Isenberg, a friend of my second wife, Melody), there are good descriptions of the struggle to get visas and having to cross the Pyrenees.

I visited Cerbère with Melody in 2002. The Pyrenees, which in my memory were so high, were now shown to be hills—still, an ordeal for those who had to cross them. Some were turned back and had to try a different route to climb.

In Barcelona, we had the number of a porter who had been hired by Jewish refugee groups. He helped us get the train across Spain. First, we went to Madrid, where we had a layover. Never one to miss a chance, my father took us to the Prado Museum. Then we continued on to Portugal. On the train, I got my fingers caught in the bathroom door. My father poured eau de cologne over the deep cuts. The next night, we arrived late in Lisbon. As I exited the station, I saw the plaza outside all lit up. I remarked that this was the most beautiful city in the world, having come from blackened-out French cities. In 2016, I returned for the first time to Lisbon, with my friend Sylvia, and had a nostalgic visit to the train station.

We hung out in Lisbon for almost a month. I celebrated my tenth birthday there. Finally, with the help of the JLC, we secured passage on an old Greek liner, *Nea Hellas*.

We crossed the Atlantic in early September just as Hitler invaded Greece to help out the beleaguered Italians. I assume we were in some danger. The first night in the early dawn, I saw a huge gray shape through our porthole. It was a British cruiser that checked us out. The trip was a blast, as it included youngsters of our Austrian group. One was our friend Kurt Sonnenfeld, with whom I was in touch until his death in 2017. Another was George Papanek, who was my closest friend and attended Swarthmore with me, and his older brother Gustav, who is still an active sociologist in Boston. George died in 2004. Fun was sneaking into the First or Second

Class. We were in steerage. On our boat was the celebrated wife of Gustav Mahler, Alma Mahler, and her then husband or companion, the famous author Franz Werfel.

On September 12, 1940, in the early dawn, we entered New York's harbor. I had my first view of the skyline. I was stunned by the skyscrapers of Lower Manhattan. It seemed like a mirage, unreal, not the comparative diminutive buildings that had been my experience in Vienna and Paris. After safely crossing the submarine-infested Atlantic, our ship collided with a Norwegian tanker just off Staten Island. It was reported in the *New York Times* the next day. My first American news story. In all the excitement, I don't remember seeing the Statue of Liberty. We docked in Hoboken just across from the Empire State Building. Our dock was right opposite midtown, and I marveled at this building, which at that time dominated the skyline. We were met there by my aunt Vally and her son John. They had immigrated with Karl Weigl, Vally's husband, in 1938.

On our first night the US, we stayed in a rooming house near Ulysses S. Grant's tomb. I think we walked to the tomb the next morning. What a coincidence that we stayed so near to where my family has lived for so many years and in an area I later represented in the New York Legislature.

What effect did being uprooted from Vienna and separated from my mother, the many changes and the presence of danger, have on my outlook of the world? Obviously a great deal. I cannot say I was constantly aware that my life was in danger as we fled Austria and then Europe. But I think I was aware that we faced risk and that my life had been upended. It was due to my father's fortitude, the support he provided, his outward calmness and his care and love that the journey to safety was not more traumatic. Throughout, I felt we would survive. But undoubtedly, these early experiences left me with anxiety I have carried all my life. I am very quick to fear the worst. If someone from the family or close to me is quite late for an appointment, I immediately have thoughts that an accident or mishap has occurred.

At the same time, these changes in my early life gave me the resilience to face unwelcome changes, whether it was adjusting to a new school, being drafted into the army out of law school, or other sudden, difficult transformations. I learned to adapt and to find a zone of safety and comfort. I probably conform more than others so as to fit in. I would seek to establish a friendship with a leader, which gave me a sense of protection and served as an entry to the larger group. But I never lost my sense of self. I believe my need to feel safe made me tougher and better able to face personal challenges but at the same time made me too self-absorbed and prone to pessimism.

## MY EARLY YEARS IN THE US

Four days after arriving in the US, Henry and I were shipped off to Cherry Lawn School, a private boarding school in Darien, Connecticut. My big disappointment was that I had been promised a trip to the World's Fair and that we would be taken there in a car that would go on a ferry. That one could be in a car on a boat astounded me. But it was not to be. I can't remember whether I ever saw the 1939–1940 World's Fair in Flushing Meadow.

Cherry Lawn promoted itself as a progressive school. The kids were mainly Jewish, and quite a few were parked there by parents who had split. So here was another adjustment. I found myself in a totally new environment, unable initially to speak or understand the language. I was still proficient in German and French but knew not a word of English.

The arrangement and payment for Henry and me to attend this school was through the generosity of Muriel Gardiner. My father was in no position to take care of us. He had no money and no job and did not speak English. She was one of the heirs of the Swift meatpacking fortune. She went to Vienna in the 1930s to be psychoanalyzed by Sigmund Freud. While there, she started a relationship with Joseph Buttinger, one of the leaders of the Austrian socialist underground with my father. At one time, I think he was the titular head. Buttinger and Gardiner married. She became a courier before the Anschluss, carrying messages from the Vienna underground to Otto Bauer, the leader of the Austrian socialists, who was in exile across the border in Czechoslovakia. She wrote an autobiography, and Melody's friend wrote a bio. She was an interesting person. Muriel and Buttinger went back to the US in 1938. She helped Austrian refugees financially and may have provided the affidavit of support we needed for the US visa.

Sadly, in the 1950s, Buttinger wrote a book about the Austrian underground in which he savaged my father for being inconsistent and not supportive of the socialist underground after the coup by the proto-fascists in 1934. It is a strange autobiography, as he wrote in the third person and gave himself a pseudonym. I met him occasionally at receptions at the Austrian consulate and exchanged a few words with him. Henry made it a point to ignore him at these receptions. I found Buttinger at that time senile. My father never forgave him.

I adapted quickly to my new environment. Having Henry there as my older brother and surrogate mother was a big plus. Within a few weeks, I was speaking English. I made friends. My closest friend was Richie Hoffman. We were inseparable. He lived around West Seventy-Second Street, where his mother ran a women's clothing store. When on vacation from school, Richie and I would meet at the Horn & Hardart Automat Cafeteria at West Seventy-Second Street and Broadway. We would go to two double features a day. The tickets cost eleven cents, and in the afternoon, there was a chaperone in the movie house, dressed in white, to prevent misbehaving. Richie and I went to Coney Island when we were back in the city on vacation and returned with queasy stomachs from the hot dogs we ate and the many rides that tossed us around and upside down. Both Richie and I were enthusiastic Yankees fans. Becoming bosom pals with Richie was one of the safety measures I seemed to have followed—making friends with popular kids. Close as Richie and I were, we lost contact after we went to college. I did not see Richie again until Nina, my first wife, and I came across his bookstall at Trinity School's annual book fair, probably in the early 1990s. He had become a dealer in books and told me he had a big collection of Black authors, which he profitably sold.

As Henry and I settled into Cherry Lawn, my father managed to enter a program the Quakers ran in Haverford for refugees with professional backgrounds, to help them learn English and to prepare them for employment. This became a turning point in our lives. Running the program was Caroline Norment, a prominent Quaker who had been dean of women at Antioch. My father and Caroline became good friends (nothing romantic). She became very important to our family. I don't know whether my father sought out the friendship, realizing its potential, or if they both developed a mutual attraction. It doesn't matter. She was our dear friend to whom we owe a great deal. She enabled Henry to go to Swarthmore, which paved the way for me. She arranged my early summers in the US and took me on a trip to see the dams of the Tennessee Valley Authority and the Smoky Mountains. We saw her often, and when she lived in New York City for a while, I would visit her and walk her dog. Caroline attended Nina's and my wedding. When we visited her a few years later in a nursing home in Baltimore, where she grew up, she had developed Alzheimer's and did not recognize me.

In the summer of 1941, after my first year at Cherry Lawn, Caroline arranged for me to stay with the Leuba family, who had a camp on a

New Hampshire lake. Mr. Leuba was a professor at Antioch. The family consisted of four kids—I think all boys. It was a lovely summer of swimming, boating, hiking, and evening campfires with singing. I roomed with Ted, who was about my age. One special occurrence I remember sheepishly was killing porcupines because the state offered twenty cents for every dead animal. Often we would be awakened at night by the cry of porcupine, and out we ran with a baseball bat to chase the hapless creature. Not very glamorous or appropriate by today's standards. Fortunately, we never faced retribution by having quills shot at us. It was a good summer.

I was at Cherry Lawn for six years—through my sophomore year. These were good years. Academically, the school was not strong, but I probably gained a decent enough education. My grades were solid. The school had a nice campus and much room to play. What I remember most is playing and fooling around. I think I was considered something of a cutup. It was there that my interest in the other sex developed. As the school considered itself progressive and supervision was not strict, we organized a kissing game around spin the bottle. It was more mechanical than sexual.

One day in April or May 1942, my father came to visit. He and Henry took me to a nearby wooded area and told me my mother had died. It was a terrible shock, as I was particularly close to my mother and never accepted the fact that I would never see her. I remember crying myself to sleep for many nights afterward. Even as I write this, tears come to my eyes.

During this time, much changed in my father's life and therefore mine. After his Haverford stint, my father moved to New York. His first accommodation was a one-room apartment, in what I remember was 44 West Ninety-Seventh Street. Henry and I stayed there during vacations. Once Henry had to make lunch for me. He served me cottage cheese covered by a melted Hershey bar. Why do I remember that so clearly? Is it that my stomach is still turning at that awful concoction? That was

Henry—so loving and caring but occasionally asserting his role as the older brother and having fun at my expense.

I don't know how my father supported himself at that time. Sometime later—maybe not until 1943—he got a job in the Office of War Information, writing material to be broadcast into the Nazi domain. He worked under Arthur Goldberg, who later became a Supreme Court justice but left the court to become ambassador to the United Nations (UN).

In the summer of 1942, I stayed with the Champney family in Yellow Springs, Ohio, the home of Antioch. This, too, was arranged by Caroline Norment. The Champneys had a son, Ken, who was about my age. These were summers of typical Midwestern kids. We would walk barefoot, pick corn in the Champneys' garden, and watch the Naval Reserve Officers Training Corps at Antioch going through their drill and playing baseball. Ken had a newspaper delivery route, which I took over at times, throwing newspapers on a porch from my bicycle.

These were the war years. But on the whole, I was little affected. There was rationing, and one had to carefully use the food stamps that came in a little book. The main war news was certainly heard and discussed, but it seemed remote.

My father, typically, became active in the circle of Austrian socialist refugees, which included a number of old friends and colleagues. He supervised the monthly publication of the Austrian information newsletter. He probably wrote most of it, perhaps more ideology than news. He frequently spoke at meetings. His speeches in German usually lasted two or more hours. (And people complained when I spoke for fifteen minutes in the Senate.) When in New York, I dutifully attended these and must have waited eagerly for him to say *schlusslich* (finally).

It was there my father met Elsa Kolari (Schweiger), a fellow immigrant who fled to the US in 1938 with her two sisters. Elsa had been a social worker in Vienna, working for the city administration. By the time she met my father, she was already working for the Jewish Welfare Agency. She had a very successful and productive career. A courtship developed. All I knew was my father had a friend Elsa who took me out at times, including to my first opera—*The Abduction of the Seraglio* by Mozart—at the old Metropolitan Opera House on West Fortieth Street.

In 1941, Elsa and her sisters were joined by their mother, Sophie Schweiger (Weisman)—I called her Babi. Babi amazingly survived the infamous *St Louis* voyage—a ship of refugees bound for Cuba, which refused to allow the refugee passengers to disembark. The ship then anchored off Florida, seeking admittance for its Jewish refugees to the US. This was shamefully refused. The ship had to return to Europe. Many of its passengers then perished in the Holocaust. The story of the voyage of the *St. Louis* has become well known as a lesson of the shameful refusal to give asylum to people fleeing to safety from murderous and dangerous places.

A shining example of human survival, marooned in Belgium, Babi made her way to the US. In 1939, Elsa was attending Case Western University in Cleveland when the *St. Louis* was anchored off Florida. While there, Babi wrote letters to Elsa, which she was apparently able to send from the ship to her daughter. Elsa read these to some of her friends at Case Western, who thought they were very interesting. Because there was a lot of press attention about the plight of the *St. Louis*, her friends suggested that Elsa send them to the local Cleveland newspaper, the *Plain Dealer*. The letters were printed, and Elsa was able to send the copies of the paper containing the letters to Babi, who by then was in a refugee camp in southern France. Somehow she went to the American consulate and was able to gain a visa to come to the US under a category that allowed writers and other professionals to gain visas. The family story is that she showed the clippings of her letters printed in the Cleveland paper to establish her qualification for the visa. She arrived in the US in late 1941 and joined her three daughters. She lived into her late eighties.

One day in 1943, with Henry present, my father told me he would marry Elsa. I cried bitterly. I was probably affected by the thought that my father would now love and take care of Elsa instead of me. Elsa turned out to be a great blessing. She and my father had such a good relationship. To me, she was not just a stepmother but a surrogate mother. Elsa and I were great friends, and I came to love her. I greatly benefited from the relationship we established.

# CHAPTER 2

# 1943–1948: ADJUSTING TO MY NEW COUNTRY

The summers of 1943 and 1944, I spent partly with friends of my father who had a farm in Ithaca, New York. These were Italian refugees from Mussolini. It was no longer an active farm. The male of the household had a business of artificially inseminating cows, and I went with him a few times on his rounds. The first summer, I took care of chickens and graded the eggs for sale. The second summer, the chickens were gone, and I worked at cleaning the chicken house. Their droppings had turned to what seemed like cement, but, showing persistency or obstinacy, I worked hard to clean the floor. Since there was no real use anymore for the chicken house, it made little sense. But it kept me busy. I was the only child there. The family did take in some guests, which at least provided some variety.

The highlight of these summers was a trip to the White Mountains in New Hampshire. In 1943, Papa and Elsa, looking for an inexpensive vacation and loving mountains, somehow found Pinkham Notch. I remember arriving late at night on a bus from Boston and finding a note guiding us to our rooms. Pinkham, in those days, was much smaller and more rustic. Joe Dodge was in charge, and we talked with him often as he joined us for the family-style meals. The day after our arrival, we were told all trails up Mount Washington were closed because a drought had created a risk of forest fires. After unsuccessfully taking a train to a place we hoped would let us get into the woods, and after a big *krach* (German for "thunder," as we called these family fights) between Papa and Elsa, we decided to hitchhike back to the base of the Auto Road. This was open and was the only way to get up Mount Washington. We trekked up the whole eight miles—far from the pleasure of a trail through the woods, but at least we were going up. Elsa and I did fine, but Papa lagged behind, especially once we got to the top and then a mile down to the hut, Lake of the Clouds, where accommodation and food were provided. It was the first time I realized my father was getting older and that, in some ways, I was now the stronger. Fortunately, the trail restriction was lifted, and we spent the week hiking.

Papa had to return after one week. Elsa and I stayed for another week. We did a lot of climbing, staying in huts, and having a grand time. One day, down at Pinkham, which we had decided would be a rest day, after lunch and feeling bored, we went up the Lion's Head trails, as Tuckerman Ravine, the more common climb, seemed too tame. It was during this week that Elsa and I bonded so strongly together. This introduction to the White Mountains and the Appalachian Mountain Club with its hut system led my family and me over many years to hike there. The White Mountains have given us so much pleasure.

In the summer of 1944, after my stay in Ithaca, we went to the White Mountains again. This time Papa and Elsa decided to upgrade, and we stayed at a small hotel in Randolph. This was at the foot of Mount Madison, and we climbed the Presidential Range from there, staying at the Madison Hut at least a couple of times. After about a week, we went to Boston and saw Henry just before he shipped off to France.

These were the years of World War II. I was certainly aware of the battles to defeat Nazi Germany. But I don't remember being that much affected. It just became a routine part of my life. When home from Cherry Lawn, we listened to the news every hour, and I am sure my father must have discussed it. In 1943, Henry was drafted after completing his first year at Swarthmore. I remember him coming to visit us when on leave. I saw him for the first time in army khakis. I don't recollect being that worried about his safety or the outcome of the war. Was I worried when the German armies in 1941 overran much of European Russia and were at the gates of Moscow, or in 1942 during the Battle of Stalingrad (a turning point in the war)? I just assumed it would all turn out well.

A change occurred in my life in 1946. Cherry Lawn asked me not to return after my sophomore year there. I am not sure whether it was my behavior or Muriel Gardiner, who had paid Henry's and my tuition, was not willing to support us anymore. With little notice, a school had to be found for me in New York City. I would stay with my father and Elsa in an apartment they had at 316 West Ninety-Fourth Street. An attempt to get me into Walden, a private school, did not pan out. I was left attending the High School of Commerce, which was located on West Sixty-Sixth Street, where Lincoln Center is now. It was not an elite high school, and it was quite a change from the more homogenous Cherry Lawn. Another big adjustment in my life.

The school was diverse. Among my circle of friends and acquaintances were Chinese, Irish, Greeks, Italians, and a few African Americans. There might have been some Latinos, but I don't remember many. This was before the large immigration of Puerto Ricans after World War II. The school was a microcosm of New York in the 1940s. The academic work was not near what my children and grandchildren faced, but it provided a decent, basic education. I did well there academically but was certainly not stimulated. I did read a lot at home, but some were trashy novels like *Forever Amber*.

As I tended to do, I made a close friendship—Morty Gilbert. His father was a doctor whose practice was with Broadway Theater types (mainly showgirls). This enabled him to get a table at the then very popular Lindy's at Fiftieth and Broadway and avoid the long lines waiting for a table. This was quite a treat—especially eating its then famous cheesecake. I often visited Morty's home, which was in a hotel on West Forty-Fifth Street. I don't think Morty came to visit me even once. One reason is that his family had a television set, which was a rarity then. Morty and I were avid Yankee fans. We played softball in Central Park at West Sixty-Sixth Street when the weather turned warmer. We would hang out with other schoolmates at the so-called penny arcades that dotted Broadway in Times Square. Occasionally there was a poker game that was held after it closed for the night in the pastry shop of my Greek friend's father. It was located where the Port Authority Bus Terminal is now, between West Fortieth and West Forty-Second Streets. At that time, there was a Greek community there. Like so much of New York, it has changed in my seventy years here. I probably got sick eating sweet pastries before a loss of money forced me home. My life was pretty typical of a kid growing up in New York.

In the summers of 1945 and 1946, Papa and Elsa rented a small cottage in Robins Rest on Fire Island. It was then very primitive. I think in the first summer we had no electricity. We had to pump water out of a well. For our shopping, we had to go to Ocean Beach in a rowboat. It was great. By the summer of 1946, Henry was out of the army and came with us. I so enjoyed diving into the waves and lolling on an almost empty beach. This too has radically changed. I assume that little cottage is gone, and houses in Robins Rest sell now for many hundreds of thousands of dollars.

In 1947, Papa was able to get back to Austria. He had strong conflicts about going since his family was in New York, and it was unlikely Henry and I would ever return. It was his sense of duty and the potential of being involved again in Austria's political life that motivated him. Elsa and I saw him off at LaGuardia Airport, where he boarded the Pan American Clipper. My father's return to Austria did not go well. He was not really welcomed back. A new generation had assumed the party's leadership, and they didn't want the old leadership to assume their previous roles. Also, Papa was further to the left than the party. And finally, he missed us and America, which he liked very much. He returned to New York in July 1948.

While he was gone, Elsa and I had almost a year alone. Depending solely on Elsa's not robust income, we rented out the living room in our two-bedroom, one-bath apartment. I was now a senior and worked on my college applications. I missed my father, but Elsa did much to fill in the void. We got on well, and I appreciated her as a surrogate mother.

I had a great summer in 1947. Once again, Henry took care of me. He and some Swarthmore College friends rented a house near Swarthmore. They were all veterans but were willing to have me join them. It was a summer of poker, bull sessions, and some paid work—a great experience in communal living with persons already in their twenties. I think I fit in well. One job we all took for a week or so was with the promotion department of the *Philadelphia Inquirer*, a major newspaper. One such event was Li'l Abner Day (a comic book character) at the old Shibe Park, home of the Philadelphia Phillies. We were dressed as hillbillies and fired off toy guns from the top of the stands.

That summer, I avoided being killed by a doctor. This is a true story, and I am very clear as to what happened. I had a foot infection and tried to see the Swarthmore College doctor. He was on vacation, so I was sent to his brother, who was also a doctor. He prescribed a toxic solution in which to soak my foot, and then, I absolutely remember, told me to drink a glass of this toxic solution. Why? Was he an anti-Semite? Did I not understand him? I don't think so. Fortunately, when I picked up the prescription, I mentioned to the pharmacist that I was to drink a glass of the toxic solution after soaking my foot. He strongly advised me not to. I wasn't sure I should listen to the pharmacist but followed his advice. And here I still am.

In early 1948, I had to make plans for college. Unlike with my children and grandchildren, there were no college visits, school counselors to guide you, tutors to prepare you for the SAT, or parents to help you write your application essay. As I think back, I am not certain this was even then required. The whole process was much easier, started in the year you planned to attend college, and was much less stressful than it has become. My only preparation for the SAT was to look through a book of vocabulary. I applied to Swarthmore, NYU, Cornell, and as a safe backup, City College of New York, which was called Harvard on the Hudson. Its free tuition attracted many Jewish refugees at that time. It has produced a number of Nobel Prize winners and enabled many successful careers. I ended up being accepted at City College of New York and NYU, waitlisted at Cornell, and I did get into my first choice, Swarthmore, and was awarded a partial scholarship, which was very important, as there was no family money with Elsa being the only breadwinner. My being admitted at a time when Swarthmore still had a quota for Jews was due to Henry attending, and his enrollment was due to Caroline Norment. The family and I owe her a great debt.

# CHAPTER 3

# 1948-1952: COLLEGE YEARS

The four years at Swarthmore were good, and as I look back, I would say *special*. I may not have said it while attending but feel it strongly now: I love Swarthmore. However, my wife, Nina, who attended Swarthmore a year after me, and I could not interest our children in even applying.

What is better in life than four years in college located in a beautiful campus setting, being intellectually stimulated, making new friends, and growing up? Not that it was always easy or that I wasn't foolish at times. And as with many aspects of life, I enjoyed and valued it more in retrospect than I did at the time.

Swarthmore had many smart students who came from elite schools. Here I was a High School of Commerce grad. I also had no money. It was a struggle for Papa, Elsa, and me to pay the tuition, which I think was only $600 a year, and I had a $300 scholarship. I had to get a paying job. Again through Henry, I got a job as a dishwasher at Inglenook—Swarthmore's premier restaurant. Henry may have worked there too. Besides providing a little money, I also received meals, which were infinitely better than the college food. So in some respects, I was something of an outsider. However, as with other situations in my life, a sense of insecurity and/or of not quite belonging also provided the drive to accommodate and achieve. For no good reason, I felt very confident academically. And I did quite well in my first year. Socially, it was more uneven. I did develop friendships, some of which lasted a lifetime.

I was active in campus life. Right from the start, I wrote for the college newspaper (sports), joined the staff of the college radio station, and in the fall of 1948, which was a presidential election, I became active in a very leftist group. We supported Henry Wallace, a third-party populist candidate. I don't remember that we did much except have long discussions. When Harry Truman won in 1948, I was actually pleased, particularly as I disliked Thomas Dewey, the Republican candidate. So early on, my allegiance switched to the Democratic Party as the more likely means to achieve social and economic change.

To show that I wasn't pigeonholed in just parts of Swarthmore life, before the annual big Swarthmore-Haverford football game, I joined a small group of fellow students to paint the Haverford College water tower with "Beat Haverford." Of course, we were captured just as we entered the campus. My colleagues were all thrown in the Haverford pond. It was November and cold. Fortunately, my capturer was a veteran who was friendly with a Swarthmore student I knew quite well. Once the connection was made, he decided to save me from the cold dunking. Our bedraggled and defeated group slunk back to Swarthmore.

As I think back on my time at Swarthmore, I am struck how I reached out to various groups (i.e., intellectuals, far-left groups, fraternity types, and jocks). It may have reflected restlessness but more my interest in the life around me. As my graduation yearbook caption said (which I did not write but was written by my friends), "friend of great and near great."

Before I entered Swarthmore, in the summer of 1948, I got my first job as a busboy/waiter in the Catskills. I did this also in the summers of 1949,

1950, and before entering Harvard Law in 1952. But my summer jobs were not in the premier Catskill resorts, like Grossinger's, the Concord, and the Nevele. These were in what was called the Borscht Belt because the guests were mainly Jewish. This was before Florida developed, air travel became part of mass transportation, the Caribbean opened up, and cruise ships became popular. These hotels I mentioned are all now gone, and the Catskills are economically depressed and hoping for renewal through a casino (good luck?). But in the late 1940s, they flourished and were known for their extensive menus stuffing their guests. They also featured top entertainment—mainly comedians. But the places I worked were small and for the less affluent, and many were refugees. Foolishly, I would get these jobs by writing to hotels, which advertised in the *Aufbau*. This was a German-language paper that flourished as a weekly when there were still many German-speaking refugees and had a decent circulation. Papa occasionally wrote for it in the 1950s. It was still around when I ran for the Senate. It always endorsed me but only after I bought an overpriced ad. I became quite friendly with its editor. It no longer exists; nor do but a handful of refugees. I should have tried to get jobs through employment agencies, which offered positions in the more prominent hotels. I would have made more money.

My first summer job was in Pine Hill, New York. I was miserably homesick and fearful as I took a bus up Route 17. Once there, I settled in and had a decent summer. My other summer jobs were in such different locations as the Jersey Shore and Connecticut. I made some money but not as much as I would have made if I had felt confident enough to pursue a job at the thriving, big hotels. Whatever I earned did help, so with my family's support, my scholarship, and working, I was just able to pay for college and leave without any debt. It was always touch and go, and at one point, a restitution payment from Austria came just in time.

The first semester of my sophomore year did not go well. I spent a lot of time playing poker and bridge. I didn't work at the Ingelnook restaurant and had odd jobs. My grades also declined. Call it the sophomore slump. My father took me to task for my mediocre grades. My family, if interested, can read more in the letters I wrote from Swarthmore and throughout the fifties, particularly on my Europe trip in 1951 and my army service. Recently, I found this trove of letters and postcards in a big envelope. These were written at a time when people communicated by letters, which sadly, in our high-tech world, have disappeared.

I picked up in the second semester and did well enough to get into Swarthmore's acclaimed honors program. In the program, you chose a major and two minors. Each semester, you had a seminar in the major and rotated the minors. I chose history for my major and political science and philosophy for my minors. The seminars met just once weekly, and for each, you had to write a paper, which was then read and discussed in the seminar. These were held in a professor's house, who provided dinner. My history seminars were particularly stimulating, especially European diplomatic history leading up to World War I, the French Revolution, and Medieval England. In the former, which I took as a senior, there was a junior named Nina Williams. Unfortunately, she missed part of the semester because of mononucleosis. When Nina and I connected in the late 1950s, and as we reviewed our Swarthmore lives, we both remembered that seminar and everyone who was in it, except each other. But that is all for a later tale.

The summer of 1951 was very special. Henry's love, generosity, and support enabled me to return to Europe for a visit. He gave me $200 to pay for my voyage and to sustain me for my eight weeks overseas. Henry, at that time, was working for the US High Commission Office in Frankfurt, Germany. This was the American HQ for the occupation of Germany, which had lasted from the end of World War II until the middle 1950s.

Henry had gone back to Europe in 1951 on a student ship, where he met Hope Jensen, who was in charge of social activity. Hope had a Fulbright scholarship and was studying in Paris. How they got together is quite a tale since Henry made it clear before he boarded that he was determined to sabotage and frustrate the social director. He was not going to be compelled or persuaded to square dance or whatever. Instead, he ended up marrying her.

The amount of $200 Henry gave me may seem very paltry today. Yet I was able to purchase a round-trip ticket on a student boat for $120 and have eighty dollars left for the two months overseas. Part of that time, I was with Henry, who took care of my expenses. The student ship, of which there were a few making the ocean crossing, was an old World War II army transport. There were dormitories, and the bunks were triple tiered. The voyage took eleven days until we landed in Le Havre. Quite a change from the current six- to nine-hour trip to any part of Europe by jet. However, it was great fun to be with a ship full of people mostly my age.

I was so excited to be returning to Europe, especially to Paris. My joy to be in Paris is expressed in the letters I wrote to my father and Elsa about my trip and arrival, which are in the trove of saved letters I mentioned earlier. It may seem strange that I should have such feelings for Paris since I was there with Papa and Henry, without my mother, as Europe became engulfed in war and we faced grave dangers. As I wrote in the chapter of our time in Paris in 1938–9, it is a tribute to how Papa created a loving home for us that Henry and I both developed this affection for Paris.

In Paris, I met Hope for the first time. A few days after arrival, Henry drove from Frankfurt to join us. Great days together. I returned with him to Frankfurt for a week. Then we came back to Paris to pick up Hope and drove to Vienna, through Switzerland and Italy. In the former, I had my first visit to the Matterhorn. How exciting. And then Venice and finally

Vienna. There, I was in great demand by the many friends of my father and mother who had managed to survive the war, like Rosa Jochmann, who endured five years in Ravensbrück. It was mainly through her efforts that my mother became so well known in Vienna and that a street and housing project are named for her. Rosa held important party positions and served in the Parliament. I would meet family friends for lunch, then at two *jauses* and a dinner.

Of all the stories and details of our trip, I will just describe my becoming enchanted by the Matterhorn. We had planned to drive to Zermatt, the town that lies at the foot of this striking mountain. We found out that you could only reach it by train, and the fare stretched our meager resources. Hope and I convinced a doubtful Henry we should drive to the next station, which was the terminus of the road, and thus pay a much cheaper fare. The drive, on a narrow road, with a sheer precipice on one side, was harrowing. Henry became furious at Hope and me for suggesting this. We made it, only to find that the clever Swiss reduced the train fare to Zermatt by only a few pennies. The next morning, I was so excited to see the mountain that I woke up at dawn. Unfortunately, it was fogged over. I started walking up in what I thought must be the direction to the Matterhorn. As I climbed higher through little clusters of huts, it seemed to get brighter, and finally, I could see just around the bend a large white object. It was the Matterhorn. What a sight. The day turned beautiful. I hiked along the base of the mountain all day. I didn't return to Zermatt until 1993 when, in spite of my sixty-plus years, I attempted to climb this most beautiful of mountains. But that story is for another day.

Henry and Hope left Vienna after a week. I stayed for another week. Next, I went to Zürich to visit more family friends before returning to Paris. Then another visit to Henry in Frankfurt and one final stay in Paris. By this time, I was running out of money. Hope, who left to join Henry in Frankfurt, gave me her Cité Universitaire identity card, on which I pasted my picture (the card checkers did not know the gender of the name Hope). I would take my evening meal there, consisting of boiled potatoes and macaroni for twelve francs—a little less than a dollar. Nevertheless, I became totally broke. I had the good idea to go to the shipping line office and plead my poverty. I was given a job cleaning bathrooms on the return voyage and a most welcome advance on my pay. What a great summer. Thank you, Henry.

My junior and senior years at Swarthmore passed well. I was really into my honor seminars. I returned to the Ingelnook but this time to the elevated position of busboy. Besides what I made on tips, I was entitled to get a free evening meal, at which I was seated as a regular guest in the dining room. Whenever I skipped an evening meal, I could make it up by bringing a guest the next time. This was quite an enticement for dates, who at least for that night could avoid the awful Swarthmore dining room. (I should point out to my grandchildren who are used to a variety of good choices in today's college cafeterias that Swarthmore then served a no-choice meal that was barely edible.)

As graduation approached, so did the question of what next? I thought I might benefit from a year off. I took the federal civil service exam but did not score high. Papa urged me to continue school. There was no question that as much as I had enjoyed academic studies, I would not proceed with an advanced degree in history or any social studies. The law did appeal. I took the Law School Admission Test and did well enough to be admitted to Harvard Law School.

I graduated Swarthmore magna cum laude. Papa and Elsa came to the graduation ceremony. It was goodbye, college, but I was ready for a change.

After another summer job as a waiter, this one in New Jersey, I started law school in the fall of 1952. I would like to say I fell immediately in love with the law. I did not. It was not a particularly good year. I was academically drained. I spent much time with some of my Swarthmore friends who were in various Harvard and Massachusetts Institute of Technology (MIT) schools. I mainly hung out with my Swarthmore friend David Deacon. He was quite special. He talked his way into Harvard Law, although he had not yet graduated from Swarthmore. David was a Marine Corps veteran who had fought in the Pacific and earned a silver star for bravery. He was already married. He spent time hanging out in bars. I would join him or seek him out, as I often became restless. He was also a compulsive gambler, but I didn't join him in that.

Law school at that time had a set curriculum. Not much changed from the nineteenth century—Torts, Property, Trust, and Corporations. The class sizes were large. You were pretty anonymous. The professors were considered like demigods. Among them were distinguished professors, including Scott, Casner, Leach, and Seavy. They were considered the leaders in their specialties, and it was their law books one studied. I was awed by them. I did my studies but without enthusiasm. As I look back, I see it as a struggle. Once I was called on in Torts. I was unprepared and didn't answer to my name. All in all, it was not a productive year. My marks reflected that. Exam week was a blur. I was more into the coronation of Queen Elizabeth II and the first ascent of Mount Everest, which occurred at the same time. I thought I could improve my performance by taking a barbiturate to increase my academic energy. This only befuddled me, and for my Property exam, I mistakenly took the test of another section. While I did manage to be in the top half of my class, it was not a good showing. During part of the year, I had a job serving room service at a local hotel. Money—the lack of it—continued to be a problem. Toward the end of the school year, I was almost broke. For the last two weeks, I lived on cans of baked beans. I remember a can cost seventeen cents. Once or twice, I splurged and bought one for nineteen cents, which contained franks.

In the fall of 1952, I became actively involved in the Adlai Stevenson campaign for president against Dwight Eisenhower. I was either the leader of the Harvard Democratic group or among its activists. I remember meeting with the local Democratic machine politicians in Cambridge, offering our services. They were not interested as they saw Stevenson as a loser who only the "eggheads," as they saw us, supported. We had meetings with Arthur Schlesinger in his home. I attended rallies. My political interest and activism had taken hold. Of course, the election turned into a disappointment. Nevertheless, it was exciting.

That summer, I first worked at a fancy lobster place on Cape Ann, south of Boston. Yachts could pull up to the restaurant, and we would serve the meals on the boats if desired. Once I served Howard Johnson, who created the restaurant chain. It was pleasant, as I mostly only worked nights and had a day off, unlike in the Catskills. We would occasionally order meals for guests who didn't exist and take a steak or lobster and tear it apart with our hands and gulf it down on the deck between serving meals. The restaurant had a big lobster tank and a "lobster boy" who would pick out the lobsters guests ordered. Once, the lobster boy was away just as I passed the tank. The maître d' asked me to fill in. I nervously reached into the big tank to avoid my hand being mangled by the claws, which at that time were just pegged. Often the pegs got loose. From then on, I avoided walking near the lobster tank. Pleasant as the job was, I wasn't making enough money, so I went back one last time to the Catskills. This time, it was to a more prestigious hotel, again in Pine Hills, where I had started my undistinguished career as waiter and busboy five years before.

In September 1953, I entered my second year of law school, determined to have a better year. But then the army intervened.

# CHAPTER 4

# 1953-1955: THE ARMY YEARS

The Korean War broke out when the North invaded the South in 1950. The US became immediately involved. So did China when Douglas MacArthur, the US commander, unwisely drove to the Chinese border. The draft was in effect, and I had to register, as did all males over eighteen. Student deferments were in effect, but these were unevenly applied, and much discretion was left to local draft boards.

I received a notice to report to the local draft board and appeared before it. I don't remember that it was other than perfunctory. In any event, the board determined I was to be drafted. One of the persons who I think was on the board I later defeated in an election for Democratic district leader in 1961. Sweet revenge. Anyway, I appealed my first case for my most important client. My appeal was rejected. I had to enter the U.S. Army. I notified Harvard Law I would have to withdraw.

On October 23, 1953, I reported for induction to the army center on Whitehall Street. It was early in the morning, and Henry accompanied me. I was given a medical, which found that my hearing was slightly impaired. Otherwise, I was fit, and my hope for some medical finding that would keep me out evaporated. We recruits were lined up and told to take one step forward. This, we were told, made us soldiers in the army and subject to its discipline. We were then bused to Fort Dix in New Jersey for processing. This included getting ill-fitting army clothes, tests, and vaccinations. There were numerous lectures. In a few weeks, I went from hearing lectures by learned professors on the law to listening to sergeants ranting about making me into a fighting soldier.

After about three days, a sergeant told us that we would have our basic training at Fort Dix. This was good news, as I would be able to visit home when I finally got a pass. But in the middle of that night, we were woken up told to get in a bus and driven to an airfield. There we boarded a plane, which was to take us to Fort Ord in California. I soon learned that rumors and what seemed like official pronouncements are legion in the Army and mainly to be discounted. The plane was a civilian aircraft that must have been under contract to the military. As I looked out the window, I saw the captain of the plane walk around, and it looked to me that he took a coin to tighten a screw on the wheels. This was my first flight. And maybe because I survived this experience, I have always been very relaxed on flights. In those days, you couldn't fly directly from coast to coast. We stopped in St. Louis and San Antonio before finally reaching Fort Ord, which was just south of the Monterey Peninsula.

When I think back on being yanked from the comfort and academic pursuit of law school into the Army as a private in basic training, it might seem unbearable. But I adjusted not only to the rigors of basic training, which were not all that terrible, but also to a different social milieu. It was not so much racial or ethnic diversity but the social background, which was such a difference. As I have throughout my life, I managed to accommodate to a dramatic change in my life. I got along well with my fellow trainees and adjusted to being in the Army. It would be two years, and I was not only going to survive but was determined to make the most of it.

I was in Fort Ord for eight weeks. There was a lot of marching and learning how to fire and take apart my rifle, which in those days was the M-1, a World War II weapon. We had shooting practice, once with a machine gun. I managed to infuriate the sergeant in charge by shooting off the stand of the target. There was also a lot of what we called "chicken shit," such as having to scrub the barrack floor, waiting in formation for hours for parades to begin, and numerous petty annoyances. All in all, it was not onerous. We were often free in the evening or on weekends. I went to the base movie house and the library. I actually managed to get some reading done. In 1983 on our family trip out west, we drove from Los Angeles to San Francisco and stopped for a visit to Fort Ord.

Was I a good soldier? No. I was more like The Good Soldier Schweik. This was a character in the book by that name about a Czech recruit in the Austrian Army in World War I who was considered very stupid but almost always succeeded in outwitting his Army superiors. It is a very funny book, and there was even an opera made of it. Nina and I read some of the book together and saw the opera. Read it for good laughs.

One of Schweik's escapades was to report frequently sick. I wasn't as inventive as Schweik but did manage once to get into the base hospital. After four weeks, we received our first pass. I went into town with some of my fellow trainees and had a few beers. Not that many. But next morning, I had stomach cramps and was given permission to go to the infirmary. It was not anything more than a stomach hangover. But the young doctor diagnosed it as possible appendicitis and ordered me to bed in the base hospital. I had a good day of rest and was taken care of. The next day, I was kicked out, and it was back to basic training.

I had one instance that could have ended with me in the stockade. One morning, my company was marched to a classroom for some lecture. As usual, we stacked our rifles outside. I was famished and took the opportunity to sneak off to get a jelly doughnut at the PX. My plan was to return just as the class ended and to blend in with my company. To my horror, when I returned, the stacked rifles, including mine, were gone, as was my company. It turned out we had been taken to the wrong classroom, so everyone left, and my rifle stood out for my not being there to pick it up. It is a serious offense to lose your rifle. Sheepishly and with dread, I went to my company's headquarters. The sergeant in charge produced my rifle and after chewing me out said I could either go before the company commander or accept a punishment of being restricted for the weekend and do cleanup work. With great relief, I chose the latter and from then on made sure not to be separated from my rifle.

At the end of what was the first part of the basic training, I received my next assignment. It was to Fort Leonard Wood in Missouri. I also was given ten days' to two weeks' leave to go there. I went to San Francisco and planned to visit some national parks on the way to my next assignment. In Frisco, I found a flophouse to stay (where there is now the upscale Embarcadero development). The next day, I walked through the city. I was in such great shape after all the marching and physical exercise of basic that I walked all the way from the waterfront to the Golden Gate Bridge and back.

My homesickness—missing Papa, Elsa, and Henry—overcame my plan to visit the national parks. I had heard that I could hitch a ride on military craft. I went to the naval station in Oakland, and after a day of waiting, I was able to hitch a ride on a plane to Palm Beach. I stayed overnight at some military installation, and the next day, I hitched a ride to Hartford. From there, a train brought me home, joyous to be back with Papa and Elsa. I had a wonderful eight or nine days. I went to Cambridge to see friends. It ended too soon. I took a train to St. Louis and then to Fort Leonard Wood. The idyll was over.

Fort Leonard Wood is one of the armpits of the world. Henry was stationed there in World War II before being shipped to Europe. It is situated in the Ozarks, which is not a place you want to be in winter. I was now in an engineer company, and to make it even more ludicrous, I was sent to electrician school. The army had found for me the area I was least skilled in and had absolutely no aptitude for. My eight weeks there were pretty miserable. We did such things as bridge building and some other endeavors that were burdensome and unpleasant. In addition, there was the usual marching, firearm training, and boring lectures. We also had a five-day bivouac in freezing weather. One day, I quickly volunteered to carry coal to the company headquarters tent to keep a stove going and avoid some miserable outdoor training in the bitter cold. To show that my services were needed, throughout the day, I shoveled enough coal for many days of heating. That stove was red-hot all day, and I kept warm by fussing around it.

I was sustained during the bivouac by a most welcome package from the Friedlanders (Elsa's sister Bertha had married Ernst Friedlander, a doctor, who worked in a VA Hospital in Augusta, Maine) containing the special bread that Babi had baked and a big salami. As I shared this, I was quite popular.

I did have my small triumphs. We had training in gas warfare. It required us to go through an enclosure in which tear gas or a weak chlorine gas was pumped as we struggled to put on our gas masks. As I had some eye ointment to treat red eyes, I smeared it heavily on my eyelids. I looked awful, as if my eyes were seriously damaged. This convinced the sergeant that I could be excused from the exercise so as not to aggravate this terrible eye condition. Once we had an exercise in climbing telephone poles. For this, we put spikes on our boots, which required that you lean outward as you climbed the poles so the spikes would stay firmly in the poles to prevent you from falling. This I found hard to do, as my instinct was to hug the pole, and I couldn't control my knees from shaking as I got higher. This resulted in the spikes not being embedded in the pole and me falling down into a sandpit at the bottom. After numerous failures and enduring the curses of the sergeant, I stepped on my glasses, which, of course, broke. Now, was this intentional? I showed my broken glasses to the sergeant and said I could not see. I was excused to get another pair. The Good Soldier Schweik would have been proud of me.

The town outside the base consisted of a number of dreary bars. It was better to stay on base, though I don't remember that it had the amenities I found in Fort Ord. I did have some weekend passes after the first weeks. Once, someone even arranged for a friend and me to have dates with coeds from a nearby college. One weekend, I joined my friend for a visit to St. Louis.

As the end neared, I waited to get my permanent assignment. I feared ending up in one of the numerous miserable bases in the South. I became quite despondent. I felt I needed some change. I went to the Jewish chaplain and convinced him to recommend me for a three-day pass, which was granted. I went off to Chicago in the hope of visiting Gerhard and Maria Piers, dear family friends. More about them later. It turned out that we just missed each other, as that weekend they were away at a conference in St. Louis. Nevertheless, I enjoyed being in a civilized place. I went to a Cubs baseball game and to a performance by the New York City Ballet. My first ballet. It was *The Firebird*. I have been a ballet lover ever since. Also, on that occasion, I had the name of one of the dancers from a fellow soldier. I went to the stage door and met her. She invited me to join her with some of the dancers for a drink—what a change from the army.

When I returned to Fort Leonard Wood, I received my next assignment. What a pleasant surprise. I was assigned to the Fifth Army Headquarters in Fort Sheridan outside of Chicago. What a break. Fort Sheridan was quite a change. It was an old base created in the late nineteenth century to house soldiers to put down strikes in Chicago, such as by the Pullman workers. The barracks were three-story brick buildings. There was a much more relaxed daily routine than in basic training. Additionally, it was a short commuter ride into Chicago. And in Chicago, there was the Piers family, who took such good care of me. I spent many weekends with them. They had a lovely apartment near the University of Chicago. The Piers were considered part of my family and treated me as one of theirs. Maria was the daughter of Karl Weigl, a composer who, after divorcing her mother, married my mother's sister Vally. Apparently, he was Vally's piano teacher, and they fell in love. The Viennese, with their nasty humor, claimed Karl divorced Maria's mother because Maria's crying as a baby interfered with his composing. Maria and Gerhard came to the US in about 1938. Both of them had distinguished careers. Maria was a psychologist and social worker who helped found and for many years ran the highly considered Erikson Institute specializing in child development. Maria was lovely, charming, and so adored by my father and brother that it became a Leichter joke, maybe to the resentment of Elsa. Gerhard was a psychiatrist who, for a while, was the president of the Chicago Psychoanalytic Institute. They were both well connected with Chicago's intelligentsia and University of Chicago professors. They would have interesting dinner meals and soirees at their home, to which I was invited. They had two young children: Peggy, who was about eight, and Matthew, who was about four. So I had the benefit of having a family in Chicago. And in the summer of 1954, when they took their vacation in Martha's Vineyard, long a favorite place of psychiatrists, they gave me the keys to their apartment.

In Fort Sheridan, I was initially assigned to the electrician shop. Fortunately, it was run by a civilian who quickly realized my limitations, so that I was mainly asked to change light bulbs. I changed the same light bulbs two or three times a day in a lounge that had a television set so that I could watch the Army-McCarthy hearings

After a few weeks, fortune smiled upon me again. The company clerk, Carmen Seminara, saw I went to Harvard Law School, from where his brother had graduated, and we struck up a friendship. Carmen was quite a manipulator of army procedures. He managed to make me the deputy company clerk. There was very little work to do, and we would spend the day reading, kibitzing, and lolling around in the company headquarters. Carmen and I became lifelong friends, and we are still in touch with each other. He pops up at various times in my life. He lives in Buffalo. He was something of a Rabelaisian figure who enjoyed life. We spent many evenings going out to local restaurants and bars. On occasion, we went to Chicago, as the army imposed no curfew. A few times in the warmer days, we went to Ravinia—Chicago's outdoor venue for classical music. When I had the Piers' apartment for much of the summer, I invited him to join me there. Once, he and I hitched a ride on military planes to spend a weekend in Washington. All in all, it was as easy and good as it could be in the army.

But then it became even better. Carmen arranged for me to go for six weeks, or maybe it was eight weeks, of Troop Information and Education training (TI&E as it was called). This was in Fort Slocum, an island off New Rochelle in Long Island Sound. So I was back in New York and able to spend weekends and some evenings with Papa and Elsa. I took the opportunity of being back east to go to Cambridge to visit with friends. The TI&E training itself was not particularly worthwhile or interesting. But, thankfully, there was no, or very little, bothersome army nonsense. And being there proved very helpful later on.

I returned to Fort Sheridan in the middle of October 1954. One year in the army had passed. Carmen and a couple of fellow soldiers met me at the station in Chicago. Carmen told me I had received an assignment to the Far East. Initially, I was upset, as my life there was so good, and the likelihood of going to Korea was real and unappealing. The Korean War was winding down, and while I was attracted by the adventure of going to

Asia, I did not want to go to Korea. It was typical of the army that after having qualified as a German-speaking interpreter (my German must have been better at that time than it is now), they would send me to Asia. I made a claim to the brass that having received the TI&E training, my job category (MOS as it was called) should be changed from electrician to education and information specialist, and my new assignment canceled. All this achieved was that I was called into headquarters and told that I could no longer work as a company clerk but would have to work as an electrician. At around this time, Carmen was discharged. So, it was not with much regret I found myself in December en route to Fort Lewis in Seattle to ship out to the Far East.

Fort Lewis was a processing center for troops being shipped to the Far East. I was there for about three weeks. The time at Fort Lewis was spent just lounging around. This is army life. You are always waiting and waiting, thinking something important is going to happen. It rarely does. But this time, it did occur. The significant event came when, one day, we were lined up to go through a barrack to get our overseas assignment. I had met a few of my Fort Leonard Wood fellow trainees, who, like me, were now being shipped to Asia. Apparently, the army needed engineers someplace, and clearly, that place was going to be Korea. No one wanted Korea. As we waited in line, we devised among ourselves a sign from those who went ahead to let those of us who were still waiting know what their assignment was. Thumbs-up, it meant Japan. Thumbs-down was Korea. The lateral motion of the hand was for Okinawa. Everyone who preceded me gave the thumbs-down sign.

When I went through for processing, I immediately said to the sergeant handing out the assignment that I was mistakenly classified as an engineer and that since I had gone to TI&E school, I was to be assigned under that classification. For good measure, I said that colonel—whoever was the commander of the TI&E school—had stated I was to be assigned as a TI&E specialist. This was, of course, not an exaggeration but a flat-out falsehood. The sergeant, who had a big book in front of him showing where soldiers were needed, looked at me as if to say, "I know this is bull." But, whether he thought there was some possibility it was true or appreciated my desperate effort to avoid going to Korea, he said, "Let me see if there is a place that needs someone both as an engineer and a troop and information specialist." He leafed through his sheaf of papers while my heart stopped and then said, "OK, you are going to central Japan," which I took to mean Tokyo. I joyously finished the processing and went out and happily made the thumbs-up sign.

After three weeks, we were told there was a ship to take us to Yokohama. So at the end of December, I boarded the *General H.B. Freeman,* a relatively small troop ship. The departure was all bathos not pathos. The pier I sailed from was right beneath the luxury hotel I stayed in fifty years later when I was in Seattle as a director of the Federal Housing Finance Board (FHFB) for a meeting. Then I was feted and attended a dinner at the home of the former mayor. But now, as a private first class in khakis, lugging a duffel bag, I boarded the ship. But who could have foreseen or even thought of fifty years on? My thoughts were on Japan. Red Cross volunteers were at the dock to give us coffee. A band showed up to play martial music, though it made sure to stay some distance away, under cover from the usual Seattle rain. There were even a few relatives waving us off (or were they brought in from central casting?). No tears though. And we the soldiers were happy to be off, knowing that no war beckoned us, as the Korean War had ended. As the ship went through Puget Sound and the lights faded, I was at the bow, looking forward, not back.

The troop ship and the voyage were miserable. We took a northern route through the Pacific in winter and encountered pretty rough seas. The next morning, as we were now in the open sea, along with most of the soldiers, I was seasick. We were chased up to the deck into the cold while the holds were cleaned. Soldiers were throwing up all over and lying on top of one another on grates to get some warmth. It was utter misery. In the hold, we slept in four-tier bunks. Mine was the top one. As I described it in a diary I kept:

> One goes to sleep in a hot, crowded hold—filled with sounds of disturbed sleepers—the smell is great—it is an effort to get into the top bunk—and hard to arrange oneself comfortably so that the life jacket does not fall off and get lost during the night—that the person ahead of me does not stick his feet into my face as I dangled my feet off the end of my bunk. The person next to me—really in the same bed as me—is coughing and makes preparatory sounds to puking. Sleep is uneasy.

Many a night I had to fight off seasickness and just made it to my bunk to avoid throwing up. I would lie perfectly still to quiet my nausea.

Yet again, I got a better deal. I went to the master sergeant and offered to put out a ship's newsletter, to which I was then detailed. Along with two companions, we were given a little space as our own office. Instead of being chased up on deck or given some miserable duty like cleaning the latrines, we could spend all day in our little cubicle. It was fun putting out the paper, which we ran off on a mimeograph machine and then handed out. I believe we had access to a wireless, which gave us current news. Once, when handing out the papers, we gave some to Philippine crewmen we ran across (then, and probably still today, navy transports use Philippine crews). In turn, they gave us a bag of oranges. We took this to the stern and devoured the oranges, skin and all, so starved were we for citrus. It seemed the army had not yet learned how to avoid scurvy.

The new year 1955 came. And so too finally did Yokohama, where we landed on or about January 10. Even though I had a fever from a bad cold, I was delighted to be off the ship and in Japan. We were put on a train to Camp Drake, a relocation transfer base. I was so excited to see the countryside with its little villages, farmers working in rice paddies, and friendly faces at crossings. It was another world.

At Drake, there was further reassignment and, to my horror, no assurance of staying in Tokyo—with a chance of still being sent to Korea. My hope was to get assigned to what was called the Finance Building in downtown Tokyo, the administrative center of the army's command. Although it was now almost ten years since the end of World War II and the capitulation of Japan, American presence was very visible. Typical of the rumors and false information that abound in the army, a group I was part of was told we would be sent to the Finance Building, only then to be told that we would be taken to the Tokyo Quartermaster Depot (TQMD), still in Tokyo but not downtown. Once there, we were told we would be again subject to further reassignment, possibly Korea. At all costs, I wanted to avoid Korea. Strange as it may now seem, in my legal practice, I went to Korea six times and loved it. However, at that time, shortly after the end of the Korea War, it was still quite backward. Thus, I decided to take matters into my own hands. I called the offices of *Stars and Stripes* to see if I could work on the army paper. No luck. I then decided to seek out the troop and information officer at TQMD. Luck was with me again. He needed someone to put out the base paper and arranged for the personnel office to assign me there.

I had another good deal. For the next seven-plus months, I put out the weekly base paper. I had an office with two Japanese secretaries. Putting out the paper was interesting. I made it into a four-page edition. I would write columns on the news of the week, what was going on at the base, things to do in Tokyo, and trips to take in Japan. I found a fellow soldier who was a cartoonist, and he filled the back page with a superhero-type character. I also ran a column on the news of the week. I had lots of free time, which allowed me to read through my first-year law books, which Papa sent me. My only problem occurred when I tried to eliminate the weekly column in my paper by the chaplain—a fire-and-brimstone type whose goal was to keep GIs from fraternizing with Japanese women by dramatizing all the ills that could come from that. His articles were so stupid I couldn't bear having them in my paper, even though eliminating his weekly nonsense meant I had to write more. The chaplain did not take this lying down. He went to the base commander and complained that I, an atheist (I had put no religious affiliation on my army personnel file), was undermining the religiosity of the troops. I was ordered to reinstate his column. Out of character, the generally supine officer to whom I reported backed me up, claiming this was a matter of freedom of the press. In a compromise, the chaplain's article was made biweekly. The paper was cited as the best in the area command, and I was taken to the Finance Building for a congratulatory handshake with the commanding general.

Army annoyances on the base were minimal. In the barrack, we chipped in a small amount weekly to pay Japanese helpers to make our beds, wash our clothes, and do KP. In fact, the Japanese seemed to do all the work on the base, which was the distribution point for supplies for troops in Japan, Okinawa, and Korea. To give you an idea, I wrote a column "Know Your Job," which led me to the various departments on the base to talk to the officer in charge. When I went to the division, which maybe was in charge of distributing toilet paper to bases throughout the Far East, I asked the major in command to describe how his office functioned. He yelled to a Japanese, "Hey, Haiko, tell the GI what we do." Like everyone else at TQMD, he relied on the Japanese, who did the work. It should have been clear to me then that the Japanese had the drive and work ethic to become an economic powerhouse.

We would fall out in the morning for reveille, and then I went to my office. After four or five in the afternoon, we went off duty and were free to leave the base. Weekends we were free. Maybe two or three times we had a parade, but that was the extent of bothersome army routine.

In typical curious and adventurous fashion, I took advantage of being in Japan by going frequently into Tokyo and also doing some traveling. Looking back, I wish I had done more, but I had limited money and didn't want to use any leave time, which if not taken could reduce my two years of service.

I loved Tokyo. It was now almost ten years since the end of the war, and the city, which had been badly destroyed, was well on the way to rebuilding and to economic renewal. It was a fairly short train ride into the heart of downtown, the Ginza. I still remember the enormous excitement I had the first time I ventured downtown by myself. It was all so different, strange, and fascinating. Besides the sights of a society that still looked as if it was in the nineteenth century, I realized the city also had a smell from the many street food vendors.

The first night, I went to Central Tokyo by shuttle service the army operated. I was excited. I walked around the Ginza and took in the sights and smells of an Asian city. It was so thrilling to be there. But when I had to return, I couldn't remember the station I had to get off to return to my base. But I did remember that it had been the naval headquarters of the Japanese during the war and was able to get directions from the hustlers who would gather around you in the Ginza, the central entertainment district, where most GIs hung out.

I was not back to the Ginza and Japan until December 2015, when I went with my friend Sylvia. She was invited to speak at the opening of a film about the Japanese consul Chiune Sugihara in Lithuania who saved her family and many thousands of Jews by giving out visas to

Japan against orders. This time, I was put up in great luxury in the Peninsula Hotel opposite the Imperial Palace. Yet another great change that sixty years had brought—as had the Ginza, now glittering with high-rise hotels and department stores. I wish that on this visit I could have generated the same excitement as my first visit in January 1955. But time and age made a difference. The thrill and enjoyments of youth are not easy to duplicate in old age.

A fellow soldier (George Nash) and I visited many parts of Tokyo. We chose some of these by picking them from areas the army said were off-limits. This designation was not because of vice. This existed mainly in the Ginza, which was not a prohibited site. The off-limits areas reflected the army's bureaucracy. As these were neighborhoods not known to the army, they were just routinely considered not safe. These were off the beaten path. There you still found old-style Japanese houses made of wood and cardboard. As we meandered, we would come across small, exquisite Japanese gardens. You could feel serenity among the carefully cultivated plants and statues of Buddha. Many nights, I went to a coffee shop, which played recorded classical music. There I became acquainted with Antonín Dvořák's string quartet, *American Quartet*, which I often asked to be played, not out of homesickness but because it is so beautiful. I also went to Kabuki plays, street festivals, and department stores. I just enjoyed walking to take in life. This has always been one way that I enjoy cities. I still find pleasure in walking through cities, even streets and neighborhoods in New York that I know so well.

George and I spent a couple of weekends in the countryside at local inns. At one, I remember we were in the hot bath, which all hotels seemed to have, buck naked in the Japanese fashion when a father came with his children, all, of course, naked. Once in, he indicated the water wasn't hot enough, though it was almost scalding. He turned on the hot water, and shortly we were forced out, looking like boiled lobsters while the Japanese family enjoyed what they considered a properly heated public bath.

I visited Yokohama, which was only an hour away, a number of times and spent a long weekend visiting Kobe and Kyoto. The latter has beautiful temples and shrines, some built in the thirteenth century. My biggest adventure was climbing Mount Fuji with one of my army colleagues. The climb started in the evening. It was July and too hot to climb during the day. We began on horseback but did most of the mountain on foot. There were huts along the way, and at one we stopped for a couple of hours of sleep. The aim is to get to the top to see the sunrise. As the mountain is covered with volcanic ash, which is very slippery, you have to follow paths that have a spine of rock to give more solid footing. There were many hikers, as this climb is also a religious expression. It was like navigating Times Square on a warm Saturday night. We did make it for the sunrise. The top was a disappointment. The entire caldera is ringed with food stalls. Trash was just thrown into the caldera. It is one of the three mountains I cherish most. So I climbed one. I tried to climb the Matterhorn (described later) and failed, and I only climbed Mount Everest in my dreams. The way down proved difficult, as we took the wrong spine/trail going down and had to traverse by sliding through the ash to find the path down to our starting point.

I made some contacts in Tokyo with locals, other than my secretaries, who were very sweet and managed some English. They would never step out of the office with me for fear that they would be viewed as my girlfriends. I did become quite friendly with one of my secretaries. After I left the army, we corresponded for a few years. Through my sister-in-law Hope, I met a professor at University of Tokyo. I also became acquainted with a student at Tokyo University and went out with him a few times and met some of his friends. He was a star pitcher for Tokyo University's baseball team. I went to a game of what was then the Japanese major league. As a Yankee fan, I found the level minor league. Yet there are now quite a few Japanese baseball players excelling in the Major Leagues.

All in all, my time in Japan was a great experience.

The army allowed me up to three months' early release to go back to school. I reapplied to Harvard Law for admission as a second-year student, which was granted. With that in hand, I was ordered released toward the end of July. However, with army inefficiency, I went to the camp to be shipped back to the States, only to be returned to TQMD after a few days. I was so near to being out, and the closer it came, the more the army grinded on me. Finally, in the middle of August, my departure actually occurred. I dreaded the thought of another troop ship crossing. It happened that one of my fellow GIs at TQMD told me he had a friend who processed returnees at the dispatch camp. He said he could arrange air travel, which was available for a few. He asked for seventy-five dollars for this. Whether I did not have the money (it may have been more than my monthly pay) or cheapness (it was also illegal), I refused to pay him. But he had given me the name of his friend, the arranger. I looked him up when I got to the dispatch camp and said I had talked with his buddy at TQMD, implying but not stating that I had paid the seventy-five dollars. This was before the days of easy communication, and I assume he was unable to check whether I had paid up. A couple of nights later, I was awakened in the middle of the night and told to get ready to fly back to the US. A final piece of good fortune. The flight to San Francisco was nice. It was a propeller plane, so we stopped in Hawaii and were taken off the plane for lunch. In San Francisco, I managed to get a flight to New York courtesy of the army, as I was to report to Camp Kilmer in New Jersey to be discharged. And there, my release occurred. By the middle of August 1955, I was a civilian and back in New York.

Maybe it was not a wasted twenty-one months. I had a lot of interesting experiences and benefited from being out of the bubble of Swarthmore and Harvard.

# CHAPTER 5

# 1955–1956: BECOMING A LAWYER

My return to Harvard Law as a second-year student was a relief and exciting after the dull intellectual twenty-one months in the army. I found a good room near the law school. I applied myself to my studies fairly well. Of my three years at Harvard Law, it was in my second year I received my best marks, unlike my disappointing first year. I was in the top quarter of my class. I don't remember whether I was enthused by my studies, but I was more conscientious.

Financially, it was not as difficult as my first year. I now had the GI Bill and received a loan from Harvard. I also had odd jobs. One was in the library of the divinity school. For pay, I became a subject of psychoanalytic/brain studies at Harvard Medical School. After one that involved getting electric shocks when I gave certain answers to questions, I stopped being a guinea pig. I worked as an usher at the Harvard-Yale football game (known as "The Game"). So I managed to get through the year without eating baked beans for weeks, as I did in my first year.

My social life was messy. I had become very attached to Helene Ferranti (Smith). She had asked to marry me in a letter while I was in the army, which I did not respond to and wasn't ready for. Whether because of my nonresponse or what had probably happened to many GIs when overseas, she had developed another relationship. I had looked forward to reinstating our relationship, which had started in Swarthmore (she was two years behind me). I didn't admit it to myself, but I was very attached to her. I had looked forward to an intimate relationship. It was more than a disappointment when, except for a few times as she vacillated between my replacement heartthrob and me, she chose the latter. I didn't take it well. I was quite distressed and behaved foolishly and badly with her. We had a final break, and for more than fifty years, we had no contact. I knew she was in the Boston area and found her through the Swarthmore alumni office in 2006. I then saw her occasionally when I went up to Wellesley. She joined us at the annual reunions I arranged with Swarthmore friends starting in 2010. We are now friends, have gone to Swarthmore together, gotten together in New York and Boston, and remain in touch by email.

My Swarthmore friend David Deacon was still in Cambridge. I hung out with him (a very interesting and appealing person but not a good influence) and some other Swarthmoreans. I visited my friend Robert Ammerman, who was getting his PhD in philosophy at Brown University. He graduated with me from Swarthmore and has remained a lifelong friend. I also developed some friends at law school who I still see. On occasions, I would leave Cambridge to be with Papa and Elsa. They had moved to Washington Heights, where so many German and Austrian refugees had settled, not to be part of the refugee community but because the move at that time was a step up from the West Side.

To find summer employment in 1956, my law school classmate and lifelong friend, Daniel Vock, joined me to find a summer job in Martha's Vineyard. We bicycled all over to find a restaurant that would hire us. No luck. Then my friend from the army, Carmen Seminara, arranged for me to be hired as a correspondent for the *Bangor Daily Commercial*. This was a daily that had existed for more than a century but had fallen on hard times.

Howard Hughes had bought it some years before with the sole purpose of defeating a Republican Maine senator, Ralph Owen Brewster. When this was accomplished, he got rid of the paper. It still had a life (barely) and a few loyal readers. Carmen, somehow, had ended up there as an advertising manager. The paper was a mess. The editor was an alcoholic, and the publisher was out of his depth. His main engagement was to tell the staff to buy at certain stores Coca-Cola to please advertisers. I was not a crusading front-page correspondent. I covered such stories as car accidents, meetings of the Rotary Club, and church bake sales.

Carmen had rented a cabin in the woods for us. We had a lively summer because he was so much fun to be with, as I noted in my description of our time together in Fort Sheridan when in the army. On occasions, we would go to Bar Harbor in the evening. One weekend, we went to Montreal. It was not a bad time. But after about a month, I had enough. I visited the Friedlanders and my parents, who were spending some time on Monhegan Island off the coast of Maine. Then I returned to New York.

I was determined to go to the Democratic National Convention (Democratic Convention, the Convention), which in August 1956 was held in Chicago. I needed money to do that. I found a job at the Brillo factory in Brooklyn and worked there for two weeks. It was an onerous work. My job was to stand at a table and, as Brillo pads came off a conveyor belt, to put them into the boxes that went to retail stores. We had two fifteen-minute breaks in an eight-hour workday. At times, I was also assigned to shovel soap into a big vat. I figured that during a workday, I must have shoveled twelve tons. On two occasions, I agreed to work a double shift. Not easy. I saw firsthand what poorly paid, low-scale work was like. But I made the money I needed.

I went to the Convention. Papa was there covering it for his Austrian and German papers. We stayed at the Piers. I loved being at the Convention.

I didn't have a pass to get into the auditorium and spent most of the day hanging out in the *New York Post* space. (It was then a progressive paper, unlike today.) It was enjoyable being there with Papa and to discuss the day's events. There was a contest between Adlai Stevenson and then New York governor W. Averell Harriman. I was a Stevenson enthusiast since my work for him in 1952. He readily won the nomination. Estes Kefauver won the vice presidential nomination after besting John F. Kennedy (JFK) in an open vote. This was the first and maybe last time that the presidential nominee did not pick the vice president candidate and left it to the Convention. This was one thing that made Stevenson so special in my eyes and that led others to consider him weak and vacillating. Although JFK lost, it projected him into the national scene and was the start of his becoming president when he defeated Richard Nixon in 1960.

On the last night of the Convention, I wrangled a pass to sit in the gallery. It was all so exciting for me. After the final gavel fell, I managed to get on the floor and ogled Carmine DeSapio, the New York Democratic boss, who led the Harriman effort. In 1960 when I became a district leader, I would meet with DeSapio as a member of the New York County executive committee. I also campaigned with Harriman when he ran for reelection as governor of New York. I have a photo that shows me taking him and Mayor Robert F. Wagner on a tour of slum housing. But that is getting ahead of the story. It is, however, appropriate to note that forty years later, I was at the Democratic Convention in Chicago as a delegate for Bill Clinton. Then I had the admittance to the Convention hall, sat among the delegates, and was invited to parties and special events. But it lacked the excitement of being a hanger-on in 1956. That is what time and age do.

# CHAPTER 6

# 1957: OUT OF ACADEMIA AND FINDING MY WAY

My third year at Harvard Law went well, though studying was now a bore. Most third-year law students find the final year a drag. I shared an apartment with Daniel Vock and two others. We often cooked at our place. It worked out well. My social life was less chaotic than in my previous year. I had a job for a while doing research for the legal office of Raytheon. I did not do as well academically as in my second year but ended up in about the top third of my class. I started interviewing for positions with law firms with no offers. I was back in New York when graduation exercises were held in June. I returned to Cambridge to be part of the colorful and traditional Harvard commencement and proudly received my diploma in 1957.

In New York, I stayed at the apartment of Papa and Elsa, who were in Europe. Hope was finishing her PhD at Radcliffe. Henry had also graduated in 1957 from Columbia Law School. We both took a bar exam review course to pass the New York Bar exam. This was essential for Henry and me since we graduated from national law schools, which did not focus on New York law. I also tried to get interviews at law firms. I must have visited up to ten without receiving much attention. There were two or possibly three problems. First, 1957 was the beginning of a recession. There was not much hiring occurring. And unlike now, when law firms stock up with many current law school graduates, law firms were nowhere near the size they are now. Secondly, I was a diffident interviewee. Whether it was a lack of confidence or not feeling comfortable in the interviews, I did not sell myself. Thirdly, there was still anti-Semitism. When I interviewed at one of the established Wall Street firms (that was where the most prestigious firms were then, known as white-shoe firms), the hiring partner took me aside, thinking he was helpful, and gave me the names of the larger Jewish firms that he said would make more sense for me. In any event, I received no job offers.

At the end of the summer, I took the bar exam. I thought I did not do well. Much to my surprise and joy, I found I had passed. In those days, you found out if you passed by reading the *New York Times*, which printed the names of those passing. By that time, I already had a job.

The other part of my summer was going to parties and out on the town with Carmen Seminara. For the third time in my life, he played an important role. Carmen and friends had rented a penthouse apartment at 244 Riverside Drive. There were frequent parties. Good fun. It was one such party that I took Nina to, and our relationship really started. But more of that later.

Toward the end of the summer and after the bar exam, I became anxious about getting a job. I went to Washington and interviewed with the IRS. Then I heard there was an opening at the Office of the General Counsel of the Navy in New York. This time I was hired. It was not my ideal job. The offices were in the Bush Terminal in Brooklyn. Reviewing contracts for the navy was not very stimulating. The head of the office and his chief assistant were Harvard Law graduates. While the work atmosphere was pleasant, this was not the job I wanted, and I soon started to look around to find a position with a law firm.

I found a position with Demov & Morris, a small real estate firm, located on West Fortieth Street and Broadway. It was not a pleasant place to work. Gene Morris, the co-senior partner, was an aggressive lawyer who was quite good at getting clients. He was the uncle of Roy Cohn and father of Dick Morris, the political consultant who played a big role in helping Bill Clinton to be reelected. *Time* magazine, at about the time of the Democratic Convention in August 1996, had a cover with a picture of Clinton, showing Dick whispering into his ear. Dick popped up at various times in my political life. I ran into him at the 1996 Convention, and he told me not to worry about Clinton winning because he had written such a terrific acceptance speech for Clinton. One or two days later, he was dismissed after a story appeared in one of the scandal magazines that he frequented prostitutes and had a foot fetish. Soon he became a Clinton hater who often appeared on *Fox News* to disparage the Clintons. He wrote a book about why Hillary Clinton would lose in 2016. He is a disgusting person, but sadly, his call was correct.

The atmosphere at Demov & Morris was hypercharged. There were some able lawyers. I don't know how many legal skills I picked up. Like most recent graduates, I was very raw. Much of my work revolved around the rent laws—not a scintillating area. Gene was not easy to work for. After I left and entered the Legislature, he reached out to me a few times and invited me to speak at a Bar Association's event he chaired.

I did not see a future there and looked around again. By answering an ad in the *Law Journal*, I was hired by Benjamin, Galton & Robbins. These were three Columbia Law School grads who had built up a decent practice. I was one of maybe four associates. The pay was not munificent. I think I started at $1,000 a month, though there was usually a $1,000 year-end bonus. The ambiance at the firm was much better. The work was also more stimulating. I argued my first cases and tried some minor ones in lower courts. It was there I was told by a more senior lawyer that one of the judges was known to be on the take. Coming out of the rarefied atmosphere of Harvard Law, I was greatly shocked. This probably was a factor in a career-long effort to insulate judges from politics by having them appointed from a small number winnowed down from a selection panel. I don't remember, whether there or at Demov & Morris, receiving much training and help to become a good lawyer. Looking back, I believe whatever legal skills I developed were mainly on my own.

# CHAPTER 7

# 1957-EARLY 1960S: BECOMING POLITICALLY ACTIVE AND GETTING MARRIED

## COMING TOGETHER WITH NINA—THROUGH THE EARLY 1960S

I barely knew Nina at Swarthmore. She was one year behind me. My impression then and later was that she was prominent and highly considered as an activist in campus affairs. We probably knew each other well enough to say hi but had no joint activities or occasions together. That is except one. When Nina and I began dating in 1957, and as we compared Swarthmore experiences, we told each other about a seminar we both took. As we named who else was in what we thought were different seminars, we remembered the other students, except for each other. We then realized we were in the same seminar, but neither of us remembered the other was there too. Obviously, we did not impress each other. One factor may have been that Nina had mononucleosis during that semester and probably missed half of it while recovering at home.

After I graduated from law school and during the summer of 1957, through Henry, I became active in a local Democratic group that was challenging the regular Democratic organization. This was the Riverside Democrats, about which there will be much more later on. Nina had already become active in the club. She was the assistant to Henry, who was the campaign manager. So we met there again as Swarthmoreans and now fellow campaign workers. We quickly became friendly.

Once more, Carmen Seminara played a role in my life. He was then working in the advertising department of the *New York World-Telegram*, one of the numerous New York City papers that have disappeared. (When I grew up in New York, there were at least seven papers. Some were morning editions, and others came out in the afternoon.) Carmen was giving one of his frequent parties and urged me and others to bring dates. The party may already have started, and there were few women (or girls as we called them then). I decided to call Nina at the Riverside Democrats and invited her to come join us. She did. It was our first date. Soon others followed. We became not just fellow alumni and coworkers but a couple. I knew this had become serious and that she had strong feelings for me when she waited up for me into the early hours of the morning on primary night, September 10, 1957. I was a poll watcher in maybe the toughest election district in the primary in which we elected our candidate, Bill Ryan, as Democratic district leader, defeating the regulars who were part of Tammany Hall. Though the polls closed at 10:00 p.m., the ballots, and at that time they were all paper ballots, had to be counted. As we argued over the ballots, which required that you place a check in a box, it became later and later. I already knew from a messenger that Ryan had won, but the counting continued its slow and argumentative way. Maybe at about 2:00 a.m. we finally finished, and I went to the club headquarters at 250 West 106th Street. Most had left, but there was Nina, obviously waiting for me. I took her home.

Our courtship then accelerated. Nina was a year younger than me. She had grown up in New York. She was youthful and exuded charm and competence and was active in many organizations. She struck me as a doer and achiever. This was attractive to me, as I had the example of my father and my mother, then my father with Elsa and Henry with Hope. These were all strong women who created an identity through their work and associations. It then seemed to me, uncertain of my future and being insecure, that whatever happened, I could still shine like the moon in the glow of Nina's sun. We enjoyed being together and the many common interests we had, not the least our involvement in the Riverside Democrats.

My plan was to settle in New York City—I never thought of any other place—and move to the Village. Papa and Elsa had moved into an apartment in Elmhurst, Queens in 1957. Queens was developing at that time, and many high-rise residences were opening. They wanted a bigger and better apartment, and Queens then seemed a step up for them. Papa had started to work at the UN, and it was an easier trip from Queens than from Washington Heights. I briefly stayed with them. Papa made it clear that he wanted me to get my own place. For a few weeks, I camped out in an apartment around West Seventy-Second Street with a not so reputable couple of friends of Carmen. With Nina's help, I relocated to West 112th Street between Broadway and Amsterdam and began over half a century as a West Sider. The apartment was a small one bedroom with a living room and a manageable kitchen.

Nina lived with her parents, Leah and George Williams, at 423 West 119th Street, on the corner of Amsterdam. Leah was a pianist who gave lessons in her home. George was an accountant and had his own practice. I was invited to meet them. Then I took Nina to meet Papa and Elsa as our courtship moved on. Our coming together was very easy. There were no traumas—no breakups and tearful reunions. We were a happy couple. One day, in February 1958, I proposed. At that time, it was still the male who was expected to take the initiative. Nina readily accepted. At a dinner at her parents', I asked for their blessing for our marriage. I was nervous.

Looking back, it seemed very traditional. George and Leah were invited to dinner by Papa and Elsa. I think all were happy that we had become engaged. There were numerous dinners given for us by Nina's relatives, and we enjoyed the attention our engagement received. Planning for the wedding was less enjoyable since, being not that traditional, I wanted a less formal affair than Nina and her parents planned. The wedding was held on July 3, 1958, at the Women's Faculty Club at Columbia University.

In the meantime, Nina and I had found an apartment at 250 West 104th Street. It was not easy getting an apartment. What one did in those days, when most apartments were still under rent control and there were few vacancies, was that on Saturday night you waited for the *Sunday Times* to be delivered to the newsstands so you could get the paper's real estate section early, to get a jump on other apartment searchers. The next day, you contacted the agent. What we probably did was go to the apartment and see if the superintendent would help out after receiving a nice tip. We only wanted to live in the Riverside Democrats area. Fortunately, we succeeded in renting an apartment on the fourth floor of this building between Broadway and West End with an elevator. It was a two-bedroom apartment with a decent-sized kitchen. I moved in before the wedding. The night before the wedding, I was so nervous that I did what at that time was my way to calm down: I went to a movie.

The wedding was quite traditional. Nina wore a white wedding gown. I refused to wear a tuxedo. Nina's family insisted that we be married by a rabbi. But there was the barest of religious service and certainly not the groom stepping on a glass to break it, as is traditional in many Jewish weddings. When I think of Kathy and Andrew's wedding on a dock and Josh and Kyra's wedding on a beach in Hawaii, how different and according to tradition was my and Nina's union. We had friends join the many family members. Nina had a large family. We invited some of the new friends we had made at the Riverside Democrats, recognizing how important the club had become in our lives. We had become such a notable couple before we married that we were constantly asked at club functions when we were going to get married, to our embarrassment. Henry was my best man, and Nina had Susan Derecskey (she was then still Brady), or was it Elinor Siner (Meiss), as her attendant. There was a band and dancing, and it turned into a fun and joyous evening once the formality of the wedding was over. The next day, Nina and I went to spend the July Fourth weekend in a cabin she had found for us to rent in Taghkanic State Park. Her father lent us his car. When we drive to the family vacation home, the Farm as we called it, on the Taconic Parkway and pass that park, I always think of Nina and me at that cabin a long time ago. We moved into our apartment as a happily married couple.

At the end of the weekend. I went back to my job at the Office of the General Counsel of the Navy. Nina took a summer job as a secretary so we would have money for the honeymoon we intended to spend in Europe. We went there in the middle of August. We had found a cheap charter flight that was advertised for unmarried couples. No one checked our status. We flew to London. This was pre-jet flight, and the plane landed in Newfoundland and Dublin before making it to London. In London, we stayed with Christoph and Gail Cornaro. Christoph Cornaro was in the Austrian foreign service and was stationed at the embassy in London. Christoph, an Austrian, was an exchange student at Swarthmore for one year. Gail Cornaro (MacMahon) was Nina's roommate at the college. They fell in love, and when Gail's family (both her parents were distinguished professors at Columbia and Vassar, respectively) took Gail to Europe in the summer of 1953, Christoph followed them. The parents did not approve of their daughter marrying an Austrian, and a Catholic at that. But marry they did. Christoph had a very successful career in the Austrian diplomatic corps, and over the years we remained friends and saw each other, usually in Vienna. I trekked with him in the Himalayas in 1989 when he was ambassador to India, and I visited them in New Delhi. Now in 1958, it was my first time in London, and as an Anglophile, it was meaningful for me to be there. I have always cherished how the British stood up to Hitler alone in the difficult years of 1940–41.

From London, we flew to Brussels to spend time with Nina's friend Jacqueline, who she knew from the Girl Scout jubilee she attended in 1947 with Susan Derecskey. They took us to the World's Fair, which that year was held in Brussels. We stayed with them in their very nice house in Charleroi. Then we flew to Vienna. As on my visit in 1951, we were treated royally by my mother's friends. I introduced Nina to Vienna, which, in the seven years since I had been there, when there were still many bombed-out buildings, had greatly recovered.

From Vienna, we went by train to Innsbruck. My mother's close friend, Rosa Jochmann, took us to the station. When we were not looking, she changed our third-class ticket to a sleeper for the overnight trip. (I don't know why it was an overnighter since the trip today takes no more than four or five hours, but probably the rail system had not yet been rebuilt.) In Innsbruck, we stayed at the Patscherkofel, a hotel you had to reach by cable car. It was perched high on one side of the Inn Valley. The next day, we had a lovely hike. As we ate our lunch looking east, we heard these loud booms. Suddenly we realized it was thunder, and as we turned around, we saw these menacing black clouds coming toward us. We raced back to our hotel just in time to avoid a fierce mountain storm. Next, we crossed the valley to stay with Christoph and Gail, who were staying in a lovely cottage Christoph's family owned.

From Innsbruck, we took a train down the Po Valley to Siena, Italy. It's a scenic trip, and Nina made drawings of the various churches we saw. Our destination was Siena. It was Nina's idea to attend Palio di Siena, the famous horse race, which is held twice annually and attracts hordes of tourists. The race is run in the town square and involves a lot of skullduggery between the various neighborhoods that race against one another. Next we went to Rome by train. We had, I think, three days in Rome. On the second day, as we attended a performance of *Aida* at the outdoor Baths of Caracalla, Nina had a bad stomach upset. I took her to the first aid room, where she was found to be suffering from food poisoning. Nina was laid up the next day, and I went through the Roman Forum in midday in a blazing sun. To the saying "Only mad dogs and Englishman go out in the midday sun," you can add "and Franz." By evening, Nina was pretty well recovered, but that night it was my turn to suffer from food poisoning. We identified a restaurant by the Spanish Steps as the source of our illness. Weak and not fully recovered, I went with Nina to the Vatican the next day. We adored the Sistine Chapel and bought pictures of some of the prophets and the Delphic Sibyl, which I so love, and which on our return we framed and hung in our bedroom.

Then it was by plane to Zürich. George and Leah were having their first European trip, and we met them there. We went boating on the Lake Zürich. It was also in Zürich that we bought our Scandinavian teak furniture, which my daughter's family still uses. With that, our idyllic honeymoon ended, and it was back to New York via London. There was a bit of excitement on the return flight. The plane developed mechanical problems and had to land in Goose Bay. We overnighted while we waited for a replacement plane, which finally came and brought us safely back. It was a lovely honeymoon and a great trip, mainly planned and arranged by Nina. I don't know how she found the hotels and pensions we stayed at, as well as plane and train schedules, at a time before the internet.

Back in New York, we had, as I look back, one of the best times of our lives together. Nina was teaching at Joan of Arc, a middle school on Ninety-Third Street on the West Side. She enjoyed teaching and would tell me stories about her favorite students, who always seemed to be the worst behaved. I went back to practice law at the Office of the General

Counsel of the Navy and then soon switched to the law firm Demov & Morris, which was not a good experience, and then to Benjamin, Galton & Robbins, which was much better. The Riverside Democrats became a focus for us but more so for me.

Nina became very active in a fledgling teacher's union, the United Federation of Teachers (UFT), which soon became the sole representative for all NYC public school teachers. She was brought into the union by Alice Marsh, who was Nina's mentor at her school. Alice gave a wedding shower for Nina, which I was allowed to attend. Alice was the UFT's representative and lobbyist when I was in the Legislature. It was somewhat uncomfortable when I voted against the UFT position on bills. But I had the union's support in my campaigns, as I was probably immunized by Nina's role (except when it mattered, in my 1974 primary for the Senate, as it could not risk alienating the leader of the Senate Democrats against whom I was running, which I understood). Nina was on the Union's executive board and was well considered as a promising member. She became friendly with the leaders, first Charles Cogan and then Al Shanker. The latter particularly became an important political figure in NYC (especially during the city's financial crisis 1975 when the public unions helped save the city from default) and later nationally when he became president of the AFT. We socialized with both and attended Al's wedding reception. Nina became the chair of the social committee. One of the first events she arranged was to have me buy two hundred tickets (was it that many? certainly a large number) to the Bolshoi Ballet's first appearance in the US. The ballet was *Romeo and Juliet* at the old Metropolitan Opera House. I got them by being first in line on the day tickets went on sale. She made them available to union members. She also arranged socials where she played the guitar and sang her favorite ballads.

But her most significant contribution was as the chair of the union's annual luncheon. This became a big affair and required much organizing, as the luncheon itself was preceded by panels on educational issues. As the union grew, Nina presided over luncheons where US Secretary of Labor Arthur Goldberg, Supreme Court Justice William Douglas, and Dr. Martin Luther King Jr. (MLK) were the recipients of an award and main speakers. There is an iconic family picture of Nina pinning a flower on MLK's jacket. She started the luncheons that are now a major two-day affair attended by most local public officials. Nina was important in the union and her work and relationships were important for me as I basked in her prominence. In those days, not having the confidence and security I developed later, I saw much of my value in being married to this achieving woman. It is a pattern in my family to marry strong women. My mother with my father, my father and Elsa, Hope for Henry, and now Nina and me. Strong, achieving women were my model.

In November 1960, just before Election Day between JFK and Nixon, the union called a strike. It was a bold move, as the union did not have nearly the membership and strength it later acquired. Nina was very much involved. She was the area coordinator for some ten or so schools. This meant organizing picketing by teachers from these schools. Her area of responsibility was East Harlem schools, and the union membership there was weak. The night before the strike, she came home in the middle of the night and woke me up to ask if I would agree to be a picketer at a school in East Harlem where she had been unable to get any of the school's teachers to agree to picket. She told me that if I appeared there and some of the teachers saw me picketing, maybe one or more would join me. I went to the school very early before teachers arrived, looking for some support. The principal stood on the steps and kept on loudly announcing that I was not from the school and pointedly added, "Children, pay no attention to him." A few teachers lingered as they passed me but then decided under the stern look of the principal to enter the school. I was left alone and felt very lonely. Then a police car pulled up, and a big police captain got out and approached me rapidly. *What now?* I thought. The captain came up to me and said in a pleading voice, "Sir, will you allow the milk delivery to be made?" Greatly relieved and now feeling powerful, I replied, "No problem." The strike turned into a success, and the union bloomed in membership. Nina also attended at least two American Federation of Teachers conferences, one was in Minneapolis, and the other in Chicago. She came back full of enthusiasm and stories. After the first, when we shortly thereafter went to the White Mountains, it took two days of hiking for her to give me a full description.

Nina and I, in those years, had an active social life. George and Leah insisted that we have dinner with them at least once a week. These were always at Butler Hall, where the Terrace restaurant is now, on the top floor of the Columbia building at West 119th Street and Morningside Drive. Like many events and activities with George, these always followed the same script. For instance, whenever we left their house and came out into the courtyard of their building, at 423 West 120th Street, we always had to wave to them as they waved back from the window of their apartment. George would have been deeply insulted if you failed to do that. Christmas Eve was the goose dinner at Papa and Elsa's. A grand affair. In the middle 1960s, Papa and Elsa moved to 2 Tudor City so he could be nearer to the UN. His work there had increased. He was now the head of *Deutsche Presse-Agentur (DPA)*, a German news agency (like the Associated Press). We frequently had dinner with him and Elsa, and Papa would take us to the UN dining room. Eventually, they moved to 180 Riverside Drive.

Henry and Hope lived near us on West End Avenue. Henry had completed Columbia Law School the same year I graduated from Harvard Law School in 1957. Henry practiced law, and Hope became a professor at Teachers College, where she has had a very successful career. Amazingly, she is still teaching full-time in 2020. They had three sons, Frederick (Fred), William (Willy), and James (Jamie). We saw them often, and over the years, there were many family get-togethers in New York, at the

Farm, and at their lovely vacation home in Elmore, Vermont. We went skiing together in Stowe and for many years attended their New Year's celebration in Vermont. All three boys now live in California, pursuing successful careers.

We also had frequent get-togethers with Nina's younger sister, Sally. She married Lester Rosenbaum, another lawyer in the family. They settled in Yorktown Heights, where we visited them. A major event was their Rosh Hashanah dinners, with Lester presiding. Sally and Lester had four children, Dan, Raymond (Ray), Steven, and Miriam. Only Dan still lives near New York City. The others have migrated to the west, just like Henry and Hope's sons.

Nina and I ate out quite a bit. Went to movies. We became enthusiasts for ballet and opera. In spite of having minimal resources, we got subscriptions to the Metropolitan Opera and to a series of various ballet companies promoted by Sol Hurok. (He was the one who brought the Bolshoi to the States and also the Moiseyev Dancers, whom we much enjoyed.) At the ballet, at the end of the performance, we would often go from our balcony seats to the orchestra to join the hardcore enthusiasts who, by their clapping, compelled more curtain calls. Nina and I were at the last performance given at the old Metropolitan Opera House in 1964, which featured highlights from popular pieces and famed performers. We hosted parties, especially at year's end, with a big Glögg Party, a spicy mulled wine, for fifty or more invitees. The nicest memories I have are of our reading books in bed about mountain climbing while I brushed her hair before turning off.

In the summer of 1959, I brought Nina to the White Mountains. She loved hiking and these mountains as much as I did. We climbed all over the range and stayed in many of the huts. Our base was Pinkham Notch. Out of many reminiscences, I will pull out this one. We had stayed at Carter Notch and the next day climbed over the Wildcats. We suddenly realized it was getting late in the afternoon, and we had to be back at Pinkham for the six o'clock dinner. In those days, you had to be on time. We decided to go straight down one of the ski slopes. These were overgrown with tall weeds and rocks. It proved a tough run down. We made it in time for dinner, but both of us had some knee problems thereafter. Throughout the year, we took some weekend trips borrowing George's car. Our life was good, and we were happy.

In the summer of 1960, Nina and I went to the White Mountains again. This time we hiked to the Crawford Notch hut and did the traverse from Lakes of the Cloud Hut to the Zealand Falls Hut in one strenuous day. From there, we went to Nantucket. Nina had been there before when she painted its classic New England church. That summer was our first visit to Elinor Siner (Meiss), a close school friend of Nina's, at her family's summer place in Elizabethtown. It was our first experience with the Adirondacks, and it was then that our interest in the North Country took hold. We spent a weekend hiking and were joined by Elinor's brother Michael. Sadly, he committed suicide a few years later.

The year 1960 was good and busy, with the election of Bill Ryan to Congress, my political activities, Nina's work in the teachers' union, the successful strike, and the campaign and election of JFK. The early 1960s continued well. In 1961, I ran and won as district leader (more of that in the next chapter). It was a hectic time. Politics took much of my attention and activity.

Nina and I participated in the Civil Rights Movement. We attended meetings that sought to change the New York law on housing discrimination. Unbelievable as it now seems, discrimination in housing was not prohibited in New York state. We worked with some very able people. Soon thereafter, New York extended civil rights protection by prohibiting discrimination in housing. We also participated in sit-ins at a White Castle franchise restaurant in the Bronx that refused to serve Negroes—the typical term for Black people at that time.

And there were interludes from our busy life. At year's end 1960, Nina and I went to Pinkham Notch to ski the Wildcat Ski Area, almost opposite Pinkham Notch. I had skied a few times. In 1947, I went to the Western Adirondacks with Elsa to one of the few ski areas in the east. It had a rope tow. Elsa was yanked getting on, fell, and broke her leg. We went to a local doctor who didn't x-ray it and said it was a sprain. Later she had to have surgery to reset the leg. On our 1960 ski trip, it was Nina who broke her leg. We were taking snowplow lessons on what seemed like an almost flat area. It looked as if Nina just sat down. But she had trouble standing up and was taken down in a sled by the ski patrol. We were advised to go to the hospital in Berlin, New Hampshire. An x-ray showed the break. The leg was put into a cast. We stayed on for a couple more days. Nina was quite cheerful. The Friedlander's were staying nearby at The Glen House, and I skied some novice slopes with them. Nina's cast allowed her to walk, and she continued teaching and many of her activities.

We both made skiing part of our life. On weekends, we went on ski bus tours to Stowe, Lake Placid, Bromley, Stratton, and for the day to Hunter Mountain. Nina progressed better than I did. On one of our tours, she won the prize for most improved skier. Jumping ahead, in February 1965, we spent Washington's birthday weekend in Lake Placid skiing Whiteface. What made it memorable is that the Kennedy clan, Robert, Jackie, and a host of youngsters, were skiing there too. Robert F. Kennedy (RFK) had just been elected as New York state senator and wanted to show that he patronized New York state resorts. There was little snow, and we all competed on a couple of runs that were skiable from the midway station. At times, this meant dodging the large group of Kennedys with ski instructors whooping it down the slope. We went to Stowe with our friends Marty and Cora Rubenstein over Christmas and New Year's 1964. We rented a place in Lake Elmore, near where the Henry and Hope Leichters have their place. When we arrived, all the snow had melted. The next day, we climbed Mount Elmore. But that night it snowed, and we had some good ski days. We kept on taking lessons and slowly improved.

In the summer of 1962, Nina and I went back to the White Mountains. This had become our country place. We both were strong hikers. On our way there, we visited Bertha, Ernst, their two small children, Steve and Tom, and Babi in Augusta, Maine. What I most remember of this visit is my first try at waterskiing. As we approached the dock, I didn't let go early enough and plowed into the dock. No serious injuries. It was at about that time that I finally gave up smoking after numerous unsuccessful tries. I had smoked since around 1948.

In the summer of 1963, we traveled to Europe again. We took the cheapest airline, Icelandic Air, which then had only landing rights in Luxembourg. From there, by train, we went to Kleine Scheidegg at the base of the Jungfrau massif in Switzerland. Nina and I, in our reading of books about mountaineering, read *The White Spider* and became fascinated with the Eiger, whose north face had been considered unclimbable until it was conquered in the early 1940s. Many lives were lost trying to climb it. When we arrived on a beautiful afternoon, we saw many people on the meadow watching the mountain. There were three groups trying to climb it. We were in heaven. The next day, we walked all over the alps (meadows). It was so beautiful. The following day, we went up to the Jungfrau Joch on the railroad that cuts through the mountains and brings you on a plateau below the majestic Jungfrau. The weather had changed. It was raining and raw. In the tunnel, our train stopped, and the engineer started yelling. It turned out one of the three climbing parties was a Japanese, who wisely turned back and used an entrance low on the mountain to get into the train tunnel. So here we were in what can exaggeratedly be called a rescue. At the end of our arrival day, Nina and I looked through the hotel's telescope at the struggling Spanish climbers. The consensus was they would not make it and were doomed. It was discomforting looking at these climbers, small figures on the vast Eiger north face, knowing they would die there. Two days later, the weather turned even worse, and they perished. Much of the romance and challenge of climbing majestic peaks is gone. Nowadays, with new equipment, the Eiger north face is climbed in a day and even during previously unclimbable winters. And these days, as many as a hundred people in one day climb Everest.

In 1981, Nina and I took the family to this region as part of our European tour. I then returned to this idyllic place in 2004 when I went with my friend and former staffer Erwin Rose. His family was then in Geneva, where his wife was stationed as a foreign service officer in the embassy. We spent two days in those beautiful mountains and took the railroad up to the Jungfrau Joch—a most beautiful sight that, when I close my eyes, I can conjure up.

From Switzerland, we went to Venice. Two days there, and then to Florence where we met up with good friends of Nina's, Bernie and Goldie. Unfortunately, it was a high Catholic holiday, and all the museums were closed. We were told to go see the synagogue. When we got there, we found it was also closed. Next we went to Vienna. There we connected with Papa and Elsa. It was my first time in Vienna with my father since 1938. We visited Mauer together, where we had lived before the Anschluss. It was a most enjoyable trip.

In November 1963, we lived through the drama of JFK's assassination. Nina and I, ironically, had tickets that night to see the *Gotterdammerung*. Like all events, it was cancelled. We connected with Papa and went to meet Elsa at the West Side Airline Terminal. (One then existed at Tenth Avenue and Forty-Second Street.) I remember Elsa coming out the door with such a sad look. We had the saddest of dinners together. Like the rest of America, we lived through these days glued to our little black-and-white TV. We watched the killing of Oswald unfolding on TV and the impressive funeral of JFK. One day, we were at Hope's looking at the TV, which showed people entering the White House to pay their respects. We briefly saw Henry with Bill Ryan. Henry was then working in Washington for the Peace Corps. What a trauma this was for the US. How different might our history have been if the assassination had not happened?

The year 1964 was highlighted by our attending the Democratic Convention in Atlantic City. I had been elected a delegate for the first time. Before going, we visited Elinor in the Adirondacks again. Nina went there before me. She and Elinor picked me up at the Plattsburgh Airport. I can still see both their bright and healthy red faces from climbing the range on a beautiful, sunny day.

The Convention was a ball. I became active on behalf of the Mississippi Freedom Party, a biracial delegation that challenged the regular Dixiecrat delegation. I met with Martin Luther King, who was there to support the Mississippi Freedom delegation. We made our room available for calls to delegates. A message was left when there was no answer to please return MLK's call. During the night, we would receive calls, like one I remembered: "This is the lieutenant governor of Nevada returning MLK's call." We would politely (and sleepily) say he was out and give our message on how MLK hoped the lieutenant governor would vote to support the Mississippi Freedom Party. There was no issue about the nomination of Lyndon Johnson, then the incumbent president. The issue of who to seat from Mississippi was finally resolved with a decision to sit half of each delegation.

This was hashed out for progressive delegates like me at a meeting in a Black church. It was packed on a very hot night, with everyone fanning themselves with a fan advertising the local funeral parlor. MLK spoke on behalf of accepting the compromise, saying there are some moral issues you cannot compromise, but on this political matter, a compromise was advisable since it established that for the first time there would be Black delegates in the Mississippi delegation. Fannie Lou Hammer, another great civil rights leader, argued against accepting this compromise in an emotional address ending with: "I am tired of sitting in the back of the bus." She carried a hand vote to reject the compromise. It didn't matter, as the delegates to the Convention, not wishing to damage the election chance of LBJ against Goldwater, overwhelmingly backed the compromise.

The 1964 election was a joy as the enthusiasm for LBJ—and fear of Goldwater—was so great and the outcome so clear. I threw myself wholeheartedly into the campaign. The membership of the Riverside Democrats rose to about a thousand. That is what the 2016 election should have been. Sadly, it was not. How the country has changed. One funny event to tell. There was a rally with Johnson in Madison Square Garden. The headquarters gave me one hundred tickets to distribute. Somehow I left these on the subway. I was filled with foreboding that they might fall into the hands of who knew who, possibly anti-LBJ demonstrators or even an assassin. Sheepishly, I told the campaign the great sin I had committed. The campaign official was totally unfazed. I then realized that they had given out so many extra tickets just to be sure there were no empty seats and that these excessive tickets might not have provided any seating or access. I did keep my junior VIP seat.

We were young, energetic, full of activities, and in love. Our life was good. But shadows were beginning to appear. Nina, somewhat abruptly, quit as chair of the union's annual conference and left its executive board. She stopped playing the cello in duets with her mother, which I so encouraged. She pretty much dropped out of the Riverside Democrats and became removed from my political aspirations and life. She was initially reluctant to have children. She did not pursue with much vigor advancement in the school system. She certainly had the qualifications to become a principal or higher. One day, she told me that after having spoken to Elsa she was going to see a therapist. I was accepting but surprised. We discussed her mood and feelings, but I did not dig down sufficiently to find out what was bothering her. Looking back, I think there might have been any one or combination of factors:

1.  She may have felt I was not paying sufficient attention to her. Nina needed attention. As I became more and more engaged with the Riverside Democrats and into politics, this probably led to resentment.
2.  She may have reacted negatively to my showing so much enthusiasm for her union work and position and other out-of-the-home activities. Nina had a reaction against what she saw as having to perform to gain love. This came from her father, George. I liked him, but he was demanding while acting as if he was very accommodating. Nina felt she had to please him and achieve what he wanted to gain his love, and that created resentment. Did she see me like her father? Was she unwilling to do what I was so enthusiastic for her to do, like her union activities or playing the cello, if she felt this was a condition to have my love?
3.  Was I emotionally supportive enough? At that time, I was so focused on my career in politics and the law and spent so much time pursuing both at the same time that I probably failed to give her the companionship and support she needed.
4.  Was it the early sign of her mental illness?

Whatever it was, or maybe none of the above, there began to develop a distance between us. I don't think we noticed it. But I became disappointed with her and probably unconsciously began to feel that this was not the woman I married or the support I expected. Did she fit the role of the strong woman I had as my model? We were still seemingly happily married and did continue many activities together. But we both gave and received less support from each other. She could at times still be the activist and achiever I wanted and had married, but the bloom was off the rose.

The year 1965 was another busy one as I made my first try for public office. Also, Nina made some significant changes. But that is all for the next chapter, which is on my early political life.

# CHAPTER 8

# 1960-1967: THE POLITICAL BUG

Politics is in my genes. Not that surprising, as I am the son of Otto and Käthe Leichter. Growing up, politics were always around me—my parents' discussions, their friends, their work, and in the lessons and education they gave me. It was not just narrow political maneuvering that was their focus but the fight for social justice that they dedicated their lives to. While I sometimes wish I had measured a meaningful life less by political involvement, I have no regret that this has been such a factor in my life.

My first political event was a rally for FDR that I attended with my father during the 1944 presidential election. We sat way up in the old Madison Square Garden. FDR did not attend. He addressed the gathering by film. I was so excited and cheered and cheered. I still remember a song we sang:

> Dewey, Dewey the White House is not for you
> With your phooey straight out of the *Daily News*

My next rally was in 1948 for Henry Wallace in 1948 in Yankee Stadium. Wallace, who had been FDR's vice president from 1936 to 1944, ran as a progressive with support from the very left wing represented by the American Labor Party (ALP), composed in part of former and current Communists. Wallace turned out not to be a factor in the election when

Harry Truman came from behind to defeat the favored Thomas Dewey. By the time of the election, I was at Swarthmore. There I joined a far-left group, the Young Progressives of America (YPA). It may have been on the FBI list of subversive organizations. Ostensibly we were for Wallace, but I don't remember our doing any campaigning. Mainly, if we did anything, it was to meet infrequently and just talk. By the time of the election, I had cooled on Wallace and was delighted at Truman's triumph.

Other than keeping up with the news, I didn't do anything of a political nature at Swarthmore. There was a fairly active student organization, part of a national student movement, the National Student Association. Nina was quite active in it and went to one or more conventions. I might have thought it too mainstream. For whatever reason, I was uninterested.

At Harvard Law School, in both 1952 and 1956, I actively campaigned for Adlai Stevenson. I was cochair of the Harvard campaign in 1956. I remember being more involved in 1952 when we had meetings with Arthur Schlessinger at his home. I went to the airport to cheer Stevenson when he came to Boston and attended a big rally for him. Maybe we had more hope in a victory in 1952. In 1956, Eisenhower was a shoo-in. I described above my going to the Democratic Convention in 1956 in Chicago. Clearly, I was already becoming a political junkie.

My involvement in local politics came in 1957 after I graduated from law school. Henry was then already engaged with a recently formed local political club, the Riverside Democrats, which became so important in my life, not just in my political future but because Nina and I connected there. The club had been formed by mostly young professionals, Columbia graduate students, and some professors, many of whom were veterans and were idealistic about changing not just their community but the world. Quite a few had been angered by the lukewarm support the Democratic organization in New York had given to Stevenson in his presidential campaign in 1956. They were also offended by the patronage-driven Democratic organization in New York City, known as Tammany Hall. Tammany had a long history and at times was very powerful in choosing governors and mayors. Illustrative is one of the mayors Tammany made. When asked whom he would appoint as police commissioner, he said, "They haven't told me yet."

Over the years, there were numerous reform efforts in the city. Fiorello La Guardia was elected by campaigning against Tammany. By 1957, it was less powerful and was basically just the Democratic organization for Manhattan. It still controlled local and judicial elections. Tammany had a ruling body called the Executive Committee, composed of one man and one woman who were chosen from each Assembly district in Manhattan in the Democratic primaries. Some of these had been divided up, but Morningside Heights and the West Side north of Ninety-Sixth Street to 125th Street and from Central Park to Riverside Drive was just one district, the 7 AD, and thus elected only one man and one woman as district leaders.

The Riverside Democrats in 1957 chose William F. Ryan (Bill) and Shirley Kaye as their district leadership slate to challenge the old line "regulars" (as they liked to call themselves) who were associated with Tammany Hall. Bill was the driving force in creating the Riverside Democrats. He was then a lawyer working in the district attorney's office. He was a dynamic campaigner and drove himself and everyone around him. He became my mentor and was a good friend to both Henry and me. Kaye had been prominent in some community issues but did not play much of a role.

I threw myself into the campaign with vigor and passion. The Riverside Democrats became like a second home. This was the springboard of my political career. But with satisfaction, there is also regret and guilt. The club was Henry's. He introduced me to it and encouraged my activism.

As always, he was the supportive brother. Yet what happened is that I pushed him aside, not consciously, but my activism was so strong that it supplanted him. In retrospect, I should have tried to make my political fortune in another political club where I would not be in competition with my brother. It turned out to be the classic case of the younger brother pushing out the older. Henry did keep active and was elected to a party position. But as it became clear that I had become more prominent in the club, he finally gave up on politics. He never expressed any resentment or showed any hurt feelings. He always was supportive of my elections. Henry did maintain many friendships among the club's founders. He and Bill and Bill's wife, Priscilla, had a particularly strong friendship.

My first assignment was to campaign in a particularly tough election district for which the club had not found anyone. This consisted of maybe as many eighty four-story brownstones between West 106$^{th}$ and 108$^{th}$ Streets east of Amsterdam Avenue. The captain for the regulars, Verbena King, elderly and with a hunched back, had held that post for many years. Although advanced in age, she was indefatigable and knew just about everyone in her election district. But I plunged in and rang doorbells and stuffed literature under doors. I gave her competition, but she won the district in the primary. After I became district leader, I recruited her for the club, and she worked for me in my campaigns in 1961 and 1963. In fact, we became quite friendly, and I visited her a couple of times. The ability to get along and even make friends with political foes is one that has served me well.

The primary was on September 10, 1957. It had been an uphill battle. At the beginning, Ryan and Kaye were given little chance, but the enthusiasm in the club and the fact that we were generally younger and harder workers than the regulars was a factor. Mainly the campaign showed Bill's drive and political instincts. He made what became known as the "Ryan Pledge." He promised that, if elected district leader, he would neither hold any patronage position nor would he as district leader hold any elected office. This struck at the heart of Tammany, where patronage had always been the oil that kept the organization and its regular clubs functioning. Joining and becoming active in one of these clubs was the door to a possible political future and a much-coveted judgeship. A number of the district leaders also held positions as legislators and congressmen. This helped to secure their control of the local organization and avoided challenges. The Ryan Pledge emphasized our commitment to democratic procedures, and, as we emphasized, no "boss" was going to make decisions for the club's members. It was a winning platform and one that I remained committed to. Even now, some sixty years later, one still hears references to the Ryan Pledge. In the Democratic primary for district leaders on September 10, Ryan and Kaye were elected. And as I described above, while Verbena King and I argued over paper ballots (no machines then), Nina waited for me at the Riverside Democrats headquarters at 250 West 106th Street. A fateful night.

With the club now established, I became the chair of the Housing Committee. It was probably my idea. I say, immodestly, that I made something of that position. At that time in Morningside Heights and the Upper West Side, there were a large number of slum buildings. Some of these were in high-rise apartment buildings. During the war, the landlords, to meet the housing needs of Columbia students (there were also many students then serving in the Reserve Officers' Training Corps) and/or to get out of rent control, had cut up the large six-to-eight room apartments, common in the West Side, into single rooms with a common kitchen and bathroom. That is how the term SRO ("single-room occupancy," still in use) became common. By the 1950s, the students were gone, and these units were rented out to poor people—mainly minorities who could not get or afford other housing. The conditions were pretty awful. There was general overcrowding, falling plaster, filth, leaks, and so on.

I began a campaign inspecting these buildings and reporting them to the city to get the Department of Buildings to issue violations against the landlords to force improvements. I did the inspections mainly on my own. I never had any safety concerns, though three particularly bad buildings at 8, 10 and 12 West 104th Street (smaller walk-ups) often had drug users hanging out. I issued reports and wrote numerous letters to the city agency in charge. I went to court in the few instances when the city took action against the landlords to point out (when the judges allowed me to) the appalling and illegal conditions. It was partly through my efforts and a tragedy at 380 West 110th Street (now and for some years a high-class coop or condo), where a young boy was killed by a malfunctioning elevator. The tabloids called it a "slum with a view." Official attention eventually came. But not that much city action came at first. I met with city officials, spoke, harangued the landlords, and issued reports. Even though my memory, especially for numbers, is now poor, I remember the address and location of some of these buildings: 140 Claremont, 512 West 112th Street, 936 West End Avenue, 873 Broadway, the Marseilles Hotel on West 103rd Street, the particularly miserable Clendening on the corner of West 103rd Street and Amsterdam, three buildings on the corner of West 103rd Street and Broadway, which were separated by a courtyard from the apartment where Nina and I had our first home on West 104th Street. All are long since gone. Partly as a result of my efforts, but probably more because of economic factors, most of these buildings were converted back to apartments. The city tore down the Clendening and rebuilt it as public housing. Similarly, the three buildings across from our apartment became public housing.

I began to draw attention for this work. City officials in the housing area came to know me. I took Governor Harriman and Mayor Robert F. Wagner on a tour of one of the SROs. There is a photograph of me with Harriman. The Riverside Democrats, and especially Bill Ryan, appreciated my work, and I became important in the club. I also organized a West Side housing group composed of representatives from the reform clubs, which were forming on the West Side, to develop city and statewide policies. And then, in about 1961, came my first mention in the *New York Times* in an article on housing in Morningside Heights.

My activities in the club grew. I tried to be there every Monday and Thursday night, which were called "Club Nights," when the club was open to people who required help with a problem—usually housing related. This continued the tradition of the regular Democratic clubs, which for decades served as something of a resource to the poor and disadvantaged. They were then explicitly or implicitly told how to vote. At the Riverside Democrats, we did not. There were also numerous club membership meetings. I was elected a member of the board of directors, which had monthly meetings, and then president. It was very time-consuming but exciting, and I made many friends and political acquaintances.

Nina was active in the club, too, but less and less. While we did many things aside from politics—family meals, opera, ballet, movies, traveling, socializing—my focus and involvement in politics became hard for her— not that I understood it then. But as I look back, I see that she was not getting the attention she needed, and Nina needed attention. She once said to me, "I am going to put on your tombstone 'He had to go to another meeting.'" For me, I saw all this activity and being involved not just in politics but in social issues that carried on the ideals and goals of my parents. I now wanted a political life and hoped for elected office; all the activity, attention, and sense of calling boosted my ego. I had found my calling, and I grew because of it. Nina once said to me some years after we were married, "You've grown into your skin." I love that.

In 1959, Ryan and Kaye were easily reelected as district leaders. In 1960, Bill Ryan challenged the congressman from our area, Ludwig Teller, who had the support of the Tammany clubs. It was a grueling campaign, and I was up to my head in it. Ryan was indefatigable. He was confident, ambitious, and politically smart. He had the support of Eleanor Roosevelt and former governor and Senator Herbert Lehman, who had by then become the face of what was called the Reform Movement. It was composed of political clubs that had formed on the West Side, East Side, and in the Village with the same goals and purpose as the Riverside Democrats. They attracted mainly younger, left-oriented professionals and idealistic persons who despised the patronage driven Tammany clubs. In or about 1958, an umbrella organization was formed, the New Democratic Coalition. FDR, Lehman, and two other prominent Democrats became the titular heads. They were partly motivated by a rebuff at The New York State Democratic Convention in 1958 by Carmine DeSapio, then still the head of the Democratic organization in Manhattan and the most powerful Democratic state leader. FDR and Lehman had always been progressives and wanted to see a Democratic Party that expressed their views and that was not just driven by political opportunism. Both of them actively supported Ryan and Manfred "Fred" Ohrenstein, who was running for the state Senate farther south. (Fred and I served together in the state Senate for many years). Their support proved invaluable. Bill and Fred scored impressive victories in the Democratic primary. They were elected in the 1960 general election in which JFK defeated Nixon.

We held a big rally for JFK at West Eighty-Sixth Street and Broadway in the November election when he bested Nixon. Thousands, including Nina and me, waited hours for him in the rain to appear. He came because Bill Ryan sought him out and convinced him to come, though he was running late and had a rally waiting in Connecticut. The story is that Bill barged in on JFK while he was shaving and told him he was weak on the West Side, and it was indispensable that he show up when people had been waiting for hours in the rain. There was initially some opposition to JFK in areas like the West Side from liberals who were uncomfortable about his father's pro-German sentiment as ambassador to Great Britain and JFK's reluctance as a senator to oppose McCarthy.

Bill was easily elected in November and inducted into Congress in January 1961. In accordance with the Ryan Pledge, he resigned as district leader. I became the candidate of the Riverside Democrats in an election to replace him held by the whole county committee of the Assembly district. Each election district elected three committee persons. I had some opposition but won easily. This was my first official position. As district leader, I was part of the executive committee of the Democratic Party in Manhattan that was still called Tammany Hall. I had meetings with DeSapio and was something of a disruptive force in the meetings of the executive committee, which had a tradition of being a rubber stamp for the county leader, then DeSapio.

The year 1961 was a turning point for the reform movement. By then, Manhattan had a number of clubs that had defeated the regular organization (as we referred to the Tammany clubs) and had elected district leaders. But these were still a minority in the executive committee of Tammany Hall. The year 1961 also held a mayoral election and Democratic primary for district leaders. The mayor was Wagner. He had been elected twice with backing from the regular county leaders of the five boroughs. These leaders decided to dump Wagner, who had become in their view too independent. Wagner turned to the reform movement for support, mainly to Eleanor and Lehman, who were both very popular, especially with the Jewish voters who comprised a significant segment of the primary voters. The regulars put up New York State Comptroller Arthur Levitt, who was a decent person. The primary for Wagner was run as a fight against the bosses.

There were a number of meetings with Wagner at Gracie Mansion (the mayor's residence at East Eighty-Eighth Street and East End Avenue). I remember one that Bill Ryan and I had with him where he was over an hour late while we waited on the veranda of Gracie Mansion, looking at the East River. There were also meetings of the reform leaders with Lehman at his duplex home at 820 Park Avenue. (Lehman came from the banking family that created Lehman Brothers and was quite wealthy. It was Lehman Brothers' collapse that was the beginning of the Great Recession of 2008, when it was no longer owned and run by the Lehmans.) Before the executive committee of the Democratic Party in Manhattan was to meet to rubber-stamp DeSapio's decision to support Levitt, we met at Lehman's home to decide how the reform leaders, as a minority in the executive committee, would make a case for Wagner. Eugenia "Gene" Flatow, who was my female coleader, and I, who were purists, felt that Wagner had come to the reform for support just out of opportunism. We told Lehman we could not support Wagner but would abstain. Lehman was shocked. But he was such a decent person that he just asked us for our reason and accepted our position. I even called some people, urging them to run as the reform candidate for mayor. But that was hopeless.

The excellent political columnist Murray Kempton (who covered me on occasion) wrote: "The Reform Movement looked all over to find a candidate to run against Mayor Wagner. They finally found him. His name is Robert Wagner." In the end, we all endorsed and campaigned for Wagner.

Flatow and I also had to be elected as district leaders in this 1961 primary. This was the election when I ran against the person who I believe was on the draft board that drafted me into the army. It was a campaign that consumed my full energy when, at the same time, I continued my legal work. There were rallies and many evenings on a sound truck. We would park the truck at a Broadway intersection and try to draw a crowd. This often proved difficult. The way to get a crowd was to have someone stop and start shouting questions or yell opposing views. That attracted some passerby, who would stop, and a small crowd would gather. When no passerby would stimulate a crowd, we used a shill to shout out questions. We had at least one rally with Lehman present. Our primary and election eve rallies were always on the southwest corner of Broadway and West 110th Street.

Wagner won the primary for the Democratic nomination, and I was elected district leader for the first time by the Democratic voters in the Assembly district. The reformers won their primaries throughout Manhattan, and DeSapio was defeated for his district leadership in the Village. Tammany and the bosses were mainly gone.

Now the reformers were the Manhattan Democratic organization. There were a lot of issues that came up. Much of this, as I look back, was silly squabbling. We had innumerable meetings, which tended to run into the early hours of the next day. When we were kicked out of whatever space we were meeting in, we would go to the restaurant Mamma Leone's, which was owned by the family of Robert Wechsler, one of our colleagues, and was part of the successful restaurant chain of Restaurant Associates. There at least our debates were leavened with pastries. DeSapio was replaced as county leader by Edward "Eddie" N. Costikyan. He was not part of the reform movement but was still independent from the old line DeSapio's organization. He was picked by Wagner, who secured the votes of the remaining so-called old-line district leaders since the reformers would not vote for him, insisting the new county leader had to be one of their own. The old-line district leaders, after having opposed Wagner, jumped at the opportunity to get into his good graces by supporting Costikyan, Wagner's choice. We reformers were so stuck in our idealism and sense of purity that we were not politically astute by trying to work with Wagner, who as mayor was still powerful. We kept our virginity but failed to be effective and gain at least some of our goals. I was chosen by the reform leaders to be one of their representatives on a leadership group of five district leaders. I was in the minority and quickly assumed the role of maverick, which I embraced in the Legislature later on. Looking back at this time before I became a legislator, I cringe at how obstreperous I was. The reformers, led in part by me, were hostile to new county leader Costikyan, which led him to rely on the few old-line district leaders who had escaped the 1961 bloodbath. How different I would manage it now. But I was filled with the idealism, certitude, and the hot blood of youth.

There were many meetings, political battles, and events to attend in addition to being district leader and taking care of the club, now that Ryan was in Washington. I still had my legal job. My absorption and time in politics was a problem for Nina, as I realized later. She never complained or tried to hold me back. Bor nor was she like Priscilla Ryan, who was so involved in Ryan's political life and worked hard for him.

Politically, 1962, for me, was defined by a hard primary Ryan faced. Because of reapportionment, his district was combined with the district of the congressman who represented Northern Manhattan. The district was drawn to favor Ryan's opponent, Congressman Herbert Zelenko, who came from a strong Tammany club. Ryan now had to run in a district unlike his initial West Side district, which went only to 125th Street to one that now went up through West Harlem to Washington Heights and Inwood. It was a grueling campaign and one that I was intimately involved in, as I was now a close confidant of Ryan. I did a lot of street campaigning and canvassing of buildings. There were three significant occurrences for me during the campaign.

I was chosen to ask Eleanor if she would endorse Ryan. Her endorsement was essential. A meeting was arranged for me to see her at her townhouse on I believe East Sixty-Eighth Street. I was told I could not be late and was limited to ten minutes. Quite punctually, I was ushered in. She greeted me warmly and asked about my family and me. Then she explained she was packing to take her uncle to Hyde Park. I could see the ten minutes passing by without my getting to ask her to support Ryan. Finally, she said, "Well, Mr. Leichter, you have something to tell or ask me." I blurted out that I and the reform movement hoped she would endorse Ryan in his primary. She answered, "Of course I will endorse Bill." I then asked if she could campaign with him, and she said she would try. And that was it. Meeting this great person, who has been rightly called the First Lady of the World, was amazing.

She kept her word and spent an afternoon campaigning for Bill Ryan. I was asked, together with Ohrenstein, who was then a state senator, to pick her up for campaign stops with Ryan. I don't know why, but we picked her up on West Eighty-Sixth Street and Columbus. I have a picture taken of Eleanor and me on West Eighty-Sixth Street. Unfortunately, the camera at that moment caught her scratching her nose. I was never able to use that photo in campaign literature, as she looked as if she was picking her nose. One of my campaign aides suggested I white out her arm in the photo, but then people looking at the photo would think her right arm had been amputated.

Ohrenstein and I had a convertible with a sound system to take her campaigning. As we drove north, a driver passing by and recognizing her yelled, "Go back to Russia." (She had her critics from the right and had recently had a spat with Cardinal Francis Spellman by supporting a strike of Catholic cemetery workers.) Ohrenstein, who was sitting in the back seat with me, stupidly said, "Wasn't that awful what that person just shouted," and foolishly repeated it for her. Sitting in the front seat and with poor hearing, she had not heard it. All she understood from Ohrenstein words was "Russia." She turned and said to Ohrenstein, "Oh! You are going to visit Russia. How wonderful."

The rally with her was stunning. As we drove through Harlem with the sound truck blaring that Eleanor Roosevelt was coming through, people rushed out of their houses to try to touch her and cheer her. A big rally was scheduled outside J. Hood Wright Park at West 176th Street and

Fort Washington Avenue, where in later years I campaigned for senator and then as senator, I frequently visited. The area then was still primarily home to Jewish immigrants. They loved Eleanor. The rally was big. We helped her stand in the back seat of the convertible as she urged support for Ryan. Considering her age and that she was then dying, this was such an act of commitment to the progressive policies to which she dedicated her life. Incredible for her to campaign for a congressman when she was a worldwide figure, the most widely known and popular woman in the world, who had just played the key role in having the UN adopt the Human Rights Convention.

What an experience to be with this great person. I am only sorry that I didn't thank her during my time with her for saving my life by fighting her husband and the State Department to get visas for Jewish refugees as World War II started, of which my family received. But when I saw her, I didn't know of her role with the visas.

Eleanor died later that year.

The other distinctive memory of the Ryan campaign in 1962 was with Lehman. He was then in his early eighties but still involved in politics. He had a longtime aide, Julius Edelstein, who was very influential with Lehman. I and others thought he controlled Lehman. Edelstein was very smart and a prodigious worker. He played a major role in forming the reform movement's umbrella organization. In his later years, we became quite friendly, and I would visit him in his home and have him over for brunch. But then in 1962, he was first deputy mayor to Wagner. He really ran the day-to-day affairs of the city. We wanted Lehman's endorsement for Ryan, but Edelstein discouraged him. I think he had never warmed to Ryan, and Wagner didn't want Ryan to win, seeing him as a possible political rival. Lehman, however, proved us wrong in believing Edelstein totally controlled him and decided to endorse Ryan. I am not sure who convinced him, but it probably was Eleanor. What weighed on him was that Ryan's opponent had voted for a bill allowing the postal service to open mail it deemed subversive or pornographic. Only two members of the House voted against that bill: Ryan and John Lindsay, then a Republican, who represented the East Side, known as the silk-stocking district. Lindsay later became a two-term mayor of New York. Lehman, knowing of Edelstein's opposition, didn't want to ask him to write the endorsement letter for Ryan, as he would have normally done. Lehman, who was in his eighties, struggled with this. Twice he called me to help him write the letter. I was flattered and, of course, delighted to help write the endorsement letter, which was widely distributed.

The endorsement of FDR and Lehman was decisive, as was our very active campaigning. Ryan won. He now represented an area not dissimilar from what became my Senate district.

In 1963, I was reelected as district leader. By then, the opposition club had folded, and this time, the election was a breeze. As district leader, I had to be sure the club functioned well. There were many political meetings and gatherings besides being active in community events. Around this time, there opened up a vacancy for a local judgeship. As district leader of the largest part of the judicial district, I could have chosen or had a major say in who would be elected to this judgeship. Instead, following my belief that judges should not be chosen by politicians, I got all the district leaders in the district to appoint a nonpartisan committee of representatives from bar associations and law deans to recommend a candidate, whom we agreed to support. Their recommendation was Martin Stecher. He still had a primary challenge, but being able to point out that he was selected not by political bosses but by a distinguished panel, he won easily. Stecher and his wife, Judy, became lifelong friends. I was able some years later to help him move up to the New York State Supreme Court. Using panels to screen candidates for judgeships has been widely accepted in Manhattan, though instead of being a panel that selects the nominee, panels now report out usually three names, opening up the process to some political maneuvering. Later, when in the Legislature, I worked to depoliticize the selection of judges by not having judges elected but chosen by the governor, from a limited list produced by, a qualified selection committee. I was not successful, though judges for the state's court of appeals, the highest judicial tribunal, are chosen in this manner under a constitutional amendment that Governor Hugh Carey initiated.

Not facing an old Tammany Club anymore, the opposition came from the radical left. One such group was the Columbia Tenants organization. This was actually a bogus outfit that claimed a thousand members but consisted of only a handful under the sway of Bruce Bailey. He was a thug who attacked me as a tool of landlords. One incident where I faced him down comes to mind. There had been a terrible crime in which a young Black boy was mutilated. Bailey put out a leaflet accusing me of being complicit in this crime and attacked the police for not having prevented this crime. He announced a march on the local police station, the Twenty-Fourth Precinct on West One Hundredth Street. Fearful of violence, I went there. Bailey had gathered some thirty supporters, including women with small children. He had a bullhorn and was accusing the police of responsibility for this awful incident by failing to protect the community. He was ranting about taking over the station. There was a line of cops standing outside. I was afraid that someone might throw a missile at the cops, who might respond with force, and people would be injured. I went into the precinct and convinced the commanding officer to come out and say to the crowd that the police would be relentless in finding the culprit of this crime. This calmed down the crowd, which then dispersed to Bailey's disappointment. Not long afterward, Bailey's head was found in a garbage can. The story is that he had been involved with some drug gangs.

Around this time, I got to know J. Raymond Jones, known as the "Harlem Fox", who was a district leader from part of Harlem. Walter White, in his book on the 1960 election, called him the smartest politician in the US. He certainly outsmarted me more than once and in what became an early political embarrassment.

Jones was then one of three male district leaders in the council district, which also comprised the Senate district. This was before "one person one vote," and each of those districts held three Assembly districts. Jones wanted to run for the council and asked for the support of the Riverside Democrats. I agreed to support him if he would support our choice if a vacancy occurred in the state Senate seat. He agreed. With our support, Jones was elected to the council. Jones was a masterful politician in back rooms but unused to local street campaigning. He was very dignified and proud, and it was difficult for me as I took him street campaigning to get him to stop strangers and shake their hands.

Shortly thereafter, a vacancy occurred for the Senate when the incumbent received a judgeship. Since this was mainly a Black area, we need to have an African American candidate. The problem was that the Riverside Club had few Blacks. One, who would have been a strong candidate, had unfortunately died young. Popular in the club was an African American, a very decent, fine person, Noel Ellison. He ran a dry cleaning store on Manhattan Avenue. It was hard to oppose him even though he lacked the background and prominence to sell to the public. I saw that it was going to be difficult to get him elected. I happened to be in Washington and met Ryan outside the floor of the House of Representatives, which was then in session. I argued with him at such length and so vociferously that Noel was not a candidate we could put forward that one of the pages, thinking Ryan was being harangued by an obstreperous constituent, came and said, "Mr. Ryan, you are needed in the chamber." Ryan was extremely loyal and insisted on the club choosing Ellison, which it did. I reluctantly went along.

Since the seat was being filled at a special election, the selection of the Democratic candidate would be made by the local Democratic committee, which consisted of persons chosen from each election district within the Senate district, maybe two hundred people. We organized for the meeting to make sure every one of our committee persons attended or gave a proxy. True to his word, Jones said he would support Ellison but that all his committee members would not. He put up as a candidate Constance Baker Motley, a distinguished civil rights lawyer with the NAACP (National Association for the Advancement of Colored People). We won narrowly nominating Ellison in the county committee vote. But then our proxies were challenged, and a lawsuit was started challenging Ellison's designation. We were fighting for an unknown person who ran a dry cleaning store against a Black woman who was distinguished for her civil rights background. It became worse when it was reported in the press that Ellison had misdemeanor convictions for taking numbers. (Before the lottery, there was a flourishing business, mainly in minority areas, of betting on numbers, and it was not uncommon for stores like Ellison's to serve as a place where people left their bets. He was a middleman.)

We were in the impossible situation of fighting for a candidate (the *Daily News* heralded with the headline: "A candidate and his record") who seemed so unqualified against a prominent civil rights attorney. Then Wagner got involved. He met with Ellison and then me and urged us to withdraw Ellison. This, we finally had to do in court. The Riverside Democrats, Ryan, and I looked pretty dumb. I did have the foresight to see we were taking a precarious path in backing Ellison, but I didn't have the political courage or political strength to keep us from making this mistake.

Motley became the senator. She later briefly was borough president of Manhattan until nominated and confirmed for the federal district court.

The main feature of 1964 was the Democratic Convention at Atlantic City, which I described in the previous chapter. In that year, Nina and I did much socializing including with our families. It was a good year. It may have been in 1964 or 1965 that Papa and Elsa moved to Tudor City to be closer to the UN. He was in his elements working as the DPA correspondent at the UN. He took us out for dinner quite often, and we would also meet him at the UN. These later years were the best ones of his life. He had a prominent position, doing what he loved best as a journalist, happy with Elsa and his growing family, and recognized in Germany and Austria, which he visited at least once every year. He took the lead in organizing a UN Correspondents Association, of which he was the president, and through the association raised money to bring an African journalist to the UN for a yearlong apprenticeship.

The year 1965 turned out to be quite turbulent. It was an election year for the mayor and city offices. There was also a special election for the Legislature. Because of legal battles over the redistricting lines, which were drawn after the 1960 census, there were elections for the Legislature in 1964, 1965, and 1966. In 1965, the court ordered another reapportionment, which required the Legislature to increase the Assembly to 165 members from its customary 150. A district was created that ran from around 110th Street to 145th Street on the West Side. It was a majority Black district. I nevertheless decided to run for the Assembly in that district. At the same time, Flatow, my district coleader, decided to run for a council position at large in Manhattan, an Ryan threw his hat into the ring for the Democratic nomination for mayor. The Riverside Democrats were overstretched, and most of the efforts by the club leaders went into the Ryan campaign.

It was not a good decision that I made to run in a Black-majority district. It was the height of the Civil Rights Movement, and as a white person running in a district designated to be represented by a Black, I was at a distinct disadvantage. Again, the Harlem Fox bested me. He put up as a candidate a young Harlem attorney, David Dinkins. Jones was committed to advancing Black political participation and power and did this by putting up well-qualified candidates who would also appeal to non-Blacks.

I did not run a good campaign. First, I had little money. Second, my reform appeal did not mean much in that district. I don't remember whether I even sent out a district-wide mailing. Jones very cleverly sent out a district-wide mailing letter for Dinkins by Kenneth Clark, the famed African American psychologist whose work was cited by the Supreme Court in the epoch-making *Brown v. Board of Education*. My later good friend Steve Solarz was attending Columbia Graduate School and lived in the district at that time. Based on the letter, he later told me he voted for Dinkins. This was some years before we met and became good friends. He enjoyed teasing me about his vote.

So I lost the primary—not bad, but it was a blow. This was the only election I ever lost, although I withdrew from a few election campaigns after putting my foot in the water and, in one case, throwing my hat into the ring. But that is for later. I still was on the ballot for November, as the Liberal Party had given me its nomination. But the Democratic nomination assured victory for Dinkins. I recovered from the loss and did not lose my appetite for politics and commitment to my policy goals.

One unexpected result is that Dinkins and I got to know each other and became politically good friends. We played tennis and had an occasional meal together. In the primary, I ran together with Basil Paterson, a candidate for the state Senate, with whom I developed a good relationship over many years. Paterson was very accomplished and became significant in New York politics. His son, David, served with me in the Senate and became governor—not very successfully. Paterson was one member of what was called the "Gang of Four," Black leaders in Harlem and influential in New York City and beyond. Besides Paterson, it included Dinkins, Charley Rangel, and Percy Sutton. I had many contacts and associations with them, and our relationships were friendly and good. Mostly, we were on the same side. Dinkins went on to become the first African American elected as mayor of New York.

In the 1965 primaries, besides my loss, Flatow lost, and so did Ryan. We had bitten off much more than we could chew. Yet I continued to be politically engaged throughout 1966 and 1967. I had found my calling.

# CHAPTER 9

# THE FAMILY: THE CHILDREN ARRIVE, BUYING A FARM, MY FATHER DIES

Around 1965, Nina and I decided we were ready for children. The problem was we could not conceive. I went to a urologist. He found that I had a low sperm count. He attributed this to what he called a varicose seal. He scheduled me for an operation. It was probably late 1965. It was performed in Mount Sinai. I might have been there for three or four days. It worked. Nina soon became pregnant. At the end of year, we went skiing to Mount Tremblant in the Laurentians, north of Montreal. Nina did not ski, as she was pregnant. Every day after skiing, she prepared a hot bath for me. It was lovely. But soon thereafter, she had a miscarriage. We were, nevertheless, encouraged. And soon she became pregnant again in April 1966.

The summer of 1966, we took another trip to Europe. We flew to Frankfurt and visited the Derecskeys in Bonn. Charles (Papi) was then working for *Time* magazine as one of its German correspondents. Their son, named Charles but always called Chaz, had recently been born, and he joined us at dinner in his bassinet. The first evening, Papi prepared pheasant under glass. What good friends throughout many years. Nina stayed with Susan and Papi while I flew to Berlin, which my wanderlust drove me to see. The city was then still divided by the wall.

I visited East Berlin and had to go through Checkpoint Charlie, which as an American I was allowed to do. It was the only time on my many passes through immigration that the official spent what seemed an eternity looking at my passport photo and then me. Finally, he waved me on. I took a taxi whose driver showed me where Hitler's chancellery and bunker had been. That part of Berlin was still in ruins. In other parts of East Berlin, I saw how gray it looked, Stalinesque drab residential blocks with no visible life on the streets. I had him take me to one of the few restaurants that catered to visitors. If my memory does not play tricks on me, it was called Moscow. There were many Russian officers at the tables. There was not anything to do afterward, so I returned to West Berlin.

To get there, I had to take the U-Bahn, Berlin's transit system, which was the only transportation system between the two parts of Berlin available to Westerners and those with special passes. This was all part of the controls to keep East Berliners from fleeing to the West. When I went to buy a UBahn ticket for my return, I sought to pay with my D-Mark's, West Berlin's currency, as I had no East German marks. The agent, an elderly woman, said she could only accept East German currency. I had been told at the border I need not change my currency. What was I to do? In my most authoritative voice, I said, "der offizier an die grenze hat mir gesagt sie müssen Ostdeutsche geld nehmen" (the officer at the border told me you must accept West German money). That was a lie. But what was I to do? There were no taxis. If I tried to walk back, I would probably be arrested as a spy. The agent looked utterly terrified. I refused to leave the counter. Then someone tapped me on the shoulder and said he would exchange my money. And back to the West I went instead of rotting in an East German jail.

I met Nina in Munich. From there, we went to Vienna to meet Papa and Elsa. It was of course special to be with them in Vienna. Many get-togethers with family friends like Rosa Jochmann. One day with friends of Elsa we drove to Austria's highest mountain. Nina decided not join us. My father was disappointed and said to me, "Pregnancy is not a sickness." Papa could be quite outspoken. Funny what one remembers. I recollect that when I got back, Nina told me she had been to the Hotel Sacher, one of Vienna's most famous hotels, and had the best omelet she ever tasted. I am a bit uncertain where Nina then went as I visited Paris. Possibly she went to visit the Cornaros in their summer place overlooking Innsbruck. I know I was in Paris alone until she joined me. My love affair with Paris continued. Then back to the States. Nina never joined in my love for Paris. I think it felt to her as if I was visiting a former mistress.

Nina's pregnancy went well. She attended birthing classes. I was a sissy and declined to be present at the birth and did not attend classes with her. It was at that time not as customary as it is now for the husband/partner to be present. Nina continued working until her sixth month. The board of education then had a policy that women must not be in the classroom when they were very visibly pregnant. How silly.

On Sunday, January 15, Nina's water broke early in the morning. We called her obstetrician, an excellent doctor. I took a quick shower and for the first time gave serious thoughts about the sex of the baby. This was before you could find out the sex while still in uterus. If available, I am not sure we would have done it. For maybe the first time, I seriously thought, *What if the baby is a girl?* Off we went to Mount Sinai. The first thing that greeted us as we went to the delivery room floor was a big sign: Welcome to Super Sunday. It was the first Super Bowl. Nina went off to be prepared, and I went downstairs to wait. And wait and wait I did. As things went so slowly, I was able to visit Nina in the delivery room. She was having contractions but not that seriously. It happened that Nina's mother, was hospitalized there at the same time. It was the first sign of the illness that led to Leah's death. I went to see her and also hoped to watch some of the Super Bowl. Between visiting Nina, her mother, waiting in the lobby, and walking the halls, I caught some of the game.

In the early evening, I was informed that it was unlikely the birth would occur that night and that I should go home. I was quite nervous and concerned. When I arrived home, I played Beethoven's Symphony No. 3, the *Eroica*, to which I am most emotionally connected of all his symphonies. Did I sleep that night? Early next morning, I returned to Mount Sinai. Still no baby. Later that that morning, or was it early afternoon, the decision was made to have a C-section for the delivery. It was a breach baby. Instead of the head being the first part, out it was the feet. We knew of this problem, and Nina had gone during her pregnancy to have the baby turned around. It didn't last, and this baby did not want to leave the comfort of the womb and face the harsh world.

After nearly forty-eight hours in the delivery room, Kathy was born. Mother and child were doing well. I had my first glimpse of Kathy as she was wheeled from the delivery room to the room for the newly born. I saw her with a tuft of black hair and seem to remember her turning her head to look at me, which, of course, could not have happened. Exciting. Kathy was brought to Nina, who was in a private room. There she held baby Kathy. George came with Leah, who was still hospitalized but could leave her bed. I went home with great relief, joy, and maybe a sense of greater responsibility. Once home, I played the *Der Rosenkavalier* opera. Papa and Elsa were in Curaçao. I sent them a telegram: "Katherine Leichter is born." There was never a question that if the baby was a girl, she would be named after my mother.

Nina was in the hospital for I think three days, unlike today when mother and baby are pushed out after what I believe is one day. Then we took

Kathy home in a little box the hospital gave us. That was her bed for at least a month. We had prepared a room in our apartment for her. Nina nursed Kathy. After a week, we took her out for the first time in a fancy baby carriage we had received from someone whose baby had outgrown it. I filmed the event on an 8-millimeter camera. It was exciting to be new parents and to hold and watch baby Kathy. Nina did not return to work during the year.

Throughout, my life in law and politics continued.

In the summer of 1967, with baby Kathy, we visited Elinor Siner (Meiss) on a Massachusetts shore. Elinor later married Joel Siner, a doctor and Swarthmore grad. From there, we went to the White Mountains for a couple of days. One day, we got one of the Pinkham Notch hut people to watch Kathy in her bassinet while we went off hiking. Up we went Lion's Head, and passing on the summit, we went around the rim of Tuckerman Ravine and down Boott Spur. We considered Tuckerman Ravine beneath us. So this was Kathy's introduction to the White Mountains. From there, we went to Augusta, Maine, where the Friedlanders lived. Babi had died in the meantime.

At the end of the year, we visited the Henry/Hope Leichters in Vermont. That was the first time we joined Henry and Hope's New Year's Eve ritual. This included melting lead, which was then put into cold water and projected on a screen to create fantastic images. It was followed by Henry's split pea soup with ham and champagne. As 1968 dawned, Nina and I went skiing at Stowe while Willy babysat Kathy.

Kathy brought us much joy. I have memories of her development. Sitting up, smiling, crawling (which she did with great alacrity), her first steps, her first birthday party—for which I cooked a beef goulash for the many Williams and Leichter family members who attended. We were doing well.

In the summer of 1968, we decided with the Derecskeys to rent a bungalow on Fire Island for July and August. They were back from Paris, and Papi was now stationed in New York. Later he switched to work for IBM, writing speeches and working in the publicity department. By then, Nina was pregnant again. We found a place in Fair Harbor, where we had a very simple two-bedroom house. Susan was often not there during the week, as she went back to help Papi write his stories. On the weekends, we were all together. Many parties. Henry and Hope were on the island for two weeks. Even though they bought their place in Lake Elmore, Vermont, they liked Fire Island so much that for a few years they arranged Fire Island visits in the summer. There were so many West Siders on the island, for instance the Kovners, which made it impossible for me to walk on the beach without someone who knew me engaging me in a political discussion. Fire Island, without its cars and the great beaches on the ocean side and with the bay on the other side for easy swimming, boating, digging clams, and so on, was a lovely experience and great for little kids. Kathy, then a year and half, could play on the beach with the many children who were around, as well as the Derecskeys' son, Chaz, her senior by four months.

I stayed only on weekends. I would arrive Friday night, taking the Long Island Rail Road to Babylon and then a shared taxi ride to the ferry. Before boarding the ferry, I would buy some delicious Manhattan clam chowder to bring to Nina and the Derecskeys and sometimes shrimp to eat as the ferry crossed to the island. To greet me, Nina would be at the dock with Kathy sitting in a red cart, which every family seemed to have to transport suitcases, food, and so forth. Sometimes she would bring me a martini. The concerns and involvement of my political and legal life would melt away. It was a fun summer. At the end, as we left, Nina took the iconic photo of Kathy sitting with Chaz in the little red cart, which I framed and kept at our vacation home. I look at it with joy and longing for days past. We were then anticipating the birth of our next child. It was a good summer.

The summer of 1968, and actually throughout the year, I was engaged in another attempt to be elected to the Legislature. I would fill Nina in on developments while taking long walks on the beach. I don't think the question came up whether I should do this. I think for both of us, maybe not for her, it seemed there was no question. I regret now that we did not have a serious discussion about how this would affect our life together. (More on my election in the next chapter.)

The pregnancy went well. My main recollection is Nina waking up frequently at night to chew on Tums. Four days after I was elected in the general election to my first public office, the Assembly, Josh came to us on November 8. It was a much easier birth. This went more traditionally. While Nina was in the delivery room, I was downstairs reading and pacing with other nervous dads. Then the call came late in the evening, or maybe it was sometimes after midnight, on the eighth. I had taken Nina to the Hospital on the seventh. The message came that it was a baby boy. I don't think I wanted a child of one sex more than another. I was just relieved that mother and baby were well.

I first saw Josh in his little box among numerous babies. Unlike Kathy, he had no hair. He was not that distinguishable from all the babies around him. I did have a scare. I overheard nurses conversing and one saying something about a problem with the Leichter boy. I finally reached the obstetrician, or maybe the pediatrician. I was assured there was no serious problem, just some congestion in the lungs, which I understand is not unusual with newly born babies. Josh was fine. I don't know when we decided on the name Joshua, but it was some days after he was born. Again, there was a happy scene in Nina's room as the family greeted the new member.

When I took Nina to Mount Sinai for the delivery, we called on Henry to stay with Kathy. It was already nighttime, and Kathy was in her crib.

As Henry recounted it, when we left to go to Mount Sinai Hospital and Kathy was alone with Henry, she greeted him by throwing up. Did she sense how her life would change? She didn't then know that it would turn out great to have a brother. How did she react when we brought Josh home? Probably surprised at how little this thing was that we had told her would be her younger sibling whom she would have fun with.

Josh lived his first months in the box the hospital gave us to take him home, just as Kathy did. The box with Josh was placed on a dresser. Nina nursed him, as she had Kathy. My recollection was that he was not a fussy baby. As he became a little older and had his own crib, he would kick his feet in excitement whenever Kathy came into view. I don't think she paid him that much attention. Josh was a lovely addition. I don't have as clear a recollection of his early days as I have of Kathy's. But I believe from early on he displayed a strong sense of himself. He asserted himself to make certain he was included in our family activities, regardless of his younger age. We were happy to have two children.

At the end of 1968, I did something I am still ashamed of. I even deliberated whether I should mention it. But I have decided to be honest and reveal warts and all. I decided I had to rest up and get mentally ready for the legislative session scheduled to start at the beginning of 1969 by going to be with the Leichters in Vermont through New Year's Eve to go skiing. Nina was left alone with toddler Kathy and baby Josh. We did have a helper—Daisy—who was with us until 1974. Nina was supportive of my going—at least there was no objection. On my part, this was so middle-European male (and probably not foreign in America then) that the mother would take care of the children, and the father was free to pursue his career. When I compare this with how supportive and caring partners Josh and Andrew were in helping to raise their children, it is even more glaring how I failed Nina then.

My absences and focus on my political life were hard on Nina. She needed more companionship. She had friends and family, but she did not have the social support that made up for my absences. At one point, Elsa suggested, when Nina went to talk to her, that she should spend at least one day out of the house to be free of the kids. I would call every day I was in Albany, but it obviously did not make up for my not being the partner that she then needed. There were no objections, but it had its effect. Nina needed not just companionship. She needed attention and to be valued. As she had given up her outside involvement (even before the children were born), there was a void in her life. Sadly, I failed to see this, though I was disappointed how she had narrowed her life. My advice: do not marry someone who is into politics and holds public office. There are some spouses like Priscilla Ryan, and others who were fully involved and active in their husband's political careers. This was part of the glue that held them together. It was not the case with Nina and me.

Already some years before we had children and as I mentioned before, Nina expressed unhappiness about our relationship. She mentioned this not so much to me but to Elsa and asked her to recommend a therapist she could see. I was quite surprised when Nina told me she wanted to see someone and that she felt some unhappiness. I don't remember that we had an in-depth conversation about what was bothering her, or if she could even articulate it. There was never a clear expression that my political focus was interfering with our relationship. Maybe it was not clear to her. But clearly it was. Elsa recommended a social work colleague of hers whom she saw in the Bronx. I was asked to and visited him once. Years later, Elsa expressed regret that she had made that recommendation.

Later, in 1969, I urged Nina to return to her position as a teacher. It did seem to me that returning to teaching, which she had always enjoyed, would be fulfilling. Also, our finances were shaky. I made $7,500 annually as an assemblyman and about that much, maybe a little more, as a lawyer.

We did have Daisy, our childcare helper, who came daily. We still managed a subscription at the Metropolitan Opera and for ballet companies that Sol Hurok brought to the States. We were enthusiastic attendees. Our lives were fairly comfortable, yet we barely squeezed by and certainly did not have any savings. We could rent a bungalow on Fire Island and pay for our children to attend nursery school and then elementary school at Bank Street. Nina was accumulating a pension as a teacher, and our medical expenses were fully paid for through her position. Her salary as a teacher may have been around what I earned as a lawyer. In so many ways, it was so much easier to get by then than it is today when couples in New York City struggle with a combined income of $250,000.

Nina did return to work at Joan of Arc. Maybe around that time, or earlier, she had taken the exam to become an assistant principal. She fell a few points short of passing. I reminded her that she had much joy in teaching in our earlier years together when she loved to tell me about her students. However, I think returning to work was not as meaningful for her now as before. Was it due to the responsibilities and care for the children, my absences, or the onset of her illness? In those years, Nina, and even earlier, when she seemed enthusiastic about teaching, was ambivalent about pursuing higher positions in the school system. Maybe because she felt it was something I wanted her to do. So the woman I hitched myself to, who I thought by her achievements would provide me with support and confidence, was gone. I was now on my own in establishing my self-esteem.

In the summer of 1969, we again rented a cabin in Fair Harbor on Fire Island. The Derecskeys could not or would not join with us. Possibly they had already moved to Washington when Papi got a job with the IBM publicity department. While our lease was for the two summer months, our finances allowed us to stay only in July, and we sublet August. In that month, we took the kids to spend a week with the Siners in Elizabethtown. How did we manage the six- or seven-hour trip on a bus with two such little ones? Elinor and Joel by then had Suzanne. Elinor was very nervous when Josh, an early crawler by then, would approach Suzanne, which he did the more he was pulled away.

It was then we decided we had enough of Fire Island and that we wanted to be in the mountains. We explored New Hampshire to be near the White Mountains that we loved. But we realized it was too long a drive. Also, since I was now a New York legislator, it made sense to have a place in New York state. In September, we started checking places for sale in the Elizabethtown area to which Elinor had introduced us. Over Columbus Day weekend, we arranged visits with some real estate agents in that area and one in Tupper Lake.

I realized that if we were to have a place in the country, I would finally have to learn to drive. I was now thirty-nine years old and still had not learned to drive. When we went away on weekends, Nina did all the driving. Usually we borrowed George's car. This was inexplicable on my part and can be explained only by a mental block. I think this is the same condition that makes me so inept with technology, beyond the difficulties that people my age have. Why I had this doubt that I could drive—really a fear—is beyond my understanding. As I prepared to learn to drive, I was mentally helped and reassured that I could do this by thinking of Nina's aunts Willy and Fofi. These were two elderly women who could barely cross a street unaided but drove without any hesitation. I told myself, "If Aunts Willy and Fofi can do it, so can I." I signed up at an AAA driving course. On my first lesson driving down Broadway, I was trying to make a right turn when a taxi from the uptown lane sought to beat me, entering the same westbound street. I knew I had the right of way and sped up to beat the taxi. The car would not move. My instructor, who had control of the vehicle, had put on the brake. He told me that while I had the right of way, "Don't challenge a taxi." I knew then that my basic assertiveness would assure my becoming not only a driver but one who could make it in New York. I passed my test on the first try and now was licensed. I became a good driver and now have probably hundreds of thousands of miles under my belt.

Columbus Day weekend, we took a bus to Albany and rented a car for the drive to Elizabethtown. Daisy stayed with the kids. There we had arranged to meet our agent, Dutch Kurtenbach. The property we had arranged to show us was a beat-up house. We asked to see other places. He then took us to a large house—built in the style of so-called Adirondack camps, set into the woods, which came to play a role in our lives but which we rejected because it was not winterized. We then were shown other places, none of which appealed to us. Dutch, seemingly out of places to show us, said hopelessly, "There is an old farm for sale in Wadhams. I don't know whether this will suit you, but let's go there." I remember my first view of Wadhams as we drove on the Elizabeth-Wadhams road down the hill to Route 22. I immediately liked its rural look. When we got to the Farm, Dutch said, "I didn't advise the residents I was showing it, so I can't take you up the driveway." He then drove us to Young's Road where we had our first glimpse of the place. It immediately clicked with me.

That night, we stayed at the Cobble Hill Motel. I had trouble sleeping, as I thought of the place that would become our second home for over fifty years. The next day, we asked Dutch to arrange for us to see the house and grounds. This he did, and we had our first real look. The house was then quite different from now. There was a big shed against the kitchen, where the patio is now. The back entrance was through a fairly lengthy, unattractive porch that led into the kitchen. The shed had two floors. The bottom was for storing carriages, and the second floor was sleeping quarters for the help. The house itself was dark, as the shed blocked all light. The dining room was painted a gruesome green, and the fireplace was bricked up and painted a loud red. The ceiling was low and covered the old beams. It was not attractive. There was a grassy area in front of the house with old maples blocking off the nearby road. In the back, there was a big barn from which there stretched more than one hundred acres of farmland. I immediately saw it as the place for us. Nina was less impressed. Dutch took us up to the little hill by the house, which we ended up calling the knoll. I recollect Nina saying that this was the place on which the house should have been built. It had a great view of the mountains, the Boquet River, which flows across the street from the house, and the village of Wadhams. After we acquired the property the knoll was the place Nina and I went to have our pre-dinner martini, watching the sunset as our children romped around.

We stayed at the Hotel Marcy in Lake Placid that night. We had arranged to see a property at Tupper Lake. We decided, with some advocacy by me, to forget about Tupper Lake and see the Farm again. It was then owned by two brothers of the Lobdell family who had owned and farmed the land for over one hundred years. We met them and toured the property, including the barns. We also met their parents. We let it be known we were interested. The price was $30,000. Next day, Columbus Day 1969, we returned to New York. On the bus from Albany, Nina and I made a list of all the pros and cons. We decided to buy it. My enthusiasm had convinced Nina. We offered $27,000. At some point, negotiations broke down, and Dutch advised us there was no sale. But then we agreed to a purchase price of $27,500 with a $7,500 down payment (all we had), and the Lobdells would give us a money purchase mortgage for $20,000 at 7 percent interest. This may seem like a high interest rate now, but that was the interest rate, or even higher, at that time. We had an engineer/architect look at the place and had an Elizabethtown attorney handle the closing, which we did not attend. He represented both the Lobdells and us. This was not unusual for the area then, as he was the only attorney around. It would be an ethical no-no now. (This attorney, who then also represented the Derecskeys when they bought their place, turned out to be an addicted gambler. The story was that he came back from the Saratoga Racetrack hitchhiking without shoes, which he had bartered away. He was later disbarred.) We were now the owners of the Farm.

Washington's birthday weekend 1970, we drove up to take possession. The house had no furniture, and all that was left, as I remember, was an old nonfunctioning refrigerator in the shed and an ice-cream sign. It was a productive weekend. We bought some secondhand appliances and arranged for Clarence White to do work in the house and watch it. We also met the Brandts, neighbors, and arranged for their daughter to babysit Kathy and Josh.

Memorial Day 1970, we had our first family weekend at the Farm. Kathy was then three and Josh was just learning to walk. We excitedly told Kathy that we now had a farm. As we drove up the driveway, she looked out and said, "That's not a farm. That's not a farm." I think her view of farms was based on the children's book of *Old MacDonald Had A Farm,* and she expected to see cows, pigs, and chicken among other farm animals. As we started unloading the car, Pat Anson, our nearest neighbor, came to apologize that her horses were on our land. We told her she could keep them there. Fortunately, the big double bed for the master bedroom, a gift from Papa and Elsa, had arrived for Nina and me to sleep in. There were no shades on the windows, and the sunlight woke me up early. I looked out the west window and saw the lilac bush in full bloom. A sense of joy flooded over me.

We spent the summer of 1970 at the Farm and every summer thereafter when Nina's school year finished. We also started coming up on long weekends. Our first summer required a lot of shopping for furniture at secondhand stores. I did some painting of furniture and cleaned the old woodburning kitchen stove. We began to settle into what for years became our Farm routine. Nina was effective in getting us engaged in the local community. She made contact with numerous neighbors. She and I joined the Grange, the local farm organization, (the initiation took a whole day and included a lot of mumble jumble). We would go to the Grange's potluck suppers. We shopped for supplies at the local Agway store run by Tom Spaulding and became friendly with his family and had them for dinner. Josh and their son Dean became playmates. We hosted numerous dinners. In 1971, we connected with Herb and Denise Scheinberg through my colleague Oliver Koppell. We became fast friends. Herb was a distinguished doctor at Montefiore Hospital and the developer for the treatment of Wilson's disease, a neurological condition. Denise, among other attributes, was an accomplished horseback rider and a gardener whose vegetables invariably won the blue ribbon at the annual Essex County Fair in Westport. We saw one another often. Herb had a little movie theater at the beautiful place they owned in Lewis and would show Charlie Chaplin movies. I played tennis with Herb on the courts outside the social center in Elizabethtown. The center was run by Bob and Carol Harsh, and they too became friends, whom we still visit when we are at the Farm. We connected with Atea Ring so the children could take riding lessons. Kathy became a rider. And then we acquired the horses from Pat Anson, and bought a pony, Phoebe, from Atea.

In 1971, Nina had the idea of entering the children's guinea pigs at the Essex County Fair. This initially perplexed the fair's management, as they had to decide whether they should be entered with the pigs or the fowls. It was the latter. Kathy and Josh garnered numerous ribbons, as well as for their collections of odd items like railroad spikes. The Farm became an essential part of our lives. Nina was the driving force and the arranger. The significant role it played in our lives we owe to her.

And then something else happened in 1970. Before we could spend the summer there, because school had not ended, we arranged for the Derecskeys to use the Farm for a week. We had told them about the camp we had seen on Cobble Hill Lane. On their return, they told us they had a surprise for us. They had bought the Cobble Hill place. Now the summers were also filled with our close friends, Papi, Susan, and their kids. Particularly during the week when I was in the city, Nina and Susan spent much time together, and Kathy and Josh had playmates in Chaz and Tom, their second child.

Our life at the Farm was so rich and important to our family. At year's end, we would go on our land and chop down a pine tree. We then decorated it. The final decoration was an angel that I placed at the top. Did we become Christians? Of course not. For me, Christmas (as it is for many) is a secular holiday, which brings joy to children. Christmas Eve, I cooked a goose. Later, Nina led us in some songs on her guitar or on the piano we had picked up at an auction. After the children went to bed, Nina and I filled their stockings, which were hung over the living room fireplace. Presents were piled under the tree. On Christmas morning, we had a gift opening followed by a pancake breakfast.

We celebrated my father's sixty-fifth birthday in 1972. The German consulate arranged for him to have a box at the Metropolitan Opera to accommodate Papa, Elsa, Henry, Hope, Nina, and me for a performance of Verdi's *A Masked Ball*. It was my first hearing of this opera, which is now one of my favorites. The consulate also arranged for a meal for us at the Grand Tier Restaurant.

Papa became a known figure in the UN. He had good relationships with the UN secretary generals. The last one, Kurt Waldheim, was an Austrian he was particularly close to. Waldheim arranged a memorial service for Papa in the UN, at which he spoke. Sadly, it came out years later that Waldheim had been an officer in the German Army with a unit guilty of war crimes. By then, he had become president of Austria. He was barred by the US and other countries from entering. The Waldheim affair became the turning point in Austria facing up to its support for Nazism after masquerading as Hitler's first victim. It led to at least a partial national cleansing. I am glad that Papa never had to endure the embarrassment of being close to someone who became so disgraced.

Already starting in the 1960s, Papa reached out to political figures for the articles he was then writing for Austrian and German newspapers and magazines. He interviewed Adlai Stevenson and Arthur Goldberg, among others. He attended a Dwight Eisenhower press conference and asked a question. This led to an admonishment by the State Department to the Austrian ambassador because he was not on the list of questioners. He became friendly with the Reuther brothers, who were the leaders of the United Automobile Workers, then one of the nation's biggest and most powerful unions. He traveled with Walter Reuther to India and managed to interview Prime Minister Jawaharlal Nehru. Papa also wrote books. He was indefatigable in his writings. I still remember how he would get up from the dining table when a thought struck him. A minute later, we would hear the typewriter sounding like a machine gun. He was a two-finger typist but as fast as anyone.

After moving to Tudor City, across from the UN, my father and Elsa bought a co-op at 118 Riverside Drive. Every Christmas Eve, he cooked a bountiful dinner highlighted by a goose. He had become an accomplished cook—unlike when he was a Herr Doktor in Vienna and probably never went into the kitchen. It was a wonderful family get-together. This was the happiest period in his life after so much turmoil. But his health was deteriorating. His heart began to weaken—possibly the same condition I have now: congestive heart failure. Then there did not exist the medications that have kept me going. Papa and Elsa took winter vacations in the Caribbean, where they received the cable with the news of Kathy's birth. He and Elsa traveled every summer to Germany and Austria to see his contacts and then to other parts of Europe, mainly the Alps for a vacation.

In 1971, Papa had a heart attack while he and Elsa were traveling in what was then Yugoslavia. He was hospitalized there for at least a couple of weeks before he was well enough to make the trip to Vienna, which family friends had arranged. He finally came back to the US. Henry and I picked him and Elsa up at JFK Airport. I was able to get the Port Authority to let us board the plane before passengers disembarked to help him out. We were quite shocked at how gaunt he looked.

On February 14, 1973, he suffered a heart attack while walking on West Eighty-Fifth Street toward Broadway. He was on the way to file a dispatch of a news article he had just written. It may be corny, but it can be said he died with his boots on, doing what he had loved his whole life—writing analyses of what was going on in the world. I was reached in Albany and came to see him at Roosevelt Hospital. But he was already comatose and shortly passed away. So I never said goodbye to him. But he has always been in my heart. Our relationship was so rich. He was a remarkable person of great strength, confidence, and caring. It was a shock even though we knew his heart was weakening. He had been such a pillar of strength. That he managed to get us out of Europe and to create for us a new life in the US was due to his strength, self-confidence, and determination. He was a loving and caring but also demanding father, though never oppressive. Our relationship was strong and loving. I depended upon him. How many times over the years since his death I have missed his counsel. And there are so many questions about his life, my mother, their personal and political lives that I sadly never asked as I busied myself with and rushed into my life. Now that I am older than he was at his death, as I think of life experiences, I wish I could share with him our lives from the vantage point of age. One great satisfaction I have is that his last fifteen or so years were his happiest and most fulfilling with Elsa, his two sons doing well and five grandchildren. He was present when I was sworn in as assemblyman. I know he was proud of me.

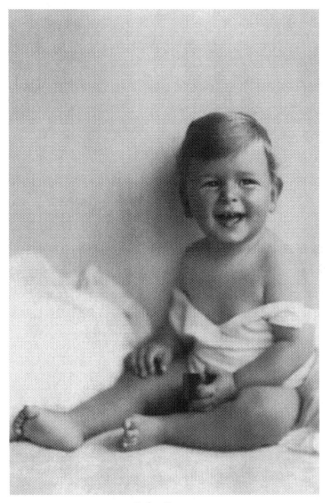

Baby Franz.

On a hike with my parents and brother in Zurich, where
we fled after the Fascist coup in Austria in 1934.

Private Franz Leichter.

Nina and I enjoying our early years together.

Campaigning with Eleanor Roosevelt.

Campaigning with Robert F. Kennedy.

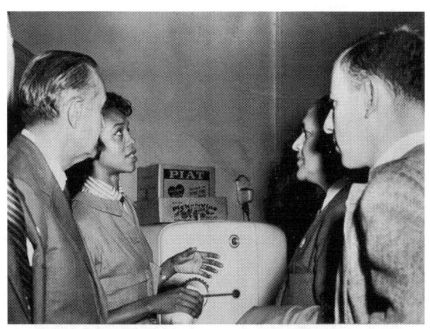

Taking Governor Averell Harriman and Secretary of Housing and Urban Development Robert Weaver on a tour of slum housing conditions.

Bus tour of the Riverside Democrats visiting
Congressman Bill Ryan in Washington D.C.

Speaking in the Assembly, which I did quite often.

Nina and me getting ready for a hike with Kathy, Josh and
our dog Cocoa! We loved these family hikes.

With Mayor Ed Koch and my colleague Assemblyman Ed Lehner,
announcing New York City's enforcement of the Pooper Scooper Law.

A flyer announcing one of the 20+ annual West Side
Community Conferences I sponsored.

Speaking at one of the numerous press conferences I held.

I loved skiing. But usually downhill with more snow.

I continued hiking into my 80s; often with my children.

I am fortunate to have a loving family.

# CHAPTER 10

# 1968-1974: IN THE LEGISLATURE

## THE UPRISING AT COLUMBIA UNIVERSITY

In the spring of 1968, there was an uprising at Columbia University, when some radical students took over the administration building—the old Low Library. The proximate cause was Columbia's plan to build a new gym in Morningside Park. This was a stupid idea because it infuriated many in the neighboring community and, among others, park lovers. It was made worse when Columbia announced that, to appease the Harlem community at the bottom of the park, it would reserve 20 percent (initially 10 percent) of the gym for the community—but separated from the rest of the gym and with a special entrance at the bottom. This was an especially offensive proposal in the inflamed environment of the Civil Rights Movement at that time.

As district leader realizing this was going to lead to growing opposition, I took the lead and prevailed upon Percy Sutton, then the Manhattan borough president, to call a meeting with representatives of the University. A high-level meeting was held, attended by some prominent Columbia University trustees and local officials, including J. Raymond Jones, then the area's councilmember. At the meeting, there occurred an event that I have relished accounting over the years. At one point, Columbia's attorney argued that people were "estopped" (legal doctrine that means, by failing to object timely one loses the right to do) from objecting as Columbia had already started excavation for the gym in Morningside Park roughly between West 116th and 112th Streets. Jones, with a usual cigar in his mouth and addressing the attorney as "dean," as he did with all the Columbia representatives (one or two Columbia deans were present), said, "Dean, I suggest you go to Morningside Avenue and tell the folks there that they are estopped from protesting." The attorney's comment and the general attitude of Columbia's representatives was one of condescension and blindness.

Sutton then arranged another, and larger, meeting at Gracie Mansion with Mayor John Lindsay. Again it was attended by high-level Columbia administrators and some of its prominent trustees. At the beginning of the meeting, Sutton called on me to state the objection to the gym and the rising community opposition. A discussion then started. Lindsay, after a few moments, said he needed to take a call. We waited for him to return. When after a good thirty minutes he still had not come back, the meeting broke off.

Fairly soon thereafter, in April 1968, the student uprising occurred based on the University's insistence on building the gym. The student revolt was led by a radical group that later became part of what was known as the SDS (Students for Democratic Society), which became prominent, especially for its violent acts protesting the Vietnam War.

The uprising ended with a police takeover of the campus in what was reported in the press and acknowledged as a police/student riot. There was a popular uproar over both the police action and Columbia's obstinacy in trying to build this gym on public parkland. Columbia's president, Grayson Kirk, was forced to resign. Columbia gave up on the gym and hired the acclaimed architect I.M. Pei (who redesigned the Louvre). He held hearings at which I testified. The distinguished Harvard Law professor Edward Cox, then issued a report that was critical of the Columbia administration. The trustees considered moving the campus to Rockland County but decided to stay in Morningside Heights. They retained I.M. Pei to design what became the Physical Fitness Center, which my New York family has made much use of. The uprising might have been avoided or ended differently if my efforts to convince Columbia that it was making a mistake had been heeded.

The year 1968 was turbulent for America. Opposition to the Vietnam War increased and was particularly strong in the Morningside and West Side community. Of course, I was involved in protests. I went to Washington to participate in marches against the war and organized the Riverside Club's participation. Bill Ryan was one of the strongest voices in opposition in the Congress. It was a heady time and a satisfying time to be actively engaged in the political arena.

In 1968, both MLK and RFK were assassinated. RFK was then running for the Democratic nomination for president. I was part of a group of reformers who held two meetings with him where we pledged our support. RFK was on the path to be selected as the Democratic nominee for president when he was shot in the evening of the day he won the important Democratic primary in California. As with the assassination of his brother, how different this country's history might have been but for their early deaths.

The Kennedy story is like a Greek tragedy. There is a Greek statement to the effect that whom the gods build up, they then destroy. The father, Joe, was an Irish kid from Boston who gained political power and great wealth, which he used to further his children's political lives. His own political ambitions to become president were thwarted by FDR and because of his known appeasement to Hitler as US ambassador to Great Britain. He saw his eldest son, who wanted to be his political heir, die on a bombing run in World War II, followed by the assassination of two of his sons.

In November 1968, I was elected to the New York State Assembly. The Assembly district was the Seventh AD, comprising the area roughly from West Ninety-Seventh Street to West 125th Street and from Riverside Drive to Central Park and Morningside Park, the home of the Riverside Democrats who held political power since 1957. It was there, after Ryan was elected to Congress, that I became the district leader in 1960 and was elected and reelected in the Democratic primaries of 1961, 1963, 1965, and 1967. During this entire time and some years before, the Assembly representative was Dan Kelly. Kelly had been elected in or about 1950 by an anti-Tammany Club, named after its leader, Bob Blakie. However, Blakie and his club were defeated by Tammany Hall regulars, whom the Riverside Democrats then defeated in 1957. Kelly and some of the former Blakie precinct captains gave support to Ryan in his 1957 election as district leader. Kelly was quite popular and had a reputation for independence and as a reformer in the Assembly. However, on social issues, like abortion and the Blue Laws, he was quite conservative and followed his Catholic teachings. He was out of step, and probably not comfortable, with the progressive views of the Riverside Democrats. I nevertheless could not challenge him for the Assembly.

# I AM ELECTED TO THE NEW YORK STATE ASSEMBLY

How I got to the Assembly requires me to go back in time to give it context. In 1964, RFK was elected as New York's state senator. In the same year, J. Raymond Jones, my nemesis the Harlem Fox (although I admired him and we had a cordial relationship), became Manhattan's Democratic leader. As a district leader, I was on the Executive Committee, composed of all the Manhattan leaders who were entitled to vote for county leader, the position that such political luminaries as William "Boss" Tweed, George Washington Plunkitt, Charles Murphy, and Carmine DeSapio had held. As he was the first African American elected to this post, which still had a certain aura because of the control Tammany once held over New York state government, we reformers did not oppose him.

In 1966, there occurred a vacancy on the surrogate's court in Manhattan. This had been a prized position, as it administered the estates of deceased residents of Manhattan, which included some very rich people. The surrogate had the authority to appoint special guardians, ostensibly to protect the interest of minors in the estate. To receive such an appointment was often good business for lawyers and became a source of patronage important to Tammany. It also imposed what I considered unnecessary expenses on estates. Mayor Fiorello La Guardia, in railing against it, called it the world's "biggest undertaker." In 1962, I held a press conference to attack this system and call for its replacement by a public guardian—a full-time position whose office would take over the function of special guardians. This was my first big publicity splash. It was widely covered, and the *Daily News* gave it editorial support with a picture of me with some fellow reform district leaders. While my proposal has never been adopted, the system of appointment has been revised and mainly taken out of politics.

When a vacancy occurred in 1966 in the surrogate's court, the regulars, led by Jones, to maintain this patronage pot, put up as a candidate a sitting New York State Supreme Court Justice. Senator RFK saw an opportunity to burnish his reform credentials and managed to get another New York State Supreme Court Justice, Samuel Silverman, to run as a reformer promising to end the patronage system I had attacked. It was a hard primary. I campaigned together with Kennedy. I also saw what an organization the RFK family still had. Money for literature was no problem. On primary day, people came down from Massachusetts to help out. Silverman won. That finished Jones, and he resigned as county leader in 1967, pushed out by RFK.

The vote to choose the next county leader was then up to the Executive Committee. The regulars, who had the majority, put up Frank Rossetti, a district leader and an assemblyman from East Harlem. The reformers fielded Shanley Egeth, who came from the Murray Hill area. Gene Flatow, my coleader, and I did not have a good political relationship with Egeth and broke ranks and voted for the regular candidate. This paved my way to the Assembly because Rossetti then backed Kelly in 1968 for a Manhattan-wide civil court seat, which he won without any opposition. The Assembly seat was now open. I never made any deal with Rossetti that in return for my supporting him as county leader he would support Kelly for the civil court. And I don't think it was even in my mind that by supporting Rossetti it would help me clear the way for the Assembly. I never discussed with Kelly if he wanted to leave the Assembly for the Court. Nevertheless, I understand people saw this as a deal I made. It is unlikely that Rossetti would have backed Kelly for the court vacancy if I had voted against him.

I was chosen as the Democratic candidate for the now open Assembly seat by the county committee for the Seventh Assembly District, as the date for the primary had already passed. The Riverside Democrats controlled the area, and it didn't prove difficult, though it still required organization to get people to turn out. In November, I faced a Republican candidate by the wonderful name of Moonray Kojima (I am not kidding). Even with my poor memory for names, how could I forget it? As the Assembly district was heavily Democratic, and I had been active as district leader, my election on November 4, 1968, was a breeze. Not that I didn't worry. I still campaigned hard. At the beginning of January 1969, I was sworn in as assemblyman and took my seat. Thus began a new chapter.

# INTRODUCING THE FIRST ABORTION RIGHTS BILL

Before I was sworn in and the session started, I was approached by a political colleague from another club who wanted me to meet with his wife about putting in a bill to remove restrictions on abortions. Abortion had become a major issue in the Legislature. New York, like most states, outlawed all abortions. In an effort to ease this restriction, a bill had been brought to a vote in the Assembly in the previous few years, which would permit abortions if two doctors certified that it was necessary for the woman's health. That bill was defeated in the Assembly and never even came to a vote in the Senate. Now I was being asked to put in a bill that would leave abortion as a woman's decision. I was convinced after hearing the arguments that this made sense.

A meeting was arranged at the home of Ruth Proskauer Smith, the daughter of a famed New York state judge who was an advisor to FDR. She was active in an effort to lift the prohibition on abortions. It was attended by Constance "Connie" Cook, a Republican assemblywoman representing Ithaca. She was a brand of Republican that has become extinct—moderate, liberal on social issues, and mildly conservative on financial issues. This was the character of the Republican Party at that time, led by Governor Nelson Rockefeller, and included moderates like Senator Jacob Javits, Attorney General Louis Lefkowitz, and others. When I think of them, it makes me shudder how far the Republicans—and the country—have moved to the right.

We discussed various possibilities and ended up agreeing to put in a clean bill that would eliminate all restrictions on abortions. I asked my neighboring West Side assemblyman, Al Blumenthal, who was the main sponsor of the two-doctor certification bill, if he minded. He scoffed at our bill. If the Legislature wouldn't pass his modest reform bill, how would it ever pass a "radical" measure leaving abortion as a woman's choice? Yet within less than two years, our bill essentially became law and undoubtedly influenced the Supreme Court in its landmark *Roe v. Wade* decision in 1973.

## BEING AN ASSEMBLYMAN

The early days in the Assembly were exciting. I tried to put together a group of new members with reform credentials who would vote as a block in choosing the new leader of the Democrats in the Assembly. In the 1968 election, which saw Richard Nixon win, the Democrats lost the majority in the Assembly. We were now choosing the minority leader. My effort to form a block of reformers was not very successful, but it brought me into contact with Steve Solarz, who became one of my closest friends. Steve had won a seat in south Brooklyn, defeating a Democrat, who had held the seat for thirty years, in a tough primary. There were others who became lifelong friends: Oliver Koppell, who was elected in 1971 as an anti-Vietnam candidate, and Ed Lehner, who was elected in 1972. Oliver was my roommate in Albany for many years.

My first speech in the Assembly was to complain that I and other freshmen Democrats had not been given adequate office equipment. Soon I was speaking more often. I was reading the bills, which almost all came from the majority. I focused on banking bills and was in frequent debates on bills that I charged would hurt consumers. One day, I argued against such a bill, and even though the majority leader, who directed Republican members, spoke in favor of this bill, I still managed to gather sufficient Republican nay votes to defeat it. That was so unusual that the *New York Times*, which in those days covered the daily proceedings of the Legislature, reported on it. In those days, while partisanship was present, it was not so prevalent and blatant as it is today. It is highly unlikely that a bill sponsored by a member of the majority would be defeated today. So I quickly made my reputation as an outspoken and independent legislator.

My first legislative session went by in a blur. The sessions then ended in late April or May. Rockefeller was a dynamic governor, and often there were major bills he proposed when we convened on Monday. A big issue was usually over the budget. But as the Democrats were in the minority, we had minimal say. We could raise questions during debates in which I was often engaged. I remember my first sessions for the comaradaerie we shared. My Assembly colleagues ranged from very able and hardworking to party hacks, ideologues of left and right, characters, and sleazeballs. It was an interesting group, and I enjoyed a good relationship with most.

It was not just with my inner circle of reform friends that I circulated; I had friendly relationships with a number of Republicans. We met at dinners and in the numerous receptions that filled most nights. In the evening, there were two or so bars where a number of legislators would show up. There, liberal Democrats would socialize with conservative Republicans over a glass of beer. It is quite different now, especially the lack of social relationships with members across the aisle (that is how you describe the other party). This seemed to change in the 1980s when I was in the Senate. Now this social mingling doesn't exist anymore. In commenting on the rabid partisanship in Congress, the lack of social relationships is pointed to as one of the causes and effects of the inability to work together legislatively.

My Assembly work and politics didn't end with the close of the session. I got myself appointed to a commission to rewrite the penal law. There were perks like a weekend retreat on an island in Lake George. In 1973, I was appointed as a member of a commission that focused on conditions in nursing homes and how political influence had played a role in lax regulations and supervision. This too proved to be fruitful in my admitted search for issues and publicity. Mainly, though, my work focused on local matters in the district and attending tenants and other community meetings. I tried to be everywhere, and no community matter was too insignificant for me to pay attention to. I continued to be deeply involved with the Riverside Democrats. Politics, not law, continued to be my main focus. It felt good holding a public office.

The demands on my time were even greater as I continued my legal work. In effect, I had two full-time jobs. And I now had a family that I enjoyed and wanted to spend time with. We did have our summers and holiday weekends at the Farm. In our first few years there, I would go up by bus on Thursday and return late Sunday. It was a grueling six-and-a-half-hour trip. When we connected with the Scheinbergs, I began to drive back and forth with Herb. Later on, I would occasionally fly into Burlington and have Nina and the children meet me at the dock of the ferry that took us across Lake Champlain. The Farm was a tonic—dinners with the Derecskeys, Scheinbergs, Siners, and sometimes local people and lots of activities—auctions, tennis, hiking, skiing, swimming.

Sometime before I became an assemblyman, my firm, Benjamin, Galton & Robbins, fell apart. The main partner, Herman Benjamin, who represented the firm's two major clients, lost them both. He left to join another firm. There was still some business, as Mel Robbins represented Mount Sinai Hospital. But the firm was in decline. Then David Galton, who never brought in much business, retired. We were joined by an attorney, Arthur Bondi, who carried on his legal work though he had become blind. Bondi was a refugee from Germany and had only minor business. The firm was renamed Robbins, Bondi & Leichter, but it was not a true partnership. While my political career was well on its way, my legal career was not doing well. Together with my legislative salary, I earned only around $30,000, and Nina as a teacher a little less. In today's 2019 dollars, that is probably near $200,000 with Nina's good, no-cost health insurance through her work as a teacher. We did not consider ourselves well off yet we managed to acquire the Farm, send our children to private school, subscribe to the Metropolitan Opera, and hire a housekeeper to help look after the children. The financial pressures on young families in the twenty-first century are much greater.

In the Assembly, I quickly found my voice. It almost seemed there were no issues I was not involved in or raising. In the years 1969–1973, I received media coverage for proposals to end surrogate patronage, treat addiction as a mental health issue through clinics instead of through the criminal system, require banks to invest in poorer neighborhoods, prohibit discrimination against gays in housing, disclose inflated rents the city was paying for day care leases, reduce criminal penalties for minor possessions of marijuana, and a bill to legalize its use under state regulation. Many of these proposals were dismissed at that time as unrealistic or dangerous. I take satisfaction in that I helped to raise these issues and that many are now accepted and became laws. For instance, Washington and Colorado led numerous states to enact marijuana decriminalization and to legalize its use under state regulation. Finally, New York legalized recreational consumption of marijuana in 2021. What I proposed in 1971, when it was considered irresponsible radicalism, is now becoming the norm in the US.

I was very keen on getting news coverage. This was my approach to becoming known and advancing my political career. It was also, I realized, the way I could bring issues before the public, which otherwise would receive little if any attention. I realized that as a member of the minority, whose bills were ignored by the majority, to be effective and have some impact, I would have to find a means to raise and advance solutions to issues which I considered important. I also wanted to raise my profile.

In 1970, in a most exciting vote, the Legislature passed the abortion rights bill. It passed in the Assembly when a Democratic, Jewish colleague from an upstate, heavily Catholic district changed his vote at the last moment. In a speech he gave as he changed his vote from against to in favor, which enabled the passage of the bill, he said, "I know this is the end of my political career, but I am doing what I think is right." It was the most courageous political act I experienced personally. It did end his political career, as he was not reelected. This was an exciting time as I worked with and championed the abortion rights groups whose lobbying and advocacy proved instrumental in New York, leading the way to a woman's right to choose. So the bill I cosponsored in 1969, which almost no one thought had any chance of passage, within two years became law and probably influenced the Supreme Court by showing there was public support for abortion rights.

In my early Assembly days, I was able to vote to create Adirondack Park Agency, protecting the area where the Farm is and whose unspoiled beauty we have enjoyed these many years. I was also active in opposing what became known as the Rockefeller Drug Laws, which imposed harsh sentences for minor possessions of narcotics. It unfortunately passed and led to the imprisonment of many, mainly minorities, in New York. It paved the way for the federal government and many states to pursue a criminal punitive approach on narcotics use instead of treating it as a public health matter. This led to mass incarceration, which is now finally a recognized national issue. Every year, I consistently voted against the death penalty, although it had strong majority support among my constituents.

With some of my reform colleagues, prompted by Steve Solarz, we held hearings on issues requiring legislative action, like reducing criminal penalties for victimless crime. We had no committees that we chaired and, as backbenchers in the minority, no legislative power to have legislation acted on. Nevertheless, these hearings secured a fair amount of media coverage. This was partially due to the novelty of legislative hearings, especially outside of Albany. Both the Senate and Assembly standing committees held almost no hearings. So when we announced our hearings, these were considered by the media as significant, ignoring or not realizing our lack of power in the Legislature. Here, too, we understood that our effectiveness depended upon our publicizing issues that we considered important but that otherwise would receive no attention. Also, in those days, it was easier to get media coverage. The *New York Times* had four reporters in Albany who, during the session, reported on almost every day's activities. CBS News had a crew in the Capitol almost every day. New York City's TV channels at that time had numerous camera crews. This is not the case now, as all these outlets have substantially reduced their personnel and coverage, and a number of the city's newspapers have disappeared. If I were in the Legislature today, very little of what I then did would be covered. This is unfortunate, as so little is now known about state and city government.

Surprisingly, we were able to attract significant witnesses to our rump hearings. For one such hearing, one of the witnesses was Mario Procaccino, who was the Democratic candidate for mayor in 1969. He made a fool of himself. When Steve asked him whether he agreed with Saint Augustine's distinction between public and private morality, he answered, "Saint Augustine was far ahead of his time."

One issue I addressed alone was discriminatory zoning in the suburbs that kept out minorities and affordable housing. Many suburban zoning laws at that time limited residential permits to single houses on one or two and sometimes even four acres to keep out minorities and affordable housing. In spite of my having no jurisdiction or role on this issue, I was able to get the county executive of Westchester to testify at a hearing I held in Westchester. Some years later, courts, led by New Jersey, struck down some of these restrictive zoning requirements.

There were not many public issues I did not get involved in. In 1971, there was a revolt at the maximum security prison, Attica Correctional Facility, which was taken over by inmates. Numerous officers were taken hostage. When Governor Rockefeller unwisely tried to take back the prison by force, some of the prison officers who had been taken hostage were killed by the state trooper sharpshooters, who obviously were not very sharp. The prison was retaken with numerous deaths. Many prisoners were forced to run a gauntlet by officers and beaten. This was the biggest prison riot ever in the US. Within two days of retaking the prison, I decided to visit and formed a group of a few legislators to join me. As members of the Legislature, we were by law authorized to visit any state prison. The correction commissioner tried to talk me out of going, but I insisted we would go. It was a depressing scene. I visited the infirmary holding many of the injured prisoners and interviewed some. I don't know what my visit achieved, but it did give me a firsthand view and allowed me to speak with more authority about the prison revolt and the Governor's response. It also spurred my interest in correction reform.

I made it my practice almost yearly when we were at the Farm to visit the Clinton Correctional Facility (by many just called Dannemora), which was outside Plattsburgh. The prison was about thirty miles from the Farm. I would go through the cell blocks and meet with the warden and inmates. It was there I ran into Martin Sostre, who was in solitary confinement. I always made it a point to have the warden take me through the solitary confinement wing. Martin was on the Amnesty International list of political prisoners. I played a role in getting him released, but that is for another chapter. I became involved in correctional issues and worked for many years with prison rights and correction reform groups. I would take my legislative friends to the Dannemora prison when they were visiting us at the Farm. Walking with Steve Solarz through the prison and passing groups of prisoners, Steve said, "They could just grab us and make us hostages to be released only if their demands were met." I answered that their demands would be met by the legislative leaders if the inmates promised to continue to hold us as hostages.

Our small group of reform legislators had fun raising issues such as the Vietnam War, by proposing resolutions putting the Legislature on record in calling for the end of American involvement in that unfortunate war. While in the minority it was nearly impossible to get your bills to the floor, resolutions had no such restrictions. Traditionally, these were mainly used to honor some community. The sponsor then presented the framed resolution signed by the speaker and maybe got some local press coverage. With my reform friends, we saw this as means to get the Assembly to vote on national and international issues. Sometimes these were framed as requests to Congress but received absolutely no attention. I forced one such resolution in 1971 to a floor debate, through parliamentary means, calling for the withdrawal of American troops from Vietnam. One of the Republican legislators, in opposing the resolution, said, "I and my family sleep very well at night because we have President Nixon at our helm and not the Leichters."

Both Steve and I also gained coverage through editorial replies on TV and radio. In those days, the local TV stations that aired editorial were required to air opposing views. I did a number of such editorials. Steve was a master of the editorial reply. Even if he found an editorial he agreed with, he would find some minor disagreements upon which to support a reply. He was called by one station a "congenital responder." As a result of all these activities, I quickly made a name for myself.

In 1969, when Procaccino secured the Democratic nomination for mayor, I broke with the party and supported Lindsay on the Liberal line. I convinced Steve to join me. Procaccino was a socially conservative Democrat, not very bright, and an old regular party stalwart. Lindsay won.

In 1971, to improve our ability to respond to bills, which came in a flurry in the last days of the session, we formed a group of seven reformers, all my friends, to pool some money and hire a counsel. We called it the study group. This worked out well and enabled us to be even more of a force in floor debates. Of our group. Peter Berle became the commissioner of the environmental department, Steve served in the Congress and made a name for himself in foreign affairs, Oliver Koppell served briefly as attorney general, Tony Olivieri, after losing a bid for lieutenant governor, became a councilmember at large for Manhattan. He had great potential but sadly died young from a brain tumor. The lawyer we hired, Eric Hirschhorn, became an undersecretary of commerce under Obama.

At this time, my staff consisted of one secretary, who worked only during the session. I managed in 1971 to have an intern from Hunter College, Elizabeth Clark. She proved so valuable that in 1972 I found a way to give her a paid position, which I told her would last only six months for the session that year. When I had a primary challenge in 1972, I knew I had to keep her. I scrambled and found money to keep her on my staff. Elizabeth worked for me for eleven years. I then helped her to attend law school. She has been a lifelong friend, as have many others of my staff. Elizabeth practiced law in St. Thomas in the Virgin Islands. I visited her a number of times, once with Nina and once with Kathy. She then relocated to Oakland and joined firms in the Bay Area. Sadly, she died much too young in 2017. By the time I left the Senate, my staff consisted of seven persons.

# I AM REAPPORTIONED OUT OF MY DISTRICT

In 1972—another turbulent year—the Legislature redrew the electoral maps through reapportionment. This always occurs two years after the decennial census, which tracks population shifts. Manhattan lost one Assembly seat. This gave the Republican and Democratic leadership, both of whom found me an irritant, the opportunity to demolish my district, combining a minor part with the neighboring Assembly district. Instead of running from West Ninety-Seventh Street to West 125th Street, my new district went from West 106th Street to West 181st Street in a narrow band east of Riverside Park. I then lived on West 104th Street, so my domicile was out of the district. This was done to keep me from seeking reelection. Legislators had to live in the district they represented to be elected. But after reapportionment, one was allowed to run for office in any part of the county. You then had one year to move into the district from which you were elected.

My district was merged into the neighboring district represented by Steve Gottlieb, with whom I was friendly and who was part of our Assembly study group. I was not going to give up on public life and certainly not to be driven out this way. I announced I would run in the new district. Gottlieb decided not to challenge me and instead challenged the Democratic minority leader of the Senate, Joseph Zaretzki. Sadly, Gottlieb allowed himself to be bought off after announcing he would run, accepting a position from Governor Rockefeller on the State Liquor Authority. Zaretzki had a close relationship with Rockefeller, who did this favor for him so he could avoid a primary. This was raised as an issue at the Senate hearing when Rockefeller was being considered for confirmation as vice president. It was also a factor when I challenged Zaretzki two years later and had to convince likely supporters that I could not be bought off.

While Gottlieb did not challenge me, I had an opponent in the Democratic primary, Alex Colgan. He had very little support. Nevertheless, I campaigned hard and won easily. I went to work in my new district, representing a much-changed constituency. Among my new neighborhoods was West Harlem, which was mainly African American, with the smallest remnants of what had been an Italian community. The northern part saw the beginning of the Latino influx, which by the time I left the Legislature was mainly Dominican. There were still some Jewish enclaves, mainly refugees from World War II, around West 181st Street, I won handedly and was reelected to the Assembly from my new district in November. I quickly went to work in this district and gained political and community supporters through my tenants' advocacy and by being very visible at community events.

## BILL RYAN DIES, AND I PASS UP TRYING TO SUCCEED HIM

Bill Ryan, my mentor and congressman since his election in 1960, also found his district significantly changed through reapportionment. In 1972, he faced a very hard primary. Reapportionment had thrown his district in with the neighboring district to the south, which was represented by Bella Abzug. Bella was a dynamo and then quite a luminary. She was one of the feminist leaders and had a passionate group of supporters. Ryan, in comparison, for all his progressive credentials, did not exude the excitement that Bella did. But Ryan had determination and conviction. People recognized he was effective if not as flashy as Bella. I remember one candidates' forum where all the candidates running for offices in the area were invited to debate their opponents. I was there debating my opponent. Ryan was there to debate Bella. He was not a rousing speaker. While he gave his talk, Bella came into the hall. Immediately you could hear people uttering her name and turning around to look at her as she went to the stage, completely upstaging Ryan in his address. I felt so bad for him. What I didn't know then was that Ryan was dying of esophageal cancer. I do remember his coming to our house to go over some campaign literature. He lifted little Kathy up, and I remember thinking then how thin and worn he looked. Nevertheless, he campaigned hard. I tried to help as much as I could but was mainly engaged in my own campaign.

Bella was a narcissist. I remember her driving down Broadway in a cavalcade shouting, "Folks, it is Bella." Another time, I saw her going into a beauty parlor to shake hands (standard for politicians but which I never could bring myself to do), shouting, "Hey, it's Bella." She certainly had the limelight. During the campaign, she appeared on the cover of *Life*. Ryan had me call the magazine to complain, which I stupidly agreed to do, of course with no effect whatsoever. So Bella had the attention. But when the votes were counted, Ryan defeated her by 65 percent to 35 percent.

But shortly after the June primary, he was hospitalized. By September, he was dead at the age of fifty. What a personal and political loss. He was my mentor and friend. A true leader. How different my political future might have been—and also that of my brother, Henry, who was personally closer to Bill—if he had survived. I think it is quite likely Ryan would have become senator for New York. It is one of those events in my life, which when I think of, I seek to avoid bemoaning the loss of what might have been and to appreciate just how fortunate I was to have him in my life.

The funeral service was held at Corpus Christi Church on West 121st Street. Henry and I—and a number of the Riverside Democrats—flew down with the family and casket to Washington for the burial. In one of the truest eulogies paid to Ryan by one of his congressional colleagues in a ceremony held in the House, he stated, as clear as I can remember, "When he could only whisper, he spoke words which we should have been shouting," referring to Ryan's opposition to the Vietnam War. His opposition was so prominent that when LBJ gave his national address announcing he would not run for another presidential term, he mentioned Ryan's opposition along with that of Senator Fulbright. What a loss.

Bill Ryan's replacement as the Democratic candidate for the congressional seat was now to be decided by the county committee for that district. Each election district chose three members. An election district was usually one or two city blocks, depending upon the population density. There may have been around three to four hundred county committee members in the congressional seat. Bella immediately announced her candidacy. When three reform legislators, who had seniority over me in public office, declined to challenge her, I indicated that I would be open to seeking the Democratic nomination. But I didn't push it hard with the club's senior leadership—those who had formed the Riverside Democrats with Bill Ryan before I joined. Unbeknownst to me, they met with Alex Rose, who was the leader of the Liberal Party. Ryan had been chosen as the Liberal Party candidate, and now it also needed to find a replacement. This was a third party, which usually aligned with the Democrats and whose support had been so essential for Robert F. Wagner's victory in 1961 and John Lindsey's in 1969. Rose was extremely influential. RFK and other nationally prominent leaders sought his advice. Out of this meeting, and I think in large part due to Rose's influence, the decision was reached to support Bill Ryan's widow, Priscilla, as the candidate to oppose Bella. And even if she lost in the county committee for the Democratic nomination, she would have the Liberal Party nomination for the general election in November. I could not oppose Priscilla and withdrew any consideration of making the race.

I felt at that time that choosing Priscilla was a mistake. She had been a loyal and active partner of Ryan's, but she was not sufficiently informed on the issues (which showed in the campaign), nor did she have the political smarts to run a winning campaign. I said in private at that time that this district was not one like those in the South where upon an incumbent's death his widow takes the seat. I was sadly proven right. Priscilla lost in the county committee for the Democratic nomination, and in November, running on the Liberal line, she had no chance. Could I have fared better? I have often run the scenario through my mind. Probably not. I might have prevailed in the club over Priscilla and convinced her to withdraw. I might have had the support of the reform clubs and thus their county committee members on the West Side, as there was quite a bit of hostility against Bella left over from the primary between her and Bill Ryan. But the majority of the county committee came from north of 137th Street and was controlled by the regulars, particularly Zaretzki, who was unlikely to support me. Also, while I have no proof of this, Bella prevailed upon Mayor Lindsay to support her, and a deal was made with Zaretzki, who as the Democratic minority leader was important to the mayor for help with the city's agenda in the Legislature. Also, Alex Rose, whose main interest was in having what he perceived as a strong candidate to get votes on the Liberal line, might not have backed me. Nevertheless, it made no sense for Priscilla to run, and if I had been the candidate and had been defeated, I would have laid down a marker. As it was, this came upon me much more quickly than I expected in 1976.

The year 1973 continued with the same hectic pitch. Still the summer was a time of relaxation and joy at the Farm. But Nina's bipolar condition began to manifest itself. This seemed to have been brought on by the death of her mother, Leah. (Although as of this writing, I am not sure whether it was 1973 or 1974 when Leah died.) And in 1973, my father died just short of his seventy-sixth birthday.

# CHAPTER 11

# 1974: AN ANNUM TERRIBILIS WITH A GOOD ENDING

In the first eight months of 1974, my wife went into a manic/depressive state and was diagnosed with bipolar disorder; another legislative reapportionment occurred that cut my new district just acquired in 1972 into three; our caretaker for Kathy and Josh left; and my law office closed, and I was out of a job.

Each of these sequentially would have been a major problem, but they all came at the same time in the early months of 1974.

Kathy and Josh were then attending Bank Street, a highly considered private school associated with a renowned teacher's college. It was located at West 112th Street just off Broadway, a block from where we lived. Even though Nina and I championed public education and Nina taught in the public school system, the public school they would have to attend, PS 165 on West 109th Street, had a poor reputation. At that time, there was no opportunity to attend a school out of the district in which you lived, as there is now. But frankly, our choosing Bank Street showed an inclination we had for private schools. Nina attended a private school through her precollege years and believed that these schools provided a better education. Our bias was shown when Kathy and Josh graduated from Bank Street, which ended at the eighth grade, and we never considered public high schools for them. We did not even have them take the test for the specialized public high schools. This was more Nina's choice, though I agreed with her.

Before starting Bank Street, both children went to a nursery school. As I remember, this was an informal arrangement mainly run by the parents, to which Nina contributed her time. There is a somewhat amusing aspect to our children attending Bank Street. The college and the school for children had been founded and existed in the Village on Bank Street; hence the name. It decided to move to Morningside Heights, partly prompted by, and maybe provided with some financial support, I suspect, by, Columbia, which probably wanted a good local elementary school available for its professors' children. To find a suitable site, Bank Street, again I suspect with Columbia's help, acquired an old residential building on West 112th Street. As the local assemblyman and with the backing of the area's militants, I opposed the demolition of good, affordable housing. Nevertheless, Bank Street School was built on that site. So it was with some embarrassment that I, and at least one other opponent of Bank Street's move to West 112th Street, sheepishly took our children to school on the first day it opened in 1972. Josh started there two years later.

Bank Street provided a good experience for both kids. It was a real joy to take them to school. Though they soon insisted on walking there by themselves, I would look out of the window of our eleventh-floor apartment and watch as Kathy clutched Josh's hand crossing West 111th Street. Nina and I loved the school. It had such a nice spirit to it. Even after they walked there by themselves, I would try to go there at the beginning of the school day to see these adorable little kids. Before classes started, there was square dancing in the hallways. It always cheered me up.

Bank Street was very convenient, as we had just moved to 610 West 111th Street, just off Broadway. As I mentioned in the last chapter, reapportionment required that I move into my new district within a year of the election, namely by November 1974. Nina and I went looking for a new home, which was not easy to find. Our apartment on West 104th Street was now out of my district. We wanted to stay in Morningside Heights. Finally, after much searching, we were able to get a very nice two-bedroom apartment on West 111th Street.

Early in the spring that year, Nina became quite manic. Later on, depression set in. It was necessary to get medical help. We found a psychiatrist who diagnosed her bipolar state. He prescribed lithium, which somewhat stabilized her. I can't remember whether she was able to continue teaching or had to take sick leave. She was not always able to take care of our children. It was obviously a very disturbing and difficult time, as I was still spending part of the week in Albany during the session. It became even more problematic when the person we had hired to take care of the children, Daisy, who had been with us since around 1970, decided to leave us. I can't remember the reason, but it was related to her family. Daisy was very nice if not very proficient. But she took good care of the kids. So here I was with a wife who was sick, no one to take care of Kathy and Josh, and facing another reapportionment that threatened my being able to continue in the Legislature.

Fortunately, Elsa found for us a replacement, Mrs. B, as we called her. She provided wonderful care for Kathy and Josh for a number of years and even cooked dinner for us. This was a real lifesaver. Later on and for some years, we also arranged for some young women (some attended Barnard) to be with the children in return for a room in our spacious apartment, after we moved to Riverside Drive.

How come I was facing another reapportionment threat in 1974, since these were by New York state law to occur only once every ten years after the census? Reapportionment had occurred in 1972, which had led to my having a far different Assembly district than the one I was first elected to in 1968. But in 1974, the US Justice Department ordered the Legislature to reapportion part of Manhattan and the Bronx. My district was in the crosshairs. Under the 1974 Civil Rights Voting Act, states and counties with a significant minority population, and where half of eligible voters were not registered, had to get preclearance from the Justice Department before making any changes in voting procedures, including reapportionment. Manhattan, the Bronx, and Brooklyn came under this stricture. Mainly because of my new district and one in East Harlem, the 1972 reapportionment plan for part of Manhattan was disapproved. The irony was that the Justice Department stated that the Assembly district I now represented was drawn to maximize the White population along the Hudson River, to the disadvantage of minorities. The opposite was the case. When the district lines were drawn in 1972, the Black assemblyman, Mark T. Southall, whose district was to the east of mine and included large parts of Harlem, did not want white voters in his district. So it was to make his district more Black, and not to make the district I ended up with more white, and not to protect me, that these lines were drawn. Absurd as it was, the Assembly leadership didn't mind drawing new lines to get rid of me.

This time, new district lines were drawn, cutting my Assembly district into thirds by creating west-east districts instead of the traditional north-south district lines. All three of the newly drawn districts were all now majority Black. I thought I could run in two of these and still win, but it would be difficult, and I didn't want to represent a district where people would ask why they were represented by that guy. I had not forgotten 1965 when I challenged David Dinkins in a district that was majority Black and lost.

As the new reapportionment lines were drawn to try to gain some leverage and input, I let it be known that if I did not have a satisfactory Assembly district to represent, I might challenge Joseph Zaretzki, the incumbent Democratic senator from Northern Manhattan. He was then, and had been for many years, the leader of the Democrats in the Senate. My threat had no effect on how the new Assembly lines were drawn. To discourage me from challenging Zaretzki, my home was put outside the lines of the new senatorial district. This also had to be redrawn due to the Department of Justice's refusal to approve part of the 1972 reapportionment plan for Manhattan. This newly drawn Senate district started on West 112th Street and went north to the Bronx boundary. I then lived at West 111th Street. In the 1972 reapportionment, I lived on West 104th Street, and the lines for the district I did succeed in representing started at West 106th Street. The new Senate lines were a blatant attempt to protect Zaretzki and to get rid of me, as I was too independent and a thorn in the side of the leadership. I was determined not to let that happen.

What happened to me twice is a good example of the misuse of reapportionment for partisan or other political reasons. In my case, it was getting rid of an independent, maverick legislator. It is a cancer on America's democracy. A fair, nonpartisan reapportionment mechanism must be established. A number of states have moved in this direction, setting up commission free of partisan prejudices.

And then, in addition, at around the same time, my law firm closed. As I set forth before, it was not a real law firm. Of the three partners when I joined the firm, only Mel Robbins was left. He had Mount Sinai Hospital as a client, but the hospital more and more used in-house counsel. He decided in April to leave and close shop.

So now I was without a job, about to lose my legislative position, with a home to hold together, two young children, and my wife having difficulty functioning. I could maybe handle one of these at a time, but as all came upon me at once within the early months of 1974, I had much to overcome.

The home situation had stabilized with the hiring of Mrs. B. Yet I had my concerns about Nina and how she would carry on. I think I minimized the seriousness of her condition and believed she would pull out of it and return to what had been normal. I probably took this attitude throughout Nina's illness. This was denial. It was one of the ways I could face her condition. Yet it may not have given her sufficient empathy. Not that I ever thought or said to her words like "shake it off." My approach was to act as far as possible as if there was no crisis. I was so determined to restore normalcy by proceeding normally. Nina's father was of great help during these days and into 1975 by spending time with her. So, somehow the family continued to hold together. I don't know how Kathy and Josh were affected nor how they remember these days when they were still very young.

I first went about finding a new law position. Among other contacts, I reached out to Hans Harnik. He too was a Viennese refugee and had become a member of the law firm of Wachtell, Manheim & Grouf. The firm had existed since just after World War I when Samuel Wachtell represented Austria at the Treaty of St. Germain, where the Habsburg Empire was eliminated. Wachtell had since died, and the firm was run by Harold Manheim and Meyer Grouf. It still represented some Austrian government interests and commercial firms. At one time, it had represented the Austrian Rothschild, who then lived in Vermont. It was a much more prosperous and solid firm than my old firm. Its offices were at the prime location of 30 Rockefeller Plaza, overlooking the skating rink. I talked myself into an offer as counsel to the firm. It worked out well over the years and gave me better financial support. More of that later.

Nina continued to be a great concern. She was manic for much of the spring and did some eccentric things like visiting in the middle of the night a disc jockey at his radio station after she had started listening to him. Her sister remembers Nina telling her how she walked down the yellow line in the middle of Amsterdam Avenue. It was not an easy time. I was very concerned.

And during this whole period, I was trying to save my political life. In spite of my efforts, I had no input into the new reapportionment lines. In one last but futile attempt, when I saw the proposed lines, I called the Assembly speaker, a Republican. This is so clear in my memory. For some years, Nina had asked our friends Victor and Sarah Kovner to use their Fire Island vacation house when Queens and Brooklyn had a special school holiday. Concerned how she was doing, I joined her there for a day. I was sitting on the Kovner's porch overlooking the Atlantic Ocean when I reached the Assembly speaker to complain about the reapportionment lines. He made some comforting sounds but, of course, did nothing. I mention this seemingly futile effort to show how I fought to remain in the Legislature.

The new reapportionment bill passed on the last day of the session, probably in the middle of May. I looked again at the new Assembly lines. The southern of the three districts, which included Morningside Heights, was winnable. No, it was not a district for me. It did end up being represented by a white woman, Marie Runyon, although it included large parts of Harlem and was definitely an overwhelming majority Black voting area. I considered her a phony radical who had built a reputation as a tenant advocate by refusing to vacate her apartment on Morningside Drive where Columbia wanted to, and eventually did, put up a building. She was ousted two years later by Ed Sullivan, who until 2002 represented this district with distinction and became very popular. He also became one of my close friends.

Finally, I decided that I would go for the Senate seat and challenge Zaretzki. The redrawn Senate district included a small slice of Morningside Heights, my home base. It did include much of the Assembly district I had started representing since 1973. It also included large parts of Harlem. I always suspected, but never really researched, whether the Legislature in sending the lines to the Justice Department for approval purposely misrepresented the number of voters to help Zaretzki by keeping the district from having to include more of Morningside Heights, my base. In any event, the main part of the Senate district included all of Washington Heights and Inwood, which Zaretzki had represented for twenty-seven years. He was then, and had been since 1966, the minority leader of the Senate and was powerful, both in Albany and also in Manhattan as a Democratic district leader aligned with Tammany Hall.

I left Albany with my friend Steve Solarz on the last day of the session, after the vote on reapportionment, to fly back to New York. Steve had a safe Assembly district but had decided to challenge the incumbent Democratic congressman who, to Steve's good fortune, had just been indicted for bribery. Good friends, we wished each other luck.

From the airport, I went to a meeting at Jerome "Jerry" Kretchmer's law office. Jerry had been a reform district leader and had served briefly with me in the Assembly before becoming for a short period the Administrator of the New York City Department of Environment. I had asked Jerry to call together reform leaders from throughout Manhattan to discuss whether I should run against Zaretzki. Maybe twenty or so people attended. The support for my running was almost unanimous. But it was really up to me to put a campaign together. In June, I held a press conference to announce I was challenging Zaretzki. The biggest and toughest challenge of my political career was on.

As soon as I announced I was in the race, the attempts to get me to drop out came. As I mentioned previously, when I decided in 1972 to run in the redrawn Assembly district, throwing me in with another assemblyman, he decided not to challenge me. Instead he announced he would run for the Senate against Zaretzki. But he was soon bought off with a lush patronage appointment to the New York State Liquor Authority, which came through Governor Rockefeller, with whom Zaretzki was close. Zaretzki, in his twenty-one years in the Senate, never had a primary. He was known to buy off challengers with a patronage job. I was determined not to fall into that trap.

The first offer was that I could become a counsel to Zaretzki during the legislative session at a salary far greater than my Assembly compensation. I turned this down. The next offer was to become counsel to Stanley Steingut, then the minority leader of the Assembly. Again my salary would be far higher, and I would only have to work during the session. In addition, Zaretzki would promise not to run again after this term, and the seat could then be mine. I turned it down. The final offer was that the African American assemblyman, Southall, who for years had represented the neighboring district, to which the top third of my Assembly district had now been joined, would withdraw, and I could have his seat. (I never found out what goodies they must have offered Southall to agree to give up his seat.) This was the northern part of the three districts into which my old district had been cut. It only included a minor northern part of my old Assembly district. I could have that seat without having to challenge an incumbent in a primary, and in two years, Zaretzki, I was told, would retire, and I could then have the Senate seat. This might have been tempting if it had been offered before I announced I would campaign for the Senate seat. Instead of campaigning during the summer, I could take care of my family. But, in addition to being determined not to be bought off, my friend Herman "Denny" Farrell wanted to run against Southall for that Assembly seat. He told me he would withdraw if I wanted to take the offer. Again I said no. I was not going to be bought off. It was on to what I knew was a tough campaign in which the political pros said I was the underdog.

I had to organize a campaign. I found a good campaign manager—my only paid staff. We located a storefront as our campaign headquarters and an office on Dyckman Street (200th Street) just off Broadway. Up went a campaign sign. I used an old political acquaintance who had become a political consultant, Frank Baraff, to do my literature. He proved very helpful, and my literature turned out well. There were small reform political clubs in northern Manhattan I had to win over and to enthuse by convincing them I was in to stay and would run a hard campaign. There were numerous people to see, endorsements to get, and a need to become acquainted with communities new to me in large areas of northern Manhattan (Washington Heights and Inwood) and Harlem. Some 80 percent of the senatorial district lay outside of areas I had represented. I had to raise money, which I was not good at and hated. And all of this had to be done as I started with a new law firm and held my family together. I don't want to sound overly dramatic. Looking back now, it seems daunting. At that time, it was just something I had to do, and any self-pity or feeling that it was too much would have been destructive.

Two things occurred that were of great help. Two persons running in primaries for Assembly seats within the Senate district were closely aligned with me. One, Denny Farrell, had been a political associate for some time. He now took on the incumbent Mark Southall, whose seat I had refused to take in one of the offers to get me out of the race against Zaretzki. This district covered much of my Harlem area, going all the way to a big public housing project at West 155th Street and the Harlem River. The other was Edward Lehner, who had won the Assembly seat for northern Manhattan as a reform candidate, after losing a hard campaign in 1970. Ed and I had then served two years together in the Assembly and became friends. While I thought he would support me, it wasn't clear whether he would have a primary, which if he did would mean he would be actively campaigning for himself and with me.

At that point, Zaretzki made a serious error. Instead of leaving Lehner alone and limiting his assistance to me, Zaretzki and his people threatened Lehner with a primary. First they told him he would have a primary opponent unless he supported Zaretzki. When Lehner said he couldn't do that, he was told it would be OK if he just stayed neutral. When Lehner turned that down too, he was told OK, support Leichter if you must, but you can't campaign actively for him. Ed said no again. Bear in mind that he had two hard primaries in 1970 and 1972. A respite and easy summer on the beach (he was then not married) must have been very tempting. In a real act of decency and friendship, he stuck with me. The Zaretzki campaign then put up a primary opponent against him for his Assembly seat. As a result, Lehner had to spend the summer campaigning against his opponent. We ran together and frequently campaigned together. He was able to introduce me to much of northern Manhattan that I was unfamiliar with and to bring me together with people who could be helpful.

Running and campaigning together with Denny and Ed also enabled me to put out joint literature and posters and have their supporters also campaign for me. This reduced the cost to me and increased my exposure and campaign workers.

Another advantage I had was that Zaretzki was seventy-four years old and had never had a primary. He was not used to or capable physically of retail campaigning, which meant going out and shaking hands and being visible. His political and community activity was centered on a political club in Washington Heights. This had once been a powerhouse. It relied upon the old Tammany system of having block captains in charge of election districts and building captains who were frequently the building's superintendents. But over the years, this organization had become sclerotic. He also was not active with community organizations and rarely showed up at community events. He relied on the traditional organization's means of meeting constituents who wanted help by being available on club nights,

Monday and Thursday, at his clubhouse. Surprisingly, as it turned out, he didn't take full advantage of the support he had from unions, almost all of whom supported him, including the UFT, the teacher's union Nina had been so active in and had helped grow. One such union, the powerful municipal union, DC 36, was headed by Victor Gottbaum, with whom I was friendly and who recognized me as a strong supporter of labor. When I went to see Victor, he said, "Franz, you know I can't support you since we have relied on Joe in the Senate. But we'll do some printing for you on the sly" (that is print campaign literature). Zaretzki also had the endorsement of the Liberal Party for November, which was an advantage in a Democratic primary for what its approval meant to some Jewish voters.

Zaretzki also had the advantage of being able to raise much more money than I did. He had the support of the Republicans in the Senate and Rockefeller, who did help him. He could have done much more. Zaretzki could have flooded the district with literature and raised enough money to have radio commercials and hire a good campaign manager. He did almost none of these. I don't think it was complacency. All he knew was that you relied on your club and its captains. His literature was mostly lousy. I remember he put out a piece titled "Eighty Ways Joe Zaretzki has made your life better." Besides being just hard to read, this list of eighty laws he claimed credit for was sent to Washington Heights and Inwood residents, who in 1974 didn't see their lives or community being better. Instead, there was significant dissatisfaction as they saw their communities change under an influx of Dominican immigrants and the City's seeming neglect. New York was then beginning to feel the economic shocks that manifested in the financial crisis of 1975.

Nevertheless, Zaretzki, because of his leadership position, having represented most of the district for many years and the backing from unions and the Rockefeller administration, was deemed the likely winner. In my mind, he was more formidable than it turned out. I threw myself into the campaign with great vigor. It was a grueling time, especially as I had to stabilize our home life and start a new job. July Fourth weekend, I drove the family to the Farm for the summer. For the first time, we saw the redone kitchen from which now one could look out at the barn and fields. The shed had been removed and became the patio. This work was done by Clarence White. He also repaneled the dining room, which had been painted an ugly green, and opened up the fireplace, which had been bricked up and had been painted a most horrible red.

Nina and the kids stayed there the whole summer. It was a difficult time for her. She was depressed during the day and felt better only in the evening after a glass of alcohol. I called every night. Henry and family made some overnight visits. She also had Susan for company, and Kathy and Josh had Chaz and Tom to play with. I came up only one weekend. And I was depressed/low then too. The Saturday I was to go to the Farm (the only time I was up there all summer, except when I brought Nina and the children there over July Fourth holiday), I looked forward to sleeping later, as there was no subway to campaign at. But I woke up at 5:30, as usual, when I heard a voice say, "You are going to lose." I was so desirous of sleep but couldn't get back to sleep after that message. I got up and went as planned to shake hands at a supermarket before flying to see the family. I had so missed everyone. It was a short weekend before returning to New York and more campaigning. One strange and funny thing happened while I was with the family. We went on a hike up Mount Joe. Going up, who comes bouncing down the trail but a *New York Post* columnist, who had promised to write a story about me. I had been unsuccessful in reaching him to remind him to do the story. And here he was for me to bug him to do the article, which he promised to do and eventually did.

It was a tough summer. The campaign consumed me totally. American campaigns are really physical endurance tests. This was certainly true in 1974. Today, retail campaigning is less important, and much more time is spent raising money and using social media. Every morning, I went to a subway stop—usually in northern Manhattan—to shake hands with voters and pass out my literature. I usually, but not always, had some volunteers with me or was joined by Lehner or Farrell, depending upon the area. I often followed this with a stop in front of a supermarket. You campaigned where the people were. I would then go to my law office. At times, I was so tired I would doze off standing up in the subway while holding onto a pole. At my office, beyond my legal work, I would dictate letters to people I had met at subway stops.

In the late afternoon, I would go back to campaigning. Often this meant going with Ed Lehner through the area's parks—Fort Tryon, Inwood, Bennett, J. Hood Wright, among others—to shake the hands of people sitting on benches. These tended to be many elderly, mainly Jewish, who could not escape us. Most Sundays, with Lehner, I would go through Fort Tryon Park where Orthodox Jews were to be found. In the evening, we would walk through Bennett Avenue, where many of these Orthodox Jews lived. They took chairs to sit outside to escape the summer heat. I spent evenings canvassing people in their homes. Friday nights, I went canvassing in public housing projects, as I avoided residences where Jews lived, who would not want to be disturbed on the Sabbath. I would go through those buildings by starting on the top floor and working my way down, ringing doorbells and hoping someone would answer so I could introduce myself. It was miserable in the summer heat. I also had numerous meetings to plan strategy, prepare literature, raise money, and spur on my supporters.

There were candidates' nights when Zaretzki and I appeared. At one in a packed auditorium in Church of The Good Shepherd in Inwood, in what had once been a predominantly Irish neighborhood and the biggest diocese in Manhattan, I had to defend my abortion stance. I pointed out that Zaretzki had taken the same position. He had his shills in the audience who would ask questions like "Senator, why is it that labor unions love you so much?" It was exhausting. But I was still young, and the adrenalin and the need to win kept me going.

Much of my campaigning was in northern Manhattan, which I had not represented. There were two distinct communities. Inwood, the northernmost part, had been primarily Irish but was changing, mainly east of Broadway, which became home to Dominicans. The other part, Washington Heights, which consisted of the area from about West 178th Street to Dyckman (200th Street), still had a significant Jewish population, many of whom were immigrants from Germany and Austria. It was humorously referred to as the Fourth Reich. You could still hear German spoken on the street. It was now mainly an older generation, as their kids had moved away.

Here, too, change was occurring. East of Broadway, Jewish delis were closing, and West 181st Street, a major thoroughfare, was losing its commercial appeal. Both communities tended to be politically more moderate while still maintaining their Democratic and New Deal commitments. I had much work to become known and gain support. In Washington Heights, there was also a significant German Orthodox Jewish community, which tended to vote in unison. I spent a lot of time courting their leadership to convince them that as a secular Jew, I would be attentive to their needs. The district also included large areas of Harlem, West Harlem, and a bit of Morningside Heights. Except for the latter, I was unknown. I had to introduce myself to the voters of a vast area of Manhattan. This required retail campaigning by greeting voters at subway stops and in parks, walking streets with volunteers and handing out campaign leaflets, going through buildings and ringing doorbells (I had a list of Democratic registrants), and mailing literature. The latter required a campaign kitty.

Campaign finances were difficult. When I started the campaign, I thought I would need $15,000. I ended up spending about $80,000. Today, in a hard-fought primary or general election for the state Senate, the cost per candidate is well over a million and a half dollars. Short of money as we approached primary day, I asked my friend Victor Kovner to take me to his friend Stewart Mott, an heir of the General Motors (GM) fortune, to try to get a significant campaign contribution. Stewart told me all his financial problems—his GM stock was down, and the large garden in his West Fifty-Seventh Street penthouse cost him more than expected. He said he could not give me a contribution, but he would cosign as guarantor for a loan. I went to my bank to borrow around $10,000. I told my bank officer that I had the guarantee of the heir to the GM fortune. He responded that he didn't know who Stewart Mott was but that the bank would give me an unsecured loan for this amount. This enabled me to scrape through with enough money to pay for the important last mailings. I still ended up with the campaign in the red.

Throughout the campaign, I was anxious. I would like to say I campaigned as the "happy warrior" (an FDR phrase). No, it was a hard, demanding ordeal. I was totally consumed by the campaign and could think of little else other than checking in on Nina and the children. I saw my campaign as a victory over an old-fashioned, patronage-driven institution that cared only for its survival and was not progressive. Looking from the vantage point of years and many more campaigns, I see this as somewhat exaggerated. But without question, I represented a more liberal, democratic approach to governing.

The first sign I was doing well was when I collected more signatures than Zaretzki on petitions to get on the ballot. Then, and still now, to be a candidate to run in a party primary, a candidate must submit to the Board of Elections a required minimum number of signatures by voters in that district. I had almost twice as many as Zaretzki. I was getting some good press coverage. And then I got the *New York Times* endorsement, which was influential and which I was able to trumpet in my last mailings. Also, the Citizens Union, a civic group, gave me its preferred rating.

My main campaign thrust was to portray Zaretzki as cozy with, and beholden to, Rockefeller and the Republicans. I tied this to the Republican attempts to weaken rent control. Zaretzki's campaign tried to paint me as a carpetbagger who lived in Morningside Heights instead of northern Manhattan. This was not a persuasive argument. As the campaign progressed, I attracted more volunteers. I also gained endorsements from public officials, including Congressman Charles Rangel, Bronx Borough President Robert Abrams, Congressman Herman Badillo, and Dinkins, among others. I arranged walking tours with them. On the Sunday before the Tuesday primary, I led a walking tour the length of my district down Broadway from West 215th Street to West 110th Street. . I had the momentum. But I was still on the knife's edge.

Nina had returned from the Farm with Josh and Kathy a few days before primary day. She was pleased to be back. Throughout the summer, she had taken care of the kids while mainly depressed. She was not capable of helping me. But being at the Farm with Kathy and Josh was what was needed.

Primary day, I spent checking in on polling places. We had volunteers outside handing out literature. It took a lot of organization to make these arrangements. We were well covered. I was full of nervous energy. Since I didn't live in the district then—we were still at West 111th Street—I couldn't vote for myself.

As the polls closed at 9:00 p.m., Nina and I checked in at a polling place in Tiemann Place. I had won strongly in a few election districts there, but as this was Morningside Heights, it didn't mean much. We then went to West 157th Street, where Denny Farrell had his clubhouse. There, someone told me I was winning in Washington Heights, Zaretzki's supposed stronghold. Excitedly, we drove up to my campaign headquarters and received confirmation that I was winning throughout northern Manhattan. If I carried northern Manhattan, my victory was assured. I won. I was as astounded as elated. CBS radio reached me for an interview. I think I was somewhat incoherent with emotion. The final results had me at about 65 percent of the vote.

Finally, a happy night. The next morning, I was taking care of Josh. For some reason, his school day started later. We played *Sorry* while the phone rang incessantly with congratulatory calls, which I did not pick up. My morning turned perfect when, at the last moment, Josh won. I then went to my law office, where I was taken out to lunch. Life was good again. I had survived.

Then came a four-day Rosh Hashanah weekend. I rented a house on Fire Island right beneath the Kovner's place in Fair Harbor. We had a lovely weekend. Nina and I started jogging, which she kept up for quite a while after we returned. She was now on lithium and pretty stable. While on Fire Island, we walked toward Ocean Beach on the beach to meet the Solarzes, who had a lovely house on the island. Steve had won his primary and was going to Congress. What a happy reunion between two good friends.

Early in 1975, I managed to move to the spacious, eight-room apartment at 448 Riverside Drive, where Kathy and her family still live. As I mentioned before, I had only one year to move into my new senatorial district. This apartment had been Bill and Priscilla Ryan's apartment. After his death, Priscilla moved to Baltimore, but she kept the apartment and rented it out to Barnard students, except for the master bedroom, which was kept for her daughter Polly's use on her infrequent visits from Florida. Priscilla was willing to rent it to me, but I would need to get rid of the Barnard students and overcome Polly's insistence that she had to have a room for her in New York City. Fortunately, I met one of the mothers of the Barnard student who was concerned about her daughter's safety living on Riverside Drive. I convinced her that her daughter and roommates would be much safer on Broadway. So I worked out switching our West 111th Street apartment for the Ryans' apartment, which has now been the family home for forty-five-plus years. Polly was just told no, she could not keep her room. The apartment was still under rent control in a building now owned by Columbia, which it had bought after the Ryans moved in. Columbia accepted me as a subtenant but would not accept me as the prime tenant. So for years, I paid my rent to Priscilla, who forwarded the rent payment to Columbia. It was not until sometime in the 1980s that I convinced Columbia to give me a lease directly and change the apartment status to rent stabilization instead of rent control. If it had continued under Priscilla's name, we would have lost the right to stay there when she died. Priscilla lived into her nineties, dying in 2017. I remember the day we moved in. After the hectic toil of moving, Nina's father, Mrs. B, and I had a drink looking out over the Hudson River and at a beautiful sunset over New Jersey—the same sunset the family has enjoyed thousands of times since. It symbolized that the year that had started with so much difficulty had come to a good ending.

The rest of 1974 went well. I was comfortable in my law firm, where I took on litigations. Some of these were on behalf of steel traders whose shipments always raised issues of timely delivery and quality. They mainly turned out successfully. In 1975, the firm's partners asked me to give up my position as senator and to become a full-fledged partner. I declined, though it would have provided me greater income and a more secure financial future. I enjoyed practicing law, but it was public service and policy that had real meaning for me.

My election in November as the Democratic candidate was assured, and I had no worries. I did make myself very visible in my new district, which I liked for its diversity. I continued to be politically active and felt much more assured. I helped Fred Ohrenstein to be chosen by the Democratic Conference in the Senate as its leader in a contest against a regular from Brooklyn. I campaigned with Hugh Carey, who was the Democratic candidate for governor. He won in November. While I was still in the minority, I could spread my wings more.

In the 1974 election, the Assembly returned a Democratic majority, which it has held ever since. The Republicans retained their majority in the Senate until 2019. So for thirty years, I served in the minority in the Legislature, about which my friend Steve Solarz took joy in teasing me—even more so when I became a director of the FHFB in 2000 and was thrust again into the minority when George W. Bush secured the presidency, thanks to the Supreme Court. If I had stayed in the Assembly, I would have become a committee chair and had much more influence in passing legislation. But being in the minority allowed me to raise issues and not be subject to party demands that, as a member of the majority, required me to vote for its bills. I was much freer in the minority and ended up prompting more significant legislation through my reports, raising issues, and strident advocacy.

The year ended well. Nina remained fairly stable on lithium and was back teaching. Kathy and Josh were well settled at the Bank Street School. We went to the Farm for Thanksgiving and at the end of the year. The kids started to ski. As we had done before, we chopped down our own Christmas tree and decorated it. The last item was an angel, which I put on the tree's crown. My determination and maybe a guardian angel had turned what started as a disastrous year into a promising future.

# CHAPTER 12

# 1975–1986: ALL IS WELL (ALMOST)

Now that I was a member of the Senate, doing well in my new law position and with a home life that was more stable, I entered into a period where life was satisfying. And it stayed that way.

I enjoyed being in the Senate. For the first time in my legislative career, there was a Democratic governor, Hugh Carey, and one with whom I had a good relationship. In the Senate, I was with a group of mainly smart colleagues, both Democrats and Republicans. The caliber of the members was quite superior to the Assembly. The Senate was more sedate, but there were not as many laughs as in the Assembly. I fit in quite well and kept my active participation in the Legislature and politics. More than any other member, I debated bills. I also issued a stream of press releases. Many Monday mornings before going to Albany, I might have a press conference or issue a release. I would then fly to Albany. In later years, I would more often go by train or drive. Usually I was in Albany Monday until Wednesday.

I was able to build up my staff. Elizabeth Clark continued as my main staff support, running my district office, which was then on West 181st Street. I next hired Tom Tedeschi, a recent Columbia graduate, to also work in my district office. Then came Glenn von Nostitz, who served as my counsel. Glenn proved very valuable in doing the research on which I based my reports for legislative action and publicity. And in Albany, as my secretary—really my assistant—I was so fortunate to have Pat Gioia. She stayed with me until I left the Senate in 1998. Throughout my career, I found some excellent staff. What has given me great satisfaction is that many of these became real friends with whom I am still in contact. Every three or so months, we have a luncheon attended by five or six former staffers.

Over the years, my staff allowance increased, and I ended up with seven people working for me in the district and in Albany. I always had some interns from colleges in both my New York City and Albany offices.

Initially, I thought that I was not doing so well in my Senate debates. Then, and even now, I would second-guess how I presented an argument. One day, the Senate employee who took care of the cloakroom, where there would be coffee and snacks, said to me, "Senator, if I am ever in trouble, you are the one I would turn to for my defense." This gave me some assurance. I continued to be probably the most frequent debater of bills. This would be initiated by asking the sponsor of a bill that was up for a vote to "Yield for questions." Since the Republicans were in the majority, it was Republican bills I was challenging. The sponsor of the bill would almost always yield to my questions. After these were concluded, I would ask the presiding officer to speak on the bill. I am sure that the Republicans found me a nuisance. Rarely did my debate lead to a Republican bill being defeated. At most, the sponsor might withdraw it to correct some flaw I had pointed out. Nevertheless, my relationships with my colleagues, both Democrats and Republicans, were good. I think there was an appreciation that I was dealing with the substance of the bills and not just trying to score political points. I was told I was one of most well-liked members of the Senate.

The year 1975 was particularly exciting. New York City and even the state were facing a severe financial crisis. The city was on the verge of having to declare bankruptcy. It was experiencing what had happened to many defaulting debtors. It had borrowed mainly short-term. But it became harder and finally impossible for the city to meet its debt obligations when interest rates rose and its revenue collection did not increase sufficiently. Then the capital market refused to buy its bonds and notes. Without the ability to borrow, the city could not meet its financial obligations. The city had just borrowed too much. The state had to step in to devise a rescue plan. But since the state had also faced a financial crisis at the beginning of 1975, it was incapable of doing so without some federal assistance to right the city's finances. At first, the Ford administration was not responsive, which led to the famous *New York Daily News* headline: "Ford to City: Drop Dead."

During the city's financial crisis in 1975, there were tense legislative sessions lasting all week. There were deadlines, usually on Friday, when, if certain bills were not passed, the city would default on its debts and be incapable of making welfare and employee payments, among others. It was a scary time. I remember the end of one week's session as a deadline approached, without action having been taken, and a necessary bill did not pass. I flew back on the state plane, which was available on call for statewide elected officials and legislative leaders, but on which I could hitch a ride if a seat was available. This time, I ended up flying back with New York's mayor, Abe Beame, and his very able deputy mayor, John Zuccoti. Beame was so shell-shocked by the city's plight that his deputy and I tried to cheer him up. Beame was quite small, and I was tempted to take him on my lap to console him.

There were all-night sessions, meetings with the very able people Carey had brought in to deal with the crisis, long, heated conferences in the Senate Democrats' caucus. One time, when the week's session had been adjourned, the Governor called everyone back into session. I was driving back to the city when a state trooper on the Thruway, assigned to look for cars with legislative license plates, which I had, stopped me, among other legislators. He told me I had to return to Albany. It was all very exciting but tense because the welfare of the city was in peril. And it was not just the city. If it had defaulted on its notes and bonds, it would have been a serious problem for the financial institutions that held these securities. It might have caused a worldwide financial crisis and a serious recession.

The crisis was overcome mainly through the leadership of Governor Carey. He cobbled together a plan to put the city under the financial control of an overseer board, which enabled it to go back in the market to issue new bonds. He muscled the unions and some of the banks to buy these. What was present then and does not exist today was a high degree of cooperation among Democrats and Republicans and not the sharp political divide that exists now—a divide that Trump as president further inflamed. A number of bills in the Senate passed only with hard-to-acquire Republican votes. A lot of credit for leadership has to be given to the Republican majority leader, Warren Anderson, who realized the stakes that were involved and pushed bills that a majority of his upstate Republicans opposed. They didn't want to do anything for New York City, which they considered profligate and might hurt them politically with a constituency that was anti-urban. They were blind to the consequences that a financial collapse of New York City and its banks would have on their communities. The city's labor unions and businesses cooperated, sometimes only after some pushing and coming to realize that the abyss the city faced would swallow them up too. It was a time when the government worked. If a similar crisis occurred today, without question it would not be resolved by bipartisan cooperation.

I thought of writing a book on how this financial and economic catastrophe was avoided, which I would have titled *When Government Worked*. I went so far as to try to enlist one of the main consultants to Carey to be my coauthor when I left my Washington post in 2006. He refused. I felt that without research support, I could not do it. I think I was also uncertain whether I had the necessary skill. It is not the only time in my life that self-doubt kept me back. But then I also wanted to travel. After all these hectic years, I didn't have the drive to engage in still another consuming endeavor. One of my Senate colleagues, who was not even in the Legislature in 1975, did write a book on this period. It is not very good.

## FAMILY LIFE

Nina did not have a good year in 1975. She took a position, still in the school system, with the former assistant principal at Joan of Arc, Edith Green, with whom we were socially friendly. This was a new program set up by the Board of Education, which Green headed. The program included a conference. Green knew Nina had run the successful UFT annual conferences and brought her on board to arrange the conference. But Nina was not functioning well in that year and could not handle the position. Her manic/depression symptoms kept coming back. Her father, George, was extremely helpful, spending much time with Nina. Even with Nina's disability and my being in Albany for a two- to three-day week (more so during the hectic 1975 crisis), the home situation was quite stable. Fortunately, we had Mrs. B. Then we hired au pair help. The first was from near Albany. I don't know how we found her. Then we had one or two Barnard students.

Nina was not able to keep her position with Edith Green, as she could not do the conference. She then was assigned or found a position in a Brooklyn school (District 15) located near Brooklyn Heights. By this time, Nina was an assistant principal for elementary schools. She still had manic periods, which made her position precarious. I don't remember if there was an actual crisis with her maintaining her job or whether it was clear to her and me that this school was not a good fit for her. Another position had to be found. Fortunately, the head of personnel at the Board of Education was someone I had a good relationship with. At my request, he had Nina transferred to an elementary school in what was considered a very good district in Queens with well-functioning schools. After a while, she was transferred to a neighboring district, also considered very desirable. In these more stable school districts, she functioned well. There were no more problems with her position in the school system. Her manic depressive condition became more manageable because of the lithium she was on. When she died, the school she last worked in, where she did well and had good relationships with her peers and students, planted a tree and named it after her.

How did Nina's condition affect me? Mainly, I tried to carry on as if Nina was her old self and we could live a normal life. I did not acknowledge to myself the severity of her illness. Somehow I tried to believe that she would recover and return to the person I had married. I continued to try to live my family's life and my own as we had before. This allowed me to function and to continue to lead a life that I found meaningful and satisfying. My denial about the true state of Nina's condition may have been necessary for my own mental state. I don't know whether this was best for Nina.

So I continued as before, deeply engaged in my political and legal life. Family life and time with my children were also important. We did have good family times together, and many of these were at the Farm: the summers, Thanksgiving, Easter egg rolls, end-of-the-year chopping down the pine tree, skiing, and so on. And we took trips to the West and a did grand tour of Europe. Nina and I together sought to maintain a family life as if nothing had changed. I don't know whether Kathy and Josh can look back on this period as a happy family time. Their remembrances may be colored by later events.

Despite all the attempts at normalcy, Nina's condition was worrisome. While the lithium provided some stability, there were episodes of mania and depression. I involved myself in her medical care: visits to doctors, taking her medication, and so on. Emotionally, though, I was drifting away. I was not able to give much empathy, about which she complained. So it became a strained marriage. We argued more. There was not much enjoyment together. She was barely involved in my political life or interested in what and how I was doing. The one thing I tried to avoid was our disagreeing about the care of the children and pitting the children or one child against the other parent. And we seemingly did not. The irony was that Nina had a strong need for attention, but as we moved into the 1980s, it became hard for me to give her that attention. Our best times were at the Farm. We socialized there a lot. We went to auctions, hiked, swam, kept horses, invited friends (once a year, I invited my staff for the weekend), continually improved the place, saving an old barn that Nina convinced me we had a duty to maintain, and more. Nina connected us to the community. She made this the family's home.

Nor did Nina's illness make her otherwise inactive. On the contrary. Once stationed in the schools in Queens, her work there went well. She was involved with Kathy and Josh's upbringing. It was more her initiative and decision that sent the children to Ethical Culture Fieldston School, a well-considered private school in the Bronx when, after the eighth grade, they graduated from Bank Street. While they were in that elementary school, Nina started writing poetry and became active with a group of Bank Street school mothers writing poetry. They published a little book. One of the mothers became a well-known poet whose work appears in the *New Yorker*. Nina's poetry can be described as whimsical. I think it gave her much pleasure to express her thoughts through this medium. These poems, and later her recordings of her thoughts, were, I think, liberating for her. She wanted us to know what was going on in her head so we would know the person with that illness. She was not ashamed by it, nor did she try to hide it.

It was during this time that Nina told me, as I mentioned before, and which I relish as a high compliment, "You have grown into your skin."

## DECISION IN 1976 NOT TO RUN FOR CONGRESS

In 1972, after Ryan's death, Bella Abzug took the congressional seat. I explained before that I half-heartedly tried to get support from reform clubs on the West Side to seek Ryan's seat on his death, but the Riverside Club's leadership was convinced to put forward Priscilla. I accepted that decision, although I considered it mistaken. My desire to be in Congress and follow Ryan's footsteps was strong.

In 1976, Bella gave up her congressional seat, to which she succeeded after Ryan's death, to run for the US Senate from New York. She was unsuccessful. This was now an open seat. A large part of the congressional district was in my Senate district, and I could expect significant support from the political clubs there. And because I had become better known, having just run an active campaign for the Senate in 1974, I had an advantage over other potential candidates. There was one in particular, Ted Weiss, who was then a council member from the West Side, who was a strong contender. Ted was a fellow reformer with whom I was on very good terms. Ted had twice carried the reform banner in running for Congress in a district in southern Manhattan. He lost two close elections, and there was sentiment in the reform movement that he was owed a shot at this seat that was now vacant. There was another potential candidate, Ronnie Eldridge, another reformer who had strong credentials with the feminist movement.

I explored whether I should run and made some initial moves to set up a campaign operation. I finally decided not to make the race. It was not political concerns that prompted my decision. It was mainly personal factors.

Nina and the children were against my running. Kathy and Josh, both under the age of ten, opposed a possible move to a new place. Washington was away from their friends and the life they knew. Nina saw more separation, as initially I would commute between Washington and New York before doing what many congressmen from New York, like my good friend Steve Solarz, did, which was to get a home in Washington for the family. But then I would often be away on weekends to return to my district for events and to remain visible. In those days, Congress was in session for a good portion of the year and met almost throughout the week. There would be a lot of separation from the family.

Weighing heavily on my decision was that just two years before, I had gone through a grueling primary fight, which was very hard on the family. Another campaign over the summer (the primaries were in September) meant Nina and the children would have another summer alone at the Farm, and I knew how hard the summer of 1974 had been for her. And while she was much better now in managing her bipolar condition, I could not be certain that she would not relapse into another depression. Could I risk this again? And Nina, unlike the wives of some of my political peers, who threw themselves fully into their husbands' political campaigns, was not involved any longer in my political activities or aspirations. Yes, we had met through our political interest in the Riverside Democrats, but Nina was no longer in my political life. Was this because she saw this as keeping me away and the abonnement that she felt? Yes, I think it was a factor. The lesson is don't marry a politician unless you have the same passion and interest as him/her.

Another consideration was my law firm. I had finally found a good home in the legal profession. And while my legal life was still second to my political, I enjoyed my legal work. My firm had been tolerant when I joined in 1974 and right away plunged into a campaign. My partners liked me, and it felt somewhat to me as a betrayal if I were now to leave. I realized if I ran for the congressional seat, I would have to leave my job. This raised financial concerns, as I was beginning to make some money. Nina and I could have managed, but it would have brought financial stress.

I would also have to give up my Senate seat that I had fought so hard to win. In 1976, I would have to run for re election to the Senate. One could not run for two positions at the same time. If I lost the congressional primary, I would have no public office and no legal position—no income. Running for Congress, as much as I wanted to be on the national stage, was a gamble.

In addition to all the above reasons for not running, I was more comfortable and settled than at any time in my life. True, Nina's condition was an issue, but she was functioning quite well. I enjoyed our home life and the pleasure that the children brought me. Did I want to put all this at risk? Did I have enough drive and self-interest to run for something I very much would have liked to do—serve in Congress—regardless of the risk, the disapproval of my family and law firm, and how unsettling it would be? Unlike now, in a time of poisoned politics, Congress was a functioning body that enabled an active member to have some real impact on national policies. It was a painful choice.

The arguments against my running were too compelling, and I announced after a while I would not seek the seat and would support Ted Weiss. As it turned out, he had no primary opponent. He served in the Congress until 1992 when he had an untimely death just as the primary season ended, giving me the third opportunity to run for Congress. But that is a story for the next chapter.

Over the years, I have not infrequently thought about the decision I made not to seek this seat in 1976 and likely to have served many years in Congress. At times, it fills me with regret. But just as now, as I lay out the arguments pro and con, I believe I made the right decision then.

My association with the law firm Wachtell, Manheim & Grouf went well. After one year there, the partners asked me to give up my legislative position and become a full-fledged partner. I declined. My involvement in public policy as a state senator and my ability to speak out on issues that were important to me had become part of who I was. I can't deny that the status and attention also were significant in my decision. However, I did have an active legal practice. My clients came through the firm at that time. I handled a number of litigations, which mainly were all settled short of a trial. In fact, I was carrying two jobs. As I look back now, I am a bit astounded that I was able to handle both.

## LEGAL WORK

In 1979, the firm took on as a client a Geneva-based lawyer who had gotten enmeshed with Investor Overseas Service (IOS), a group of mutual funds created by Bernie Cornfeld, who started by selling insurance in Germany to US servicemen. For a while, IOS was wildly successful, and Cornfeld, a poor kid, I think from the Bronx, was flamboyantly wealthy. It all came crashing down in the late 1970s, leaving many disgruntled investors. Our client, Schertenlieb, represented some of the unhappy French and Swiss investors. But he also represented some persons seeking to gain some of IOS's assets. If he succeeded on their behalf, it might have reduced the assets available to his Swiss clients, whose investments had been seriously reduced in value. It was a clear conflict of interest. While probably not criminal under US laws, it had landed him in a jail in Geneva.

His wife came to my firm, and I took on his case. This involved a claim that his New York lawyer was the cause of his problem by making false accusations against him in Geneva, which had led to his incarceration. I had to go to Geneva and then to Paris. I was delighted to go back to Europe for the first time since Nina and I had been there in 1966. Nina was not supportive about my going; I assume it reflected her issue with abandonment. I was hurt by her attitude since this was important for my legal practice, and travel was appealing to me.

The Schertenleib case was interesting and consuming. It took me to Europe three more times. On the first trip, I visited him in jail, accompanied by his aggressive wife. When we came to the big jail door, which looked like the entrance to a feudal castle, Mrs. Schertenleib would yell into the intercom, "C'est le advocate Senator Leichter." The big door would creep open. I would then discuss the case with Schertenleib in a conference room. This went on for four to five full days. When it came lunchtime, a officer would come in and ask Schertenleib what he wanted to order from a choice of mouthwatering dishes. He was in a special section of the jail for incarcerated bankers and lawyers who were well treated. Maybe they paid for special consideration. Mrs. S and I had to go out and eat a poor lunch in a little brasserie and then return for the rest of the afternoon. While in Geneva, Schertenleib's lawyer and I met with the prosecutor to argue for his release on bail. We were unsuccessful. The prosecutor struck me like the police inspector Jaures in *Les Miserables*. I heard later from my Geneva attorney that he was offended by my bright tie.

Schertenleib's problems, aside from his apparent conflict of interest, were manifold in the narrow-minded Geneva legal community. First, he was Jewish; second, he had not been born in Geneva; third, he married a loud

Greek woman who wore gold shoes; fourth, he drove a fancy French sports car instead of the expected black Mercedes; fifth, and most damning, unlike most Geneva attorneys I encountered, he worked past 5:00 p.m. and was assiduous in gaining business. He told me, and I believe him, that he held an account for the queen, or was it a princess, of Saudi Arabia of many hundreds of thousand Swiss francs. As most of his assets had been seized, he was relieved to get her money out of Switzerland in time.

I brought a lawsuit in the federal courts in New York against the NY attorney, Jerome Traum, whom Schertenleib claimed, and I so stated in my complaint, had by false accusations landed him in jail. I was met with a motion to dismiss on the grounds of forum non conveniens—the doctrine that a case should be dismissed if it is brought in a forum that is inconvenient because the material events occurred in another more convenient forum where the witnesses are and whose law would apply. It was true that the events on which my lawsuit was based occurred in Switzerland, where many of the witnesses were and whose law would apply. But I had a very good answer to why I did not bring my lawsuit in Switzerland. Under Swiss law, which governed because the wrong, as my client claimed, occurred there, one had to sue a defendant in his place of domicile, which was New York. After submitting many affidavits and briefs, at the last moment, Traum, through his lawyers, stated he would submit himself to the jurisdiction of a Geneva court. I vigorously contested whether a Geneva court would accept jurisdiction. Based on Traum agreeing to submit to the jurisdiction of the Geneva court, the district judge ruled against Schertenleib and dismissed my suit. I appealed to the second circuit, which affirmed the dismissal in a lengthy opinion. Those of you, if any are interested, can Google the case of *Schertenleib v. Traum*, which was often cited as one of the leading cases on forum non conveniens.

What happened to Schertenleib? He finally got bail. He and his wife visited us in New York, and Kathy and Josh babysat their child. I appeared for him at his trial in Geneva. It was a fiasco, as Traum and I were testifying at the same time. This turned out to be a debate between us. The prosecutor, who under Swiss law sits with the judges and lay jurors, stated dismissively, addressing the panel, "You see, gentlemen, you can never get lawyers to agree." That was it. Schertenleib was convicted and sentenced to eight years of imprisonment. But I was told he fled Geneva and settled on the Côte d'Azur, where he had purchased a villa. I never heard from him or his wife in the gold shoes.

## FAMILY TRAVELS

In summer of 1981, Nina and I took the children on a grand tour of Europe. We flew into Amsterdam and stayed with Nina's friend, a retired professor of astronomy from Swarthmore. Next we visited and stayed with Nina's friend Jacqueline (a friend from the Girl Scout Jamboree Nina attended in Sweden in 1948), who lived with her husband in Charleroi, Belgium. From there to Paris to stay with the Derecskeys. Papi had a position with IBM in Paris. We were there for the July 14 French Independence Day and watched the big parade on the Champs-Élysées. A lovely reunion and time together with our closest friends.

From Paris, we took trains to Grindelwald in the Jungfrau section of the Swiss Alps, near where Nina and I had been in 1963 to see the Eiger. We had two beautiful days riding the trams and cog railroad up to the Jungfraujoch. Josh and I even got in a tennis match in the shadow of these magnificent mountains. The third day, the weather turned bad. The next day, we took a train through the Alps to Milan. There we rented a car and drove to Venice, stopping at the stunning, well-preserved medieval hilltop village, Bergamo. One could not drive up. You had to hike to the top of the village, where we found a good restaurant. I mention this because Nina and Kathy—or was it Josh? Certainly not me—ate rabbit. Then two or three days in Venice, including a day at the Lido. And on to Vienna by daylong train trip, which at one point because of a landslide required us to cover a distance by bus. In Austria, we visited the Cornaros in their lovely summer residence in the Tyrol and then had some days with them in Vienna. We visited Leichter family friends. With Rosa Jochmann, we went to the cemetery, where there was then a gravestone for my mother. This was before a plaque with her and my father's name was installed in a site for prominent Austrians. Finally, back to the US via Amsterdam.

It was a glorious trip. Nina did much of the arrangements and reservations for transportation and hotels when we did not have friends to stay with. One of the nicest parts of the trip for me was the family time we had together on the numerous train trips in our compartment. I think back with pleasure how we managed the train trips with all our luggage. Mostly I passed the luggage through the train window when we arrived at our destination. I would hand the big bags from the compartment to Josh on the platform.

In the summer of 1983, we took a trip through America's Southwest. Nina and the children flew to Austin. I was already in San Antonio attending a legislative conference. Nina's relatives, Leon and Barbara Schmidt, picked me up in San Antonio. On the way to Austin, we stopped at the LBJ Ranch. The Schmidts were related to Nina's mother and had prospered in retail with a big department store, Yaring. Because Yaring had advertised on LBJ TV stations, we had special access to the ranch and were given a grand tour. Interestingly, we met with the caretakers of the ranch. The man at that time was immobilized in a wheelchair. But the wife told us stories about LBJ. She recounted how when he came back after his presidency, he had her teenage son help him on the ranch. He worked him hard—just as he had his staff as senator and president—and refused his request to join his baseball team for a game. In Austin, we stayed with Barbara and Leon and were feted by the whole Schmidt clan. There were no better hosts then the Schmidts. I had three further visits later to Austin, one with Kathy when she went to raise some money for her film.

From Austin, we flew to Las Vegas. While Nina and I were checking in at the Circus resort, with our backs turned, Kathy and Josh started playing slot machines with nickels. Las Vegas was fun, and as the saying goes: what happens in Las Vegas stays in Las Vegas. We flew from there to a ranch on the rim of the Grand Canyon. Next day, we rode horses/mules from the rim down five thousand or so feet to the Colorado River. There we boarded a raft for a white water journey of three, or was it four, days. Just magnificent to go down the Colorado River. The views of the canyon walls were stunning. Each turn of the river brought a new view. At night, we stayed in tents on the river edge. The rafts were operated by young Mormons. One took a liking to Kathy and followed her to our next visit at a national park. Unfortunately, on our last day on the river, it rained—an unusual occurrence. We rafted into Lake Mead. A bus took us back to Las Vegas.

We then rented a car and drove to and stayed at two gorgeous national parks, Zion and Bryce. At Bryce, everyone except me went for a tour on horses. I unwisely decided to go on my own by foot. It was difficult hiking in the hundred-plus-degree heat. Back to Las Vegas and a flight to Los Angeles. We stayed there maybe two days and then spent two days driving to San Francisco. On the way, we drove through my old army base, Fort Ord, where I had my first eight weeks of basic training. We spent a couple of days sightseeing in beautiful San Francisco—a city I could live in if I had to leave New York. It was my first time back since my army days in 1953. Nina had to fly back before the three of us, as school was starting. I drove with Kathy and Josh to Yosemite, where we stayed in a cabin for three nights. We climbed Half Dome—but from the back and not the sheer face. We visited the giant sequoia forest. So impressive. Finally, back to San Francisco to catch a red-eye home.

In 1984, I was elected as a delegate to the Democratic Convention, which was held in San Francisco. The whole family went, and Kathy brought along a friend. We all stayed in one room at the Hyatt Embarcadero, where the New York delegation was housed. Being at the Convention was a ball. There were parties, events, and sightseeing, and as a delegate, I had lots of invites. The Convention itself was, as these have become, a showcase for the Democratic ticket of Mondale and Ferraro. The primaries had already decided that Mondale would be the candidate. During the primary, there was an event for Mondale at Zabar's. Kathy joined me. There is a picture of her with her mouth open, whooping it up for Mondale. I was able to bring Kathy and Josh onto the floor of the Convention.

We rented a car and drove north. On the way, we went to a redwood forest. We stopped for two days at Crater Lake. What a beautiful place. Although it was the middle of July, one could not drive around the lake because the roads were still snowed in. One day, Kathy and I climbed what I believe was a mountain named Baker. From here, we drove to Euclid, Oregon, to visit with relatives of Nina, where we stayed overnight. Then on to the Snake River for a white water rafting trip of some three days. It wasn't as stunning as the Grand Canyon, and I don't remember much white water, but it was fun. On disembarking, we drove to Boise, Idaho, where we boarded a flight back home. As with the Europe trip, Nina did much of the arranging. Another wonderful family trip.

# MY FRIEND FROM THE WHITE ROSE

In 1985 or maybe 1986, I met Franz Mueller, who became a good friend. Franz was special. He was a member of the White Rose, a small group of mostly young students who formed an opposition group to the Nazis. It was inspired by and led by the siblings Hans and Sophie Scholl. They printed and distributed leaflets opposing the Nazis and describing their brutality, including the killing of Jews in the East. Instead of slogans and hyperbole, the leaflets were reasoned arguments drawing on German thinkers and history. The Scholls were arrested when they threw leaflets from a balcony in the University of Munich. They were shortly executed in February 1943. Most of the members of the White Rose were arrested and mainly executed. Franz and a colleague were tried before the rump court the Nazis established. Because they were fifteen or sixteen years old, the Nazis were concerned about public revulsion if they were executed and instead sentenced them to imprisonment. By being sent to a regular prison instead of a concentration camp, they survived to the end of the war.

Franz formed a foundation in the name of the White Rose. For the rest of his life, Franz ran the foundation and worked so that the White Rose would be remembered. There are hundreds of schools in Germany named after one or both Scholls. In the sad history of how most Germans succumbed to Hitler, the White Rose stands out for its courage.

My meeting Franz was pure serendipity. I was in Koblenz, Germany, on a legal case and decided it was high time I visited a concentration camp memorial. I hoped to find one near Frankfurt. I had the strange experience of telephoning the offices of the Jewish community center in Frankfurt and asking if it could direct me to a concentration camp. The nearest were Bergen Belsen by Hamburg or Dachau near Munich. I decided to visit Dachau near Munich. I knew the name of a professor at City College of New York who had organized a protest when President Regan visited a cemetery where members of the Gestapo were buried. I called him. Luckily, I reached him in his office. He gave me the name of Franz Mueller, who, fortunately, I also reached by phone. He agreed to take me the next day to the memorial on the site of the concentration camp. I flew down to Munich to meet him. He was on the board of the governing body for the Dachau memorial and gave me a daylong tour of that despicable place. It was very moving and depressing. Out of this tour, we developed a friendship. I visited Franz and his wife, Britta, a number of times in Munich. On his invitation, I attended a conference in Hamburg where I was the keynote speaker.

Franz organized with Henry and me a daylong conference on the Scholls and my mother in Vienna in 1988. Josh flew in from London to attend. He was in London for his semester overseas. Afterward, Josh and I went skiing in Kitzbühel. Henry and I invited Franz and Britta to join us in Vienna in 2004 for the event surrounding the publishing of my father's book, *Briefe ohne Antwort (Letters without an Answer)*.

Franz was honored by the Friends of Yad Vashem at its annual dinner in New York, a very prestigious award and event to which he invited me as his guest. He was very gregarious and at his house or at his friends', there were always parties I was invited to when I visited him. Through Franz, I got to know Otto von Bismarck's grandson (more likely the great-grandson). He told me about some of his experiences. He was a pilot in the Luftwaffe and was shot down over Stalingrad. He became a fervent anti-Nazi.

Franz joined me in two visits I made to the Ravensbrück, including in 1995, the fiftieth-year commemoration of the liberation of the camp. It was extremely emotional for me to see numerous survivors and to join with the Austrian contingent in a memorial march to the nearby lake where the Nazis threw the ashes of their victims. I last saw Franz when he met me in Berlin after I came back from Hungary and Poland, and for the second time with him, I visited this infamous place.

His family, a boy and a girl, visited us in Wadhams and then visited Henry and Hope in Vermont. When Josh went on his European tour with friends during his semester abroad in England, they stayed with the Muellers. And years later, when Josh and Dana were traveling in Europe with baby Memphis, they also stayed with the Muellers. My relationship with him was so gratifying. I so admired what he did as a member of the White Rose. It was an honor for me to have him as a friend.

## LEGISLATIVE ENDEAVORS

While active in my legal practice, I was also an active legislator. I succeeded in bringing a number of issues to public attention and achieving legislative and executive action. I saw my role as something of a muckraker. To do that, one had to find the issues, do the research and fact digging, and then be persuasive by seeking a way to publicize it. I was getting much publicity and admit that I sought and enjoyed it. But without bringing these issues to the public's attention, no action would be taken. So my publicizing these issues was not merely publicity seeking. Even though I was not chair of a committee, and as a member of the minority in the Senate I was hampered in passing bills, I think I made an impact. One bill I managed to pass, solely because of the determined work of a counsel who was with me for one year, was of some significance. It required staff of hospitals and nursing homes to report any abuse of patients with a penalty for failing to do so. I don't know how well that law is being enforced, but it is a means to protect patients, particularly those in nursing homes.

One of my first efforts that received coverage was of a New York City program to provide leases for day care centers. I was able to show that the rents were often inflated for the benefit of landlords with political connections who gave campaign contributions. This occurred during the John Lindsay administration, which used these leases to reward supporters while he was flirting with running for president as a Democrat.

Banking abuses were always high on my list. I attacked redlining by banks. This referred to banks refusing to make loans in less affluent communities by drawing a red line around neighborhoods where the banks would not provide mortgages. I pointed out that people in redlined communities deposited money in banks, but none of this money was made available to them and the communities in which they lived. I worked with Governor Carey to have New York pass one of the first laws to prohibit this practice.

Over the years, I also criticized banks for not having branches in poorer communities, harming small businesses and making it difficult for thousands to have accessible banking service. To make the point and use leverage, I opposed bank mergers and requests banks made for regulatory approvals unless commitments of financing were made to underserved banking communities. I was only mildly successful, but I think the drumbeat of bad publicity did have some positive effect.

While still in the Assembly and continuing as a senator, I worked to free Martin Sostre from prison. Martin was, at that time, the only person imprisoned in America who was included in Amnesty International's list of prisoners of conscience. There was a national and even international campaign to free him. Martin had been a drug dealer in Manhattan and was sent to jail. In jail, he became what is characterized as a Black militant. Out of prison and no longer dealing in drugs, he relocated to Buffalo and opened a bookstore with books by and about Blacks and Asians. Some of the authors were probably radicals. The Buffalo police framed him by planting drugs, for which he was arrested and sentenced to a long prison term. I vaguely knew his name when I went on one of my visits to the prison, Dannemora. I always asked to be taken to the solitary confinement wing. Martin was in one of the cells, and as I walked by, he asked who I was. When I identified myself, he gave me some legal papers. These were one of the many lawsuits Martin brought against the state's prison system. He was effective in bringing these proceedings in federal courts through habeas corpus petitions. This usually required that he was taken to the federal court where he had filed his lawsuit. I began looking into his case and corresponded with him. It was evident he had been falsely convicted. I appreciated his fight against his mistreatment in prison.

Needless to say, the officers detested him. Whenever his lawyer or anyone else visited him, he was always subject to a strip search, which, since he was locked in his cell most of the time, was done only punitively. Martin always fought off the officers even though he was small and slight. After one of these instances, the prison got the local district attorney to charge him with assaulting the officers. At his trial in Plattsburgh, I appeared as a character witness. It didn't help Martin, as the local jury convicted him, and he was given an additional sentence.

I joined with many others to urge Governor Carey to pardon him or give him clemency. There was something of a movement for Martin, and I remember seeing "Free Sostre" graffiti in the subway. One day, Governor Carey called me to say he was commuting Sostre's sentences and he could go free. That Carey informed me was a recognition of how active I had been on behalf of Sostre. I knew at that time that he was in the federal prison in Manhattan because of another pending habeas corpus proceeding he had initiated. I called Martin. I believe I was the first to give him this welcome news. But there was still a problem I helped to resolve. To be released, Martin had to go back to the state prison where he was incarcerated, which was Danemora. He refused. He told me, "They'll kill me." I could not convince him that this would not happen. Negotiations, in which I participated with the commissioner of corrections, led to an agreement that he would be released from a correctional institution nearer to New York City. I think it was Great Meadow. If I remember, he was not required to stay there and was released as soon as he arrived there.

There was a postscript on Martin that was not so gratifying. He married a woman with whom I became friendly and who was and still is active in the Broadway Democrats. They had two sons. Martin worked as a real estate representative. In one of his buildings, he apparently was involved in an altercation in which a person was shot. Martin was the prime suspect. He then went into hiding and for two and a half years disappeared. He was found in the New York University law library and arrested and charged with assault. I went to court when he was arraigned, but I was not involved in his defense. There was a trial, and he was acquitted, or maybe the charges were dropped. Martin went back to his family. He lived until the age of ninety and died recently.

## CREATING RIVERBANK PARK

In 1977, Carey's budget cut out funds to build a park on top of the water sewage plant that was being built on the Hudson shore between West 135th and West 145th Street. The plant had initially been planned for the area around West Seventy-Second Street. The move to West Harlem was done for what I suspect was to avoid placing such a large plant on the shores of a wealthier neighborhood. West Harlem was chosen as a no-problem area. Rockefeller approved this move. To placate the West Harlem community, Rockefeller agreed to build a park on top of the plant. Carey's action threatened this. I held a press conference criticizing the budget cut. I organized support in the community and worked with other elected officials to counter the elimination of the park. Carey finally agreed to restore the money, but with each succeeding budget, I made sure the money for the park was included.

I was actively involved in planning for the park. Some changes had to be made. The initial plans called for tall trees, which would require more topsoil than the roof could handle. There were numerous meetings with community groups, the architect, and the state's Park Commission, since this was a state and not a city park. Issues were fought over where to place the tennis courts, whether to have more basketball courts, the size of the swimming pool, and others. Mainly through the patience and ability of Elizabeth Clark, my first staff hire, working with community groups, we were able to reach agreements between the community and the state. The park, named Riverbank, was opened in about 1991. It is visited by more than three million people a year. Most people who were involved with the long battle to get it built credit me with getting it done. One of the rewards I received was that my grandchildren have used the park.

In 2018, it was named after Denny Farrell. Denny was the assemblyman representing the park. He and I were not just political allies but friends. When I ran for the Senate in 1974, I ran together with Denny, who was first elected that year to the Assembly. He was very helpful in getting Carey to restore the money for the park but otherwise was not that involved. Why was it named after him? Denny was physically fading in 2018 and could not run for another term. He had by then served forty-three years in the Assembly, holding for many years the important position of chair of the Ways and Means Committee. He was also New York county leader (the post Boss Tweed and Carmine DeSapio had held). Denny's campaign to win the county leader position was planned in my home.

Denny was well liked, and his leaving the Legislature brought forth many deserved honors. The naming of Riverbank after him was due to Governor Andrew Cuomo wanting to name the new Tappan Zee Bridge after his father, the former governor Mario Cuomo. The Legislature balked. So to overcome this opposition, the governor cleverly agreed to name one state park after a Democratic assemblyman and another one after a Republican senator. Denny was the perfect choice as the Assembly member for whom to name a state park. So Cuomo, by combining all three in one bill, was able to get it through the Legislature. The former Tappan Zee Bridge now bears the name of Mario Cuomo. Previously, it was named after Governor Malcolm Wilson. I expect it will continue by all who use it to be called the Tappan Zee Bridge. Cuomo had a big event renaming Riverbank as the Denny Farrell Riverbank State Park. Of course, I attended. I can't say it didn't bother me not to be recognized for what I had done to create the park. But I was so fond of Denny and our relationship was so good that I am glad he is remembered by his name adorning the park. Sadly, he died a year afterward.

For many years, after the park was completed, I tried to get the city, which operated the plant underneath the park, to solve the problem of odors emanating from the plant. These did not affect the park but were a nuisance to the neighboring residences. I issued reports showing the plant was overused. I even made this argument as a basis for scuttling Trump's plan to build what is now Riverside South or to compel a reduction in the number of units and the height of the buildings as the sewage from these buildings would flow through the plant, which as I showed was often over capacity. I was not successful. The buildings went up. Though not owned by Trump, they bore his name—that is until after the November 2016 election when the residents voted to remove his name from the buildings. Even today, as you drive down the West Side Highway in the summer with your window down, you get the smell, somewhat faintly, from the plant.

## POOPER SCOOPER LAW AND CORPORATE WELFARE

Together with my friend and Assembly colleague Ed Lehner, in 1978 we sponsored the canine waste law, more popularly known as the pooper scooper law. The law requires dog owners to clean up after their pets. We held some press conferences to publicize the law, in which our dog, Cocoa, appeared. The law was a novelty and drew quite a bit of attention. It has been a great success, and for all I did and achieved in the Legislature, this gets the most attention and praise. Lehner and I, in recognition, received a prestigious award from the Municipal Art Society. *New York* magazine, in its issue in 2000 on the fifty (or was it one hundred) best things that happened in New York City in the previous century, listed our law. Ed Koch, then the mayor, told me that on a visit to Paris, at a fancy dinner for the Parisian elite, hosted by the mayor of Paris, Jacque Chirac, asked him publicly, "Eddie, tell us how you *reed* New York of dog *sheet*." The truth is when I asked Koch to support our bill before passage, he refused for fear of the wrath of dog owners, who can be a very determined group. But he did support the enforcement of the law. New York is definitely cleaner. Other cities have now enacted such a law—but not, I think, Paris.

In 1981, I took on a state program that gave subsidies to businesses that claimed to have created or retained jobs, which might otherwise go to other states. The retained part was an enormous loophole. The program was administered by the Job Incentive Board. I succeeded in getting some attention to what a wasteful program this was when I held a press conference in front of Tiffany & Co., which wanted a subsidy for building another floor on its store at East Fifty-Seventh Street. I pointed out that Tiffany & Co. had made a business decision to have additional space not prompted by the state's incentive and that it was not going to move its flagship store to Weehawken in New Jersey. I then attacked other such unjustified subsidies, challenging the claim that jobs that would be retained. I even sued the Job Incentive Board. In 1983, Governor Mario Cuomo agreed to end the program. This was a good achievement.

# THE RETURN OF THE SWEATSHOP

In 1981, I publicized that sweatshops producing garments were having a resurgence in New York City. In 1911, there had been a tragic fire in a garment sweatshop, the Triangle Shirtwaist Factory. Sweatshops were then common, hiring recent immigrants at low wages. Hundreds died, unable to escape because management had locked the doors. This created a public uproar leading to workers' protection laws. The common belief in the 1980s was that sweatshops were a thing of the past. Walking through the upper part of my district, I noticed signs advertising for sewing machine operators. This aroused my curiosity, and I went into one of the places that had such a sign outside. What I saw shocked me. In the basement of a residential building, I saw maybe up to twenty women crowded together over sewing machines. There were electrical wires wound around leaking pipes. There was no safe egress in case of fire. I began to inspect other such places. I directed my counsel, Glenn von Nostitz, to work on this issue. He did a terrific job in locating numerous such places. I then held a press conference charging that sweatshops were back. This received much coverage. A number of TV stations asked me to take them on tours of these shops. It was then pretty easy to gain access. But one time as Glenn and I toured a Chinatown sweatshop, a burly man came up and almost threw us down the stairs. I believe he was part of the Mafia that was behind many of these sweatshops.

We were able to locate on West 165th Street a sweatshop where a dress had been made by poorly paid machine operators. We were able to follow its path through middlemen to its sale with a big markup in a Macy's store in a New Jersey mall. We showed how the low wages enabled the dress to fetch a very profitable sale price. It was as if the garment factories in Bangladesh had found a home in New York. I held numerous press conferences, issued more reports, and proposed legislation. Some did pass.

Studies and investigations I did with my staff showed us that the sweatshops were really dependent upon the truckers, who tended to be run by organized crime. Unless the truckers were willing to carry the finished goods, one could not get them to market. The truckers also supplied the owners of the sweatshops with the sewing machines. These were only a step above the workers. Often, like their employees, they were immigrants.

I had on my staff Mike Weber, who did outstanding research. Mike would disappear for weeks on end but then would show up with some worthwhile research. He had examined the garment-trucking business and came to the conclusion that it was run by the Mafia and that its main boss was Tom Gambino. I issued this as a report. I was roundly criticized for making a McCarthyism-like attack and ethnic slur. Tom Gambino was the nephew of a real mobster by the name of Gambino. I was accused of defaming him just because of his name. Both the International Ladies Garment Workers (ILGWU) and garment business interests criticized me. Tom Gambino was considered an upright businessman who had been honored numerous times by the garment industry. How could I attack such a reputable businessman just because of his last name?

The ILGWU, once a very dominant, progressive New York union, had been organized and headed by a legendary leader, David Dubinsky. It was a good union, but to organize garment workers, it had made a deal with the truckers not to intrude on their arrangements or to organize them. This arrangement allowed organized crime to continue its role in the industry and allowed it to become the basis for the reemergence of the sweatshops.

One factor I did not mention in my reports and releases but which it is appropriate to point out now concerns globalization. As more and more clothes were made in cheap labor countries like China, Bangladesh, Honduras, and others, legitimate unionized shops, of which there once were so many in New York, went out of business. Sweatshops, with their low wages, could still exist and in fact blossomed, fed by immigrants whose need for work enabled their exploitation. This showed some of the harm of free trade and globalization, which, however, unlike many of my progressive cohorts, I don't condemn, as I see it as inevitable and impossible to roll back. One must also consider some real benefits from globalization like one billion people brought out of abject poverty. The harm to those adversely affected by globalization, particularly in the US, could have been mitigated by government support programs. But any such programs, like extended unemployment, were blocked by the Republicans.

A year or so after I received so much abuse for naming Tom Gambino as part of the Mafia, he was indicted for racketeering by the New York attorney general, Robert Abrams, who had been a colleague and a good friend. He was then indicted by the Manhattan District Attorney, Robert Morgenthau. He pleaded guilty and served jail time. The Mafia's control over the trucking industry was broken. So I was proven right. I have no idea whether my report on Gambino prompted the prosecutors to act. I should note that none of the people who attacked me for accusing such an "upright citizen" as Tom Gambino as being part of organized crime ever apologized or admitted I was right. But the spotlight I brought on the remerging sweatshops did lead to laws being passed, and many of the neighborhood sweatshops closed. I don't know what is the situation now, thirty years after my disclosures?

# ENDING A MULTI-BILLION-DOLLAR CONSUMER SCAN

In 1983, I achieved for bank customers a major consumer protection. For years', banks had delayed clearing deposited checks by not timely putting the money they received from the banks on which checks were drawn into their customers' accounts. They held that money for some days before crediting their customers' accounts on the grounds that there might have been some fraud and that the bank forwarding the money may ask for its return. This was a spurious argument, as the incidences of fraud were negligible. The total withheld from their customers' accounts amounted to billions in profits for the banks over a year. This money they delayed putting into their customers' accounts, called a float, the banks invested or lent out for their own benefit. Withholding for days the monies the bank had received from the intended account at times resulted in the amount the customer thought he/she had in their account, after having deposited a check, not in fact being there yet. Rightfully believing that their account held the deposited amount, that customer might write a check to pay the rent, or pay some other indebtedness, knowing he/she deposited sufficient funds into their account. But because the bank had held on to the money it had received some days before, instead of timely crediting the customer's bank account, the rent check, for instance, would be returned for insufficient funds. The customer might then face fees both from the landlord and the bank and possibly even eviction.

I had been railing against this practice for some time but with little attention. To make the point, I devised a scheme. I arranged to have some fellow legislators and staffers join with me, as state employees, to take our paychecks, issued to us on the same day and drawn on the state, and deposit them, also all on the same day, into the different banks where we each had an account. We then checked with our bank to see when the money from the checks was actually put into our accounts. Some banks took as long as eleven days, some nine, and others different days. No bank timely put the money into the designated accounts when they received the money from the state. The banks' claim that they had to wait for some days to be sure there was no fraud or insolvency, which might lead the bank on which the check was drawn to demand the return of the monies forwarded, made no sense since these were government checks. Even if the checks deposited were not government checks, I was able to show that, in almost all instances, banks received the monies from the banks on which the checks were drawn days before they actually put the money into their customers' accounts, with almost no instances of fraud and a demand that the money be returned to the issuing bank. I called this the nation's biggest consumer fraud.

As a consequence, and with the help of my friend, Assemblyman Denny Farrell, who was then the chair of the Assembly Banking Committee, legislation passed that required the Banking Department to set guidelines. The result was a regulation requiring banks to clear (that is deposit) in their customer's account any check of $1,000 dollars or less on the day the check is deposited. Checks for larger amounts banks could hold for five days, except for the first $1,000. This action by New York State also prompted the federal government to impose restrictions on banks failing to clear their customers' checks in a timely manner solely to create a float for their benefit. I testified before a House Banking Committee on this issue. Federal action was taken along the lines New York had pioneered.

## AND OTHER ISSUES

I received attention for what I charged were wasteful subsidies to businesses statewide and to real estate interests in New York City. My point was that the state subsidies failed to create the promised jobs, and the subsidies that went for commercial and residential buildings in New York City were unnecessary and a drain on the public purse. I held numerous press conferences, as I saw this as the way to draw attention to the issue and create public support. Some changes tightening up these subsidies were made both by the city and the state. I became known as one of the main voices criticizing corporate welfare.

In the middle of the 1980s, my counsel, Glenn von Nostitz, came up with a brilliant idea. We would do a survey that rated banks on how they treated their depositors on such criteria as interest paid, fees, and other charges. Glenn did the research, which we published annually by naming the best bank for consumers. Our survey announcing the best bank for consumers always got good coverage. We also printed a little brochure with the ratings, which I mailed it out to my constituents. For one or two years, the best bank was Amalgamated, which was a union-run bank. It placed ads in newspapers boasting of being number one in a survey by Senator Leichter. It even had a radio commercial with two funny, well-known actors boasting that their bank was rated number one. Unfortunately, after working for me for twelve years, Glenn was hired away by Mark Green, who had been named New York City commissioner of consumer affairs in 1990 and who appropriated the survey.

There were numerous other matters I raised and held news conferences on. Many of these involved tenants' rights, but they were as varied as gun laws, protective gear for boxers (on which I held a hearing and had top boxers testify—they were against my proposal that professional boxers wear the same headgear as boxers in college), the subway system, and trucks carrying inflammable material across the George Washington Bridge into my district. I held so many press conferences that one roundup news item referred humorously to me as starting each day by leaving a press release in the city hall newsroom. It was not far from the truth.

I was very active in opposing Westway in the 1980s. This was to be a subterranean arterial highway under the east bank of the Hudson River along the Manhattan shore, with a park on top. It would have replaced the elevated West Side Highway. My main objection was to the cost and that federal money, numbering in the billions, would be better spent on mass transit. There were other objections. The main and fiercest opponent of what had been named Westway was Marcie Bienstock, with whom I worked closely. Her concern was the degrading effect such a tunneled highway would have on the Hudson and its fish stock. It was indeed this argument that led a court to strike down Westway. This opened the way for the creation of the Hudson River Park (HRP). The state had acquired land for the projected highway and now had to figure out what to do with it. I worked with various commissions and groups to come up with a replacement plan with a park. Sadly, Marcie opposed the HRP and was a real thorn in my side and attacked me when I pushed a bill for a park. That is for a later chapter.

## AN ABORTED CAMPAIGN THAT LEADS ME TO SHOW THE INFLUENCE OF BIG MONEY

In 1985, spurred by a bit of hubris, I decided to challenge the sitting New York City comptroller, Jay Goldin, for this citywide position. I first had a poll taken. This was a waste of money because it inquired mainly about name recognition, citywide, which in spite of my press coverage was minimal. What the poll should have focused on were issues. And there were a number of potent issues, which did prompt me to enter the race and might, under different circumstances and if properly presented, have been the basis for a meaningful campaign. I sadly must say looking back that I was unprepared not just financially but in understanding that a citywide campaign was not like running for the Senate. Despite my years in politics, I was somewhat naïve and not sufficiently hardened to the realities of New York City politics.

Goldin had something of a reputation of a sleaze. He bore some responsibility for the city's near decline into bankruptcy in 1975, and he and Mayor Beame just escaped being criminally charged by the Securities Exchange Commission (SEC) for selling city securities with false and/ or inadequate information about the city's finances. They were criticized in an SEC report. Goldin had received favorable loans from banks that depended upon the goodwill of the comptroller and had received large campaign contributions from real estate interests that depended upon his vote in what was then the Board of Estimate, which passed on land use matters. (The Board was subsequently found to be unconstitutional by the courts under one person one vote and was abolished, with an empowered city council assuming most of the land use authority.) And there were other issues to develop.

In April 1985, I announced that I was a candidate for the position of comptroller. I realized it was an uphill fight, but I was energized. I hired a press person, and, as I mentioned, I had a pollster. But this was pretty much my support, other than my staff, who could not devote work hours to the campaign. The main problem I faced was raising money. To get significant campaign contributions, one had to show a realistic chance of winning. But to have such a possibility, one had to have a decent campaign kitty or show the ability to raise money. It was a catch-22. When I entered the race, my good friend Steve Solarz told me, "Franz, you are going to have to spend 90 percent of your time raising money. You can do a subway, a press conference or so in the morning, a bit of campaigning in the evening, and the rest of the time spent raising money." This was something I hated to do, was not good at, and I frankly didn't have the connections that would allow me to raise needed funds for a citywide campaign.

Mentioning Steve, and to show what a good friend he was, he supported me, although he was also a friend of Goldin's and could have pleaded that he would need to stay out of a fight between two friends. He had even gone on a rafting trip with Goldin in New Guinea. I was invited to join but declined. Nevertheless, Steve endorsed me. Very different from my friend Oliver Koppell, who was my roommate in Albany. Oliver failed to endorse me in his Riverdale Club because its district leader, who had worked for Goldin, was lining up the club for Goldin. On the club's endorsement night, he was silent. To her credit, his wife, Lorraine, spoke and campaigned for me. A study in political decency and weakness.

I held some news conferences raising questions about Goldin's campaign contributions from developers who benefited from his official action. There was really much more to develop. But much of my energy went into trying to raise money and win the support of Democratic clubs. The reform movement at that time had an umbrella organization, the New Democratic Coalition, in which all Reform Democratic clubs were represented. It held a convention to choose between me and Goldin. I narrowly lost. This was a big blow since I was running as the Reform candidate.

I was not able to project myself as a competitive opponent to Goldin. It clearly was an uphill struggle. The media didn't take me that seriously, and my coverage was not that good, which deprived me of appearing as a real challenger. In the same week that I announced my candidacy, the *New York Times*, a couple of days before my press conference announcement, (which was known in advance) ran a favorable piece on Goldin. My announcement was in one of the back pages of what then was the Metro section. I think this was done very deliberately because some of the *Times* editorial board were critical of my opposition to subsidized development, especially in the Times Square area, where the *Times* planned to, and did, build a new headquarters building. Yes, politics and self-interest do affect news coverage.

After I dropped out, in an article in the *Daily News* about my lonely campaign, Ken Auletta, who is an author of books on New York and now writes for the *New Yorker*, wrote:

> This year no one better knows the frustration of trying to drum up press coverage than State Senator Franz Leichter. On April 17 he announced his candidacy

for city comptroller, challenging incumbent Harrison Goldin. Just 37 days later Leichter withdrew. Leichter had done something unusual: He stole the press' job probing the way Goldin used, or abused, his office. With few exceptions ... the media yawned. "I just felt that when the press didn't follow up, I just couldn't raise the money," explains Leichter. So he retreated, taking with him the serious questions he had raised.

I finally decided to end my campaign when a former state senator, with whom I was friendly, came to give me a check for $3,000. That was a very nice contribution from someone I did not know. My friend told me that this check came through Donald Trump, and the donor was in Chicago. There is nothing illegal for someone, like Trump, soliciting campaign contributions. However, if this was Trump's money disguised as someone else's, it would be illegal. I also recognized that Trump was hedging his campaign bet. He gave much more to Goldin, his A candidate, but just in case I might win, he wanted me, the B candidate, to be aware of his contribution. I realized once I was fully committed to the race, my need for campaign funding might tempt me to accept questionable contributions.

I think I also dropped out because I didn't have the fire in the belly to commit myself to a campaign I was likely to lose. Some urged me to stay in the race because, even if I lost, I would make a name for myself. Many if not most candidates lose their first campaign. This was not sufficiently appealing to me. I have thought of my decision at times, as I am prone to review my past actions. At times, I regretted I did not stay in because there might have been just enough dirt on Golden to have upended the race. But if I had, it would have succeeded only with the knowledge of campaigning and the self-control I acquired later. I might have been too risk averse. But there was also consideration of the family—namely Nina. She would have another lonely summer at the Farm. Kathy had started college, and I don't remember now whether she planned an entire summer at the Farm. When I announced I would drop out of the campaign, I was actually relieved.

But I wasn't going to give up on my effort to limit the role of money in decisions by the city on land-use issues and elections. My brief campaign for comptroller had shown me how money is raised through favorable actions by city officials. These mainly concerned land-use issues that came before the Board of Estimate. On the Board, the mayor, city comptroller, and president of the council each had two votes, and each of the five borough presidents had one vote. I issued a detailed report in December 1985 showing how much in campaign contributions had been given by major real estate and financial interests to board members, but mainly to the mayor and comptroller. I followed this up with specific reports about donors and the city business they had. This received wide coverage. By lifting the log and showing what was underneath, I was instrumental in getting the city in 1988 to institute a system of public financing of campaigns. This has been effective in decreasing the role of money in campaigns for public office in New York City.

My research into campaign contributions had shown the appearance of conflict of interest by top city officials. This research was done mainly by my staff and particularly Mike Weber, whom I mentioned above for uncovering Thomas Gambino's mob connection. He uncovered that a front group run by two brothers (Bernstein) for the Philippine dictator Ferdinand Marcos had given $35,000 in campaign contributions to Mayor Koch and Comptroller Goldin. At that time, the Marcos interests wanted permission to build a forty-five-story office building on Sixth Avenue and West Forty-Sixth Street. Based in part on my research, Steve Solarz, who then headed the subcommittee of Pacific Affairs in the House of Representatives, held a hearing at which he compelled testimony from the Bernstein brothers. The aim was to show how Marcos had looted the Philippines and was now investing in New York real estate. I went to the hearing with one of my law partners to help Steve. With Marcos out and the Bernsteins unmasked, as well as the stench of the campaign contributions to Koch and Goldin, the Marcos development on West Forty-Sixth Street collapsed.

Based on my staff's good work, I was able to issue a report and hold a press conference, which showed large campaign contributions to the members of the Board of Estimate at around the time it voted on land matters affecting these contributors.

## PRESENT AT THE END OF MARCOS'S REIGN

When in about March 1986 Ferdinand Marcos was overthrown as president of the Philippines, Steve Solarz, who had been a strong critic of Marcos and a supporter of democratic rule, asked me to join him in a congressional trip to Manila a few days after what was called the Yellow Revolution—the colors worn by demonstrators—ended Marcos's despotism. Marcos's departure was achieved through street demonstrations, in a peaceful change, which was also called the People's Revolution. It was an exciting time to be in Manila shortly after the revolution and an exhilarating visit.

Steve was recognized as a hero, and the new president, Corazon Aquino, hailed him as the Lafayette of the Philippines. Steve had gone to the Philippines when Aquino's husband was assassinated by what everyone assumes was on the order of Marcos. He met then and other times with opposition leaders and was outspoken in getting the US and other nations to oppose Marcos's dictatorial regime. We were feted and had interesting meetings in our stay in Manila, including with President Aquino. During this trip, we were shown the presidential palace, where we saw Imelda Marcos's bedroom. I have a photo of me and Congressman Gary Ackerman, a former Senate colleague, sitting on Imelda's immense bed.

She was known for having three thousand pairs of shoes, which we also saw on the tour of the palace. A great trip. I made some acquaintances with Philippine leaders and was invited to some events to speak when they visited New York.

## PERSONAL MATTERS

The year 1986 was also one of personal issues. In 1982, I met Melody Anderson when she was in Albany on a lobbying trip. She was running a women's support group at that time. Later that year, we started a relationship that continued—with some breaks—until about March 1986. Melody was twenty-one years younger than me, very attractive, and fun to be with. My attraction to her and the development of our relationship filled a void in my life. She brought out in me excitement and a torrent of words. I was happy to be with her. What her attraction was for me only she could have answered. But I am fairly certain it was not because I was a senator. She was married at that time but soon moved out and got her own apartment. She was in love with me. She must have understood at that time that I was not ready to leave Nina.

By 1986, my marriage with Nina was not going well. Nina's condition was hard for me to adjust to, and I found her difficult at times to be with. I did not feel much love, nor did she show much interest, and she certainly did not share what was important to me—my political life. I was more alert to her work in school than she was to my work. I may have felt it as abandonment. And she did not turn out to be the achieving woman I thought I married. This was unfair, because she carried on well in many respects in spite of her awful disease. But abandonment is part of my psychological makeup—a feeling that probably developed that my mother, not being in my childhood life, had abandoned me. Factually absurd. Yet that is how a mindset can develop in a young child.

It was hard for me to show much empathy to Nina, though I was involved and concerned about Nina's care. And we did carry on much of our customary home life and visits to the Farm. Kathy was by then attending Cornell, and Josh was getting ready to enter Wesleyan University. Early in 1986, I came close to ending the marriage and moving on with Melody. Nina and I went to marriage counselling, but this provided little help. I told Nina I was ready to move out. Yet I could not do it. It was a combination of feelings for Nina, the unhappiness she showed, realizing that she should not be left alone, the effect on the children, and the disruption in our lives. I ended the relationship with Melody and told Nina we needed to stay together.

Throughout, I felt very alone and had no one to help me. I had friends but did not have the openness to discuss this with them and seek advice. I did talk to Henry, without much help. I don't remember talking to Elsa in any depth. She may have been away as the decision loomed. Looking back, with all the troubles in the ensuing years and the tragic ending, I am glad I did not carry through on my desire to leave and instead stayed with Nina. I am sorry for the pain I caused her.

In part, in an effort to rebuild our relationship, I proposed a trip to France, which would coincide with my being in Germany on a case I had taken on for a pharmaceutical company. We went in the summer of 1986. I met Nina in Strasbourg. We spent some time in the Alsace region, though unfortunately, Nina got sick by eating a traditional meal of various sausages and sauerkraut. Nevertheless, we had lovely days driving through the region, which we found very interesting and beautiful. We then went to Dijon, visiting old castles and vineyards. From there, we drove to Paris and enjoyed, at least I did, the City of Lights.

An eventful decade, 1975 through 1986.

# CHAPTER 13

# 1987-1994: BUSY LEGISLATING AND LAWYERING

The eight years from 1987 through 1994 pretty much followed my life during the previous period. The biggest change was probably in my law practice. I was more involved in my legal work and changed law firms in 1989. My legislative activities continued much the same.

## INTERESTING LEGAL WORK AND CHANGE OF FIRMS

In my firm, Wachtell, Manheim & Grouf, I took on some more high-profile cases and did more international travel. I described in the last chapter how I represented the Geneva attorney who ended up sentenced to jail. Starting in 1985, I represented a German pharmaceutical firm. This case took me to Germany a few times. It ended up in arbitration which went against my client. The case took much time and earned my firm a good fee. But unfortunately, I lost.

I had a very interesting case representing a Brazilian bank, Banco do Nordeste, which had been swindled out of a few million dollars. This took me to Rio de Janeiro three times. On my first trip, I was able to identify the main swindler. I set up a meeting with him. He was a no-show. But I knew his address. With my fellow attorney, who was with the Washington firm from which my firm got this business, and two bankers from the bank I represented, we went to his home in the fancy Ipanema Beach area. The Brazilian bankers were quite nervous at my determination to corner the mastermind of the swindle. The concierge wouldn't let us go up. I noticed a staircase, which seemed like it was for delivery and servants, and told my bankers to ask if we could go up the stairs. The concierge looked surprised and shrugged his shoulders, as if to say, "Go ahead if you want to use the stairs." Up we went—I think it was the third floor. I rang at the back door, which was for deliveries. A maid opened the door with some surprise to see our group of four white men. She called the owner, who was the person who had stood me up. He looked uncomfortable but invited us in. It was a beautiful apartment with a view of the beach and ocean. On the wall hung a fine tapestry. I thought, *So that is where my client's money went.* He was very suave and said he was sorry to have forgotten our meeting. We arranged lunch the next day. He did show up this time. But aside from a good meal, I got nothing from him.

I then sued two Israeli banks that had failed to honor a letter of credit that the swindlers had used to get what was about a $3 million advance from my client's bank. I lost on the technical rules that apply to letters of credit all the way through New York State's highest court, the court of appeals. I was stymied. But then a piece of luck went my way. One of the participating swindlers was a US citizen who had filed for bankruptcy. As I had also sued him for fraud, he had to list my client as a creditor in his bankruptcy proceeding. While debts can be discharged in bankruptcy, a claim based on fraud, as mine was, could not. I spoke to his attorney and told him I would never agree to his being discharged in bankruptcy unless he gave me an affidavit admitting to the swindle. He agreed to confess and gave me an affidavit of what had occurred.

It turned out he was double-crossed by the Brazilian swindler in what initially was to be only a ruse to gain a loan on low interest and to invest it at higher return before repaying the loan. However, the loan was never repaid, and a phony shipment was made, which led the Israeli banks to dishonor the letter of credit. The affidavit gave a full description of what had happened and established a clear case for a recovery against the Brazilian mastermind swindler and also the basis for his criminal prosecution. The affidavit also established the role of a notary public in Rio (in many Latin countries, this is a very responsible and prestigious position). He had falsely certified the authenticity of the signatures on the letter of credit. I took the affidavit to my clients in Rio. I am fairly certain no action was taken. Probably there were some payoffs in a country sadly known for its corruption. A strange postscript. I became somewhat friendly with the American from whom I got the affidavit and who, with my acquiescence, was now out of bankruptcy. We had a few lunches together. More surprisingly, he did business again with the Brazilian who had double-crossed him. Last I heard, he was suing the Brazilian. No honor or good sense among thieves.

During this time, I also acquired a Brazilian client, Jorge La Salvia. I represented him in a number of matters. He was a wheeler-dealer and very much engaged in the Brazilian way of doing business. I went, on his matters, a few times to Brazil. I loved going to Rio. I traveled first class and stayed in the best hotels on Copacabana Beach. Disregarding my socialist instincts, I admit to enjoying comfort. Once in Rio, he offered to pay my way to Manaus, the city in the Amazon jungle. I very much wanted to see it. But it was a long trip in this large country, and I felt I needed to return, probably because of some meaningless community meeting. I thought I would do that on my next trip, but the opportunity never came again.

Jorge La Salvia became an important client. I had various matters for him. I knew he was a wheeler-dealer who had too little regard for laws. At times I had to discourage him from some scheme or other. So it was not surprising when in 1993 he asked me to help his friend Paulo César Farias. He had been campaign treasurer for Brazilian President Fernando Collor de Mello and during his presidency was a powerful politician. I had met him briefly when I sought to help Hyundai establish dealerships or engage in car manufacturing in Brazil. La Salvia told me that since the impeachment of President Collor for corruption, the persons who had engineered the impeachment were now after Paulo. He had gone into hiding in Uruguay where he did not feel safe. He now sought refuge in Great Britain. Could I get a British barrister to help him to immigrate? I went to London and arranged for a lawyer to represent Paulo. Then La Salvia asked me to hire a private plane to bring Paulo from Uruguay to Antigua, where he would meet up with the British lawyer who would bring him safely into England. I made these arrangements.

I was not asked to go to Uruguay, but my sense of adventure and disregard for risk led me to decide to join Paulo's friends whom I met in New York and were to help Paulo leave Uruguay. What was the risk? La Salvia told me there were people who were looking for Paulo to assassinate him and the Uruguay government was likely to appease the new Brazilian government by finding Paulo and returning him to Brazil. Nevertheless, I flew down to Montevideo in the private plane I had secured. As we approached the city I went into the cockpit and saw a fascinating view of Montevideo with the lights of Buenos Aires in the distance. We arrived late at night. La Salvia met us and took us to our hotel.

The next day someone was charged with showing me the city while arrangements were made to get Paulo to the plane. I connected with La Salvia, Paulo and his friends in the afternoon and we went in a convoy of cars to the airport. I became a bit apprehensive as I saw we were being followed by a red Volkswagen. I wondered if it were someone from the Uruguayan authorities because there was tension over whether the

Uruguayan authorities would stop us. I was not apprised of whatever arrangements had been made, but I would not be surprised if it involved some payoffs. This was after all South America. Without any problem we reached the airport and boarded our private plane, whose pilots I had told to be ready to leave in the afternoon. Once airborne, champagne was served.

We flew to Antigua. Arriving late at night, we met the British lawyer and agreed to meet at breakfast. I spent part of the next day enjoying the tropical pleasure of a beach and going on a long walk with Paulo. I found him charming and interesting. Among other stories he told me about his trips to Cuba and friendship with Fidel Castro. He and his entourage, which now included the British lawyer, left on a commercial flight for London. I stayed until next day and flew back on a commercial flight, the private plane having returned to New York earlier.

Meanwhile, Brazil had secured an arrest warrant through Interpol of Paulo. He was to keep a low profile in London. I shortly learned from La Salvia that he continued going out to dinners and shows. When he realized someone had recognized him he fled to Thailand, I was told. I then explored with La Salvia whether he could find refuge in Austria, which has very limited extradition. I met La Salvia in Vienna in 1995, and we made some arrangements to purchase a home for Paulo in the city. But, before we could do anything further, Paulo, again due to carelessness, was arrested in Thailand. I found out in a strange way. I was at JFK Airport waiting to board a plane to Seoul. While waiting, I checked with my office and was told there was a call for me from Thailand. I had a number and placed a call and reached Paulo's wife (at least I assumed that's who it was). She asked if I could help. I told her I could not immediately go to Bangkok but would after I finished my Korean trip. Then the line went dead, and I had to rush to catch my flight. Later I learned that Paulo had been extradited to Brazil.

That's not the end of the story. La Salvia asked me a year or two later to open a bank account in New York for Paulo, which required we get him to sign some papers. I don't know why we didn't do it by fax but instead I sent a law colleague to Brazil. He met with Paulo in jail. In June 1996 I learned that Paulo had been shot and killed by his lover, whom, according to the official story he refused to marry, and who then committed suicide. The common belief is that both were murdered, and a Brazilian parliamentary committee so claimed. Likely, he knew too much about Brazilian corruption, which sadly burdens a country of lovely people that should be prosperous.

I also had a matter that took me to São Paulo for a deposition. And I went there again with one of my New York Korean friends/clients, who was trying to do a deal to get a dealership to sell Hyundai cars in Brazil. I brought him together with La Salvia, who was then close to one of Brazil's top politicians. We flew on a private jet from Rio to Brasília and then to São Paulo. Although I devoted much time to trying to get Hyundai and later Kia to enter the Brazilian market, nothing came of it.

I was mostly unsuccessful in trying to create business opportunities for my clients. I went to Korea maybe six times for La Salvia and at other times with my Korean friends in New York. Two of these times, I also involved my good friend Steve Solarz, who had left Congress at the end of 1992. Steve was now using his many contacts, mainly in Asia, to act as a business consultant based on the many friendships he had formed with persons who were outcasts and had asylum in the US but with change of governments were now the leaders of their country.

Through another failed business effort, I became friendly with the representative of Hyundai in New York. He invited me to one of the gala dinners in Washington surrounding Bill Clinton's inauguration. There I was seated at a table with the founder of Hyundai. Actually, I had met him in Seoul the previous year through Steve. The next day, with Steve, we met him regarding La Salvia's effort to get a Hyundai dealership for Argentina. He said we needed to see his brother, who was running the automobile subsidiary, and he scheduled a meeting for us. So off we went to Seoul. I managed to get Steve a fee of $25,000 to join us for that meeting. Nothing came of it. Yet these were busy, good, and satisfying days.

Fortuitously, I picked up an excellent Mexican client, the Mexican government development bank, Nacional Financiera (Nafinsa). My firm had some connection with a larger Washington firm that would refer matters to us that required handling in New York. One such matter was a simple collection matter involving a New York property, which I resolved successfully. This so pleased the counsel of Nafinsa that he sent me some significant matters. These took me to Mexico City a few times. More important, these were well-paid matters, which proved very helpful when in 1989 I switched law firms.

Wachtell, Manheim & Grouf, where I had been since 1974, while it had some very good lawyers and was a firm I enjoyed being part of, wasn't doing particularly well financially. Our situation was not helped when we moved to a larger and more expensive space in 30 Rockefeller Plaza. One day, as I came to the office, I was told that the main rainmaker at the firm, the son of the Grouf in the firm's name, had decided to leave for another firm. I considered this a death knell for the firm. Unfortunately, I had to look for another firm and again was anxious about my legal future and how I was going to make enough money to maintain my family's well-being. I was sorry to make a move, as the firm had been a good home, and I had been treated well. Both Kathy and Josh interned there for a short period.

Fortunately, I was able to make a connection through David Sweet, who had worked in Albany for my colleague, later a judge, Ed Lehner. David is a friend and my personal lawyer. Through him, I became a counsel to the firm he was a partner in, Walter, Conston, Alexander & Green. This was a much larger firm of maybe some fifty or sixty lawyers, which represented a number of substantial German firms. The founding partner, Walter, had been a lawyer in Munich before the Nazi era. When the Nazis came into power, as a Jew, Walter was forced to flee to the US. Here he first worked as an accountant. After the war, he was contacted by some of his former clients, at a time when they were still struggling as Germany rebuilt, and could not attract or afford better known firms. He became a lawyer when he realized his clients needed legal representation. He built up a good practice, and through mergers, he created what was then, especially for me, a fairly large firm, although considered a medium- sized firm. (This was before major firms, which now consist of thousands of lawyers with offices throughout the world—an aspect of globalization.) Joining any firm meant you had to bring some business with you. Fortunately, I had my Mexican client and few others as a selling point. It must have been around July or August 1989 that I made the move. Again, the change turned out well. Initially, I brought in what was then considered good business. I made more money and was treated well. There were some fallow years in the middle 1990s, but that is for later.

I continued to have interesting cases. One such matter was representing the hotel chain Best Western. It had cancelled the franchise of a hotel/motel in Albany for not meeting its standards. The hotel sued on the ground that my client had violated federal antidiscrimination laws. It claimed that the cancellation was because the hotel had taken in Black families on welfare. The suit dragged on with all the legal features of litigation—motions, depositions, court appearances, and so on. For this case, and one or two other matters for Best Western, I went to Phoenix and Tucson.

As the trial date approached and I started reviewing depositions, which I should have looked through earlier, I noticed that the AAA had inspected this hotel shortly before the inspection by Best Western that led to the cancellation of the franchise. I managed, through AAA's Albany lobbyist, to get the report, which confirmed my client's decision to cancel the franchise for the poor condition of the property, and to provide a witness to authenticate the report. When I presented this news to my opposing lawyer, he knew I had him and agreed to drop the case. As I had brought a counterclaim for Best Western, I refused to drop my claim until his client agreed to pay a decent sum to settle. I think it was $200,000. Best Western's representatives and witnesses were already in New York for the trial, which was to start the next day. We all went out and had a celebratory, fancy meal at my client's expense. The next day in court, I was able to tell the judge that the case had been settled. This was one of my major legal victories, as I not only saved Best Western from the injury to its brand if it had been found to have violated the fair housing laws but also was able to get it a nice monetary reward for my client.

As I have made clear, I loved traveling. And while these business trips tended to be short and did not permit for much sightseeing, I enjoyed the change from my legislative work. But it also meant that I had two jobs. It gives me real satisfaction that I was able to carry on an active legal practice while at the same time being a very visible and active legislator. At times, it felt as if I was on a tightrope, balancing my legislative and legal commitments. There were times when I had a court date scheduled for a day when I had to be in Albany for an important vote. But somehow I managed to work it out.

One time, I was in Paris when my office reached me to let me know that I was urgently needed that night for a vote on funding for the Metropolitan Transit Authority. My meetings in Paris were over fortunately, and I was able to get a flight arriving in JFK Airport in the early evening. Arrangements were made to have the state plane ready for me at LaGuardia Airport to bring me to Albany. Nina met me in JFK to get me to the state plane. When I landed in Albany holding my suitcase, I rushed to the Senate chamber. It was closed. The session had been cancelled. So I started the day on the Champs-Élysées in Paris and ended up on State Street in Albany.

One other time when my client, La Salvia, wanted me to go to London to meet a British solicitor. I was up at the Farm, as it was the summer. I told him I had to be back two days later in New York, and I could only do this if I flew back on the Concorde. I rushed back from the Farm to catch a Virgin Atlantic flight to London, where I stayed just one day. The next day, I flew back on the Concorde. For those who may read this and don't know what that was, it was a supersonic jet. I left London at 7:30 p.m. and arrived at JFK at 5:30 p.m. The flight took around four hours. What was the rush to get back? It was the annual dinner of the Bronx Democratic Organization. Hardly an urgent event to rush back to from London. I did enjoy the flight on the Concorde, which suspended service after a crash and because it was not economical. My business trips were all first class, and I stayed at five-star hotels courtesy of my clients. I do miss that, as I am now squeezed into economy on my flights.

## TO ASIA AND TREKKING IN THE HIMALAYAS

The first of my numerous trips to Seoul, Korea, was in 1989, arranged by my Korean friends in New York. This trip was very special. I first flew to Hong Kong from San Francisco. I left the latter only a few hours before the big earthquake that hit the city in October. I was fascinated with Hong Kong. From there, I went to Seoul to meet my Korean hosts. I am not sure what the purpose of the trip was. I think they wanted to show off that they had a senator in tow. We met a few politicians, including one who later became president. Here, too, I was enthralled by an oriental city.

Next I flew to Kathmandu for the Nepalese trek I had arranged with a travel agency in New York. Being there was entering a world of centuries ago. After two days, I flew to Pokahara to meet up with Christoph Cornaro. As you might remember from previous chapters, he was married to one of Nina's college roommates and best friends, Gail. I had invited him to join me in the Himalayan trek. He was then the Austrian ambassador to India. Christoph had to be back in New Delhi for Austrian Independence Day celebration on October 26 and was able to join me for only four days.

The trek was one of the most enjoyable events in my life. I had arranged for us to go to what is known as the Annapurna Sanctuary. While I had always been attracted to Mount Everest, a trek there would take too long, and my reading up on the Himalayas had described the Annapurna trek as more beautiful. When Nina and I had our mountain-reading period in the early years of our marriage, we fantasized about going to Everest. We thought maybe with $35,000 we could do it. That was still a time of expeditions with tens and hundreds of porters and Sherpas. Now, in 1989, trekking had become easy. For the trek, I arranged for two Sherpas. We added four porters in Pokhara. I don't remember the cost, but it was not nearly $35,000.

The day after arriving, we met our Sherpa guides. Before we left, I had the first glimpse of Machapuchare—the fishtail mountain that we continually saw on the trek and that forms part of the Annapurna Sanctuary. It is sacred, and no one is allowed to climb it. Off we went. At a place where workers gathered, we picked up the four porters. The first day was just a long, fairly flat walk. That evening as Christoph and I had dinner— cooked by the Sherpas—I saw high in the sky what I took to be a white cloud. As the sky cleared, I saw it was the peak of a mountain. I was in fairy land.

I will not go through every day's trek, though they remain fairly fresh in my mind. I'll just touch on a few highlights. The next day, we went up six thousand feet, mostly steps avoiding being pushed off by caravans of mules carrying goods up and down. Either the next or the following day, we were woken up around four or five and taken up to a viewpoint from which you saw the first rays of the sun hit some of the highest eight-thousand-meter peaks—among them Dhaulagiri and the Annapurna's peaks. It was stunning to see these mountains turn pink and orange as the rays of the sun hit them. Maybe the most beautiful sight I ever saw.

After three full days, Christoph, with one Sherpa and a porter, left to return to Pokahara. Christoph had to be back in New Delhi for the Austrian Independence Day celebration at the embassy. I continued on for a few days with one Sherpa and three porters. I felt a bit silly having this entourage when on the trail I saw young, single women trekking all by themselves. But it was very comfortable having this support group. The Sherpa was so caring. He would walk right behind me to catch me if I slipped. He was fairly small and maybe in his thirties or forties. He had only a pair of sneakers and walked so effortlessly and so quietly that at times I would look behind me to see if he was still there. He always was.

One day, we had a porter rebellion over some issue I did not understand, as no one spoke English. The upshot was that the porters who carried all the food and equipment did not follow us. I had to wait for my lunch. Eventually, they showed up, and all was resolved when I said I would buy them a bottle of brandy, which was available from the rest houses along the way. I loved being in the Himalayas and did well going up and down multiple times, surrounded by majestic peaks.

After a few days, we reached the Sanctuary, which is surrounded by glorious peaks, including Annapurna—a fabled mountain in climbing lore—and Machapuchare. Just stunning. We were maybe at fourteen thousand feet, and it was cold. I didn't want to sleep in my tent, so my Sherpa arranged for me to sleep in a guesthouse. There were no beds. I shared a plank with an Israeli couple. I slept so well and think of it as, on too many nights now, I turn and twist sleeplessly in my comfortable bed. The next day, as we headed down (still some ups), it rained. My Sherpa again put me into a guesthouse. There I ran into a group of three or four Harvard female students who were having their semester abroad in Nepal. We spent a good portion of the night playing hearts. In our globalized world, things get scrambled—and even more so now with the internet.

One other special remembrance. The next day, my Sherpa led me off the trail to a hot spring that was just a few feet from a roaring brook. After days of not bathing, it was so delicious to soak in the spring and listen to the rushing waters of the brook. On the way back to the trail, a number of leeches fastened on me, which my dutiful Sherpa noticed and knocked off. Good days on the way back to Pokhara. From there, I flew back to Kathmandu.

I next flew to New Delhi to visit the Cornaros. For an inexplicable reason, my visa to India was valid only for the next day. It took me quite some time and a gathering of ten or more police officers, who had a lengthy, animated discussion, until I was finally allowed out of the airport. Christoph was away, and I spent some time with Gail. I went out with her for a delicious Indian meal. Unfortunately, I overate. That night, I was hit with a double whammy. I threw up because of too much food, and I also had diarrhea as a result of drinking polluted water on the last day of my trek. I know what happened. We stopped at a tea house for some refreshment. It took forever to get the tea, and I impatiently asked the waitress when my tea was coming. She brought it right away, which probably meant the water had not been sufficiently boiled. It was not the only time my impatience had consequences. The significance of all this uninteresting description of my digestive tract is the problem it caused on my next-day trip to see the

Taj Mahal. I had to get up very early to catch a special train to Agra, on which breakfast was served. I felt so sick that just to look at food brought back the nausea.

At Agra, I had arranged for a guide. Weak and miserable as I felt, I had a full day of sightseeing but carried on motivated by the interest and beauty of what I was seeing. The day tour ended with a visit to the Taj Mahal. Often, when a place or an event you read or hear about is so positively described, you tend to build up your anticipation. When you finally see and/or experience it, your high expectations are not met. This was not true of my seeing the Taj Mahal. It is a work of exceptional beauty that literally took my breath away.

It has been my experience that, at times, when aware of your body because of some ailment or infirmity, you are more sensitive to your surroundings. Whatever, I survived the day, including watching a snake charmer and declining the suggestion that I pet the dancing cobra. On the return train, I was even able to eat a little food. I enjoyed my remaining days in New Delhi, sightseeing and being invited to dinner by a banker I had met cashing some traveler's checks. Back to the US via Hong Kong. What a great trip.

# MORE OF MY LEGISLATIVE EXPERIENCE AND HELPING TO SAVE MILLIONS OF ACRES IN NORTHERN QUÉBEC FROM BEING FLOODED

My legislative work continued much as before. I issued reports, which my excellent staff worked on, held press conferences, and sent out releases. My focus was on ethics reform in the Legislature, campaign finance, the subway system, unreasonable state subsidies for businesses, some more work on exposing sweatshops, and legislation to protect their workers.

I especially focused on what I called corporate welfare, unjustifiable subsidies to allegedly keep or create jobs in New York. As I pointed out, these subsidies were not needed, and often, the promised jobs never materialized. In one instance, I succeeded in having Mayor Giuliani freeze a subsidy to a bank when I pointed out it had cut jobs after getting a previous hefty subsidy through tax abatements. I continued showing how campaign contributions were made by businesses and individuals who wanted favorable action from the governor or the Legislature. This led to one of my spiffs with Donald Trump, who was the biggest contributor to elected officials. This is described in the addendum.

I continued to strongly oppose the death penalty and support abortion rights. I still called out excessive bank fees and issued the annual report on which banks were best or worst for consumers. In 1993, the *New York Times* ran a feature on me with the title "Leichter, the Senate Minority of One, Finds An Audience Beyond Albany." The article captured my philosophy that as a member of the minority in the Senate, I was unable to pass meaningful legislation under my name, but by publicizing issues, I could create change. And on some issues, like banking, wasteful, pointless government subsidies, and furthering the New York City public campaign-financing system through my reports on contributions to public officials, I did cause change. Throughout, I sought to avoid the herd mentality and peer pressure that leads so many legislators to just go along.

I also made a name for myself by being the only legislator on the last day/night of the legislative session to get up and ask for an explanation and to challenge many bills. The *Times* quoted me as saying, "Bills drop on our desks like fall leaves." A terrible practice of the Legislature, which I believe still exists, is that on the last few days of the session, and especially the last day, which usually runs until the sun comes up, the calendar for passage is filled with literally hundreds of bills. These are bills that have been held up by both chambers and sometimes due to the governor's involvement, mostly as leverage in negotiating which bills will be passed by both chambers. Thus a bill the Republican majority wants is held up in the Assembly to trade its passage for a bill the Assembly wants the Senate to act on. This gamesmanship goes on throughout the session as the leaders of both houses hold up these bills as their bargaining chips. The result is this flood of bills at the end of session as the legislative leaders and the governor make their deals swapping bills. The legislators are not given time to read and mostly do not understand the substance of the bills. To slow down the process, I rose to ask questions and debate many of these bills. This did not please my colleagues, who wanted to go home to bed, but I think they accepted my purpose and sincerity in doing this.

The advantage of being in the minority was that I felt pretty free to tackle any issue that caught my attention and not be concerned if I departed from positions that most Democrats took. If I had been in the majority, I would have been under more pressure to support Democratic bills and positions. But I would have retained my independence.

In 1992 and 1993, I became engaged in an effort to save millions of acres in northern Québec of land occupied by indigenous people from being dammed and becoming a large reservoir to produce hydroelectric power. This led to two interesting trips to Hudson Bay, followed by a Québec-government-sponsored trip to Québec City. How did this involve New York state one may ask? The state had signed a letter of intent to purchase billions of dollars' worth of electricity from Hydro Québec, the large and powerful utility. To increase its electricity output, it needed to develop more hydroelectric power. It had previously flooded a large area to create its first hydroelectric project. Now it planned to flood an area the size of France, which it needed to achieve its goal, as the area was fairly flat. The land flooded was home of the Cree, part of the First Nation, which is how the Canadians refer to what we call Native Americans. This project would also cause environmental damage and even risks to the food chain because of the mercury that would be released from the drowned vegetation.

I was approached by a raft company manager who was organizing a raft trip down the Great Whale River to protest this development that would submerge so much land and rivers and lakes. It would also flood burial and hunting grounds of the Cree. He gathered together a group that included another legislator, Robert F. Kennedy Jr., and his brother Michael (sons of the late RFK). I brought Nina along. We left from Montreal to fly to Great Whale, the town at the mouth of the Great Whale River, on the shores of Hudson Bay.

We were met by the leadership of the Cree. The town had been built by Hydro Québec, and the house we stayed in and the ones we saw were comfortable with modern appliances, including bigger and newer television sets than we had. Hydro Québec had done this to accommodate First Nation people who had been forced out of their villages and encampments when it created its first hydro project, which flooded millions of acres and displaced the residents. But the effect of this supposed largess was to erode the culture of the First People. They now had a high rate of alcoholism, drug use, teenage pregnancy, and obesity. The leadership wanted its people to return to its traditions of hunting, fishing, and spending weeks in the bush living in teepees. They saw further flooding as taking away their lands and traditional livelihood as well as flooding their burial grounds. One interesting feature of the town of Great Whale was that it is also populated by Inuits, a different native people who live mainly by fishing in the sea. They have their own part of the town and government. There seemed little connection or cooperation with the Cree. We met some of the Inuits. There were really two separate towns comprising Great Whale.

We spent about five days rafting and camping out along the river. We flew around in what was called a float plane as we surveyed the land that was threatened by flooding. It is a beautiful place with much greenery, bluffs along the river, and many streams and ponds. At night, we saw wondrous northern lights. It was as if the whole sky was ablaze—a sight I will never forget. The area had one big drawback—black flies and, in the evening, mosquitoes. They were ferocious. You needed to wear a head net, and even then, some of the bugs would get in and feast on your blood. This really made impossible the tourism we thought we might engender by rafting down this otherwise beautiful river and its challenging white water.

It was great fun and interesting. I particularly remember one night around the campfire when both Nina and Michael sang ballads. The Kennedy brothers were like caricatures of the Kennedys. Both Robert and Michael had brought their ten-year-old sons. They were continually jumping into the river or throwing their kids in. On one occasion, as we got into the float plane to go to another location, Nina said she had left her purse. I said I'd get it. Before I could move, both Kennedy brothers jumped up and bumped into each other rushing to get it. On our last night, we played our Cree hosts in softball under the northern lights. The Kennedys were super competitive, exhorting our team as if it was the World Series. I was put into right field.

I became friendly with Robert, who headed the Riverkeepers—an effort to keep the Hudson unpolluted. We worked together on some environmental issues in addition to saving the land of the Crees. He came to Nina's funeral. Michael, sadly, died not long afterward playing football while skiing without a helmet and crashing into a tree.

Hydro Québec, learning of our group's existence, invited us to see their first project and flew us there—impressive engineering but devastating to the environment. I recollect that at that time, or maybe on another occasion, Kennedy Jr. gave a speech. You could close your eyes and think it was JFK or RFK speaking. I thought he was very talented. At different times, I urged him to run for the New York Senate or the US Senate. He declined. He was a prominent environmentalist but seems to have faded now from public view and unfortunately is an active leader in the anti-vaccination movement.

The next year, we repeated our rafting trip on the Great Whale River. This time, Nina did not go along. I decided not to bring a tent and to sleep in the tepee the Cree would build. After an evening meal where we were served bear meat and Canadian goose (tough and unlike the goose I would cook), I turned in with about ten Cree. The snoring was deafening. I got out and crawled into the tent of my colleague, Suzi Oppenheimer, and her husband. Fortunately, there was room for me, and I slept with them the rest of the trip.

After our trips, I joined with other colleagues and some of the environmental community to defeat Hydro Québec's plans. To build this enormous project, it needed to have a firm contract with New York State to buy the electricity that would be generated. Based on such a contract, Hydro Québec could get the financing it needed for the project. We had to convince Governor Mario Cuomo not to enter into a binding contract.

The environmental community opposed the project. The first Hydro Québec development had led, among other negative consequences, to an increase in mercury pollution because of the millions of trees and bushes that were flooded and decayed. The mercury ended up in the food chain. There were rallies and protest meetings at which Kennedy Jr. and I spoke. It never became a hot-button environmental issue, but I felt strongly about it not only for the harm to the environment but the devastation to the life and culture of the Cree. Some of the Cree leadership came to New York to state their protest. I arranged for them to meet David Dinkins, who was then mayor. We raised the issue in the Legislature and put pressure on Governor Cuomo not to enter into a final contract. And, indeed,

Cuomo cancelled the deal. He did so, he claimed, because of economic consideration. But I think our protest and advocacy played a key role.

Still trying to overcome our opposition, Hydro Québec flew some of us in a chartered plane to Québec City for a weekend. We met with Québec government officials, were given tours, and feted. The Québec government at the time, though not autonomous from Canada, was elected on a separatist platform for this predominant French-speaking state and threatened to secede from Canada. Of course, our opposition to the plan did not change. One nice consequence of the trip was that Erwin Rose, on my staff, and since then a lifelong friend, met his wife, Jan Levin. She was employed in an office the Québec government maintained in New York. She left that job and entered the US diplomatic service. She has had overseas postings, including Israel and Switzerland, where I visited their family. Her next posting is in Havana, and with luck, I will visit her there. (Since then, because of the deteriorating relationship between Trump, US, and Cuba and strange hearing damage to US diplomats, her posting has been cancelled.)

One nice personal footnote to this adventure: Nina had become acquainted in Great Whale with one of the school teachers. Upon our return, she gathered books that she sent to Great Whale for use in its school. In return, we received what I guess you could call a tapestry, which was made by the Cree. It hangs over the sink at the Farm.

## VISITING KATHY IN PARIS AND MORE FAMILY EVENTS

I visited Kathy when she had her semester abroad in Paris. I believe it was 1988. I had combined the visit with a trip to my German clients. The plan was for me to fly to Paris and spend the weekend with her. I would then go to my clients in Koblenz. However, in 1998 you needed a visa to enter France; my travel agent failed to inform me. When I went to the airport with Nina, to see me off, I was not allowed on the plane. I could have rescheduled the flight for the next day after getting a visa. I just didn't feel like going back home, so instead I arranged a direct trip to Frankfurt in Germany and from there to fly to Kathy in Paris. I knew Frankfurt fairly well and thought it would be easy to get a visa there.

When I arrived at the French consulate, my heart dropped as I saw a long line. It was Friday, and the guard advised me to come back Monday. I was frantic. I wanted to see Kathy, and my suitcase had already been checked to Paris, so I had no clothes. (I believe I was flying Pan Am first class, and you had the privilege of checking your suitcase as you exited your car.) And Monday, I had to meet my clients. I forced myself into the building and found there a room full of people seeking visas. It was like a scene from 1939 with Jews desperately seeking visas, except now it was tourists and American soldiers on leave wanting to enjoy Paris. Somehow I managed to push my way in and got to see the person in charge. I told her I was a New York state senator, which I rarely did, but I was desperate, and that my daughter was staying with Guy Vadepied, a member of the French Parliament. She answered, "I don't care if she is staying with the French president. I need more staff." But she took pity on me. I got the visa, rushed back to the airport to catch my flight to Paris, found my suitcase there, and, best of all, spent the weekend with Kathy.

Throughout this time, and starting in the 1970s, Nina and I introduced Kathy and Josh to skiing. It became a regular feature of our family. We started them on Paleface and Otis Mountain, neither of which exist anymore. Then as they got older and more proficient, we went to Snowball in Middlebury and Gore Mountain. We were then finally ready for our local, more challenging, and frequently miserably cold mountain, Whiteface. We went skiing on trips at the Farm over the end-of-the-year

239

holidays, Washington's birthday weekend, and when the snow lasted, even at Easter. Friends and family members would join us occasionally. We would also ski at Stowe with the Hope/Henry Leichters.

The Farm was the center of much of our social life. We had numerous friends visit us for weekends. In 1980, when the Winter Olympics were held at Lake Placid, we invited Steve and Nina Solarz and Sarah and Victor Kovner to join us for a weekend and to go to some of the events. The Henry Leichters came to visit. As Henry had been the lawyer for the Austrian Olympic team and had arranged for the construction of its welcoming center in Lake Placid, we had use of the facility and the good food it provided. We were included in cheering the Austrian medal winners, of which there were quite a few for such a small country. While there, I was invited to appear on Austrian television on a panel with a former great Austrian Olympic star. It was about the US withdrawing from the Moscow Summer Olympics because of Russia's invasion of Afghanistan. I was to defend the US decision. Not that easy, as my poor German and the hostile position of the other panelists left the US poorly defended.

After the weekend, Nina went back to school, and guests left. I stayed the whole week at the Farm with Kathy, Josh, and Jamie Leichter. We went to some events, which was made easier by my having a pass that allowed me to drive into Lake Placid itself when most vehicular traffic was prohibited. This experience was typical of the continuing activity in our lives, not only at the Farm but also in New York. This mainly reflected my restlessness but also my zest for life. I enjoyed being active and busy.

Home life with Nina became more lonesome as we entered the decade of the 1990s, and there was less to bind us together with Kathy and Josh gone. Nina continued in the school system as an assistant principal in a Queens elementary school. She did well there, and I think she was appreciated. In or about 1992, she retired. It was her decision. I neither encouraged nor discouraged her. Her bipolar condition remained pretty well under control until she retired, although there were occasional manic and depressive periods. I can't say we were emotionally close. We did do numerous things together, like any other couple—see friends, attend movies and cultural events—and there was always the Farm.

Elsa, whom I considered my stepmother, was an important part of my life. We were very close, and she was someone I turned to for advice. I saw her frequently, but she was out of the country every summer and at times in the winter. Though well into her eighties, she was very active and traveled a lot. For some years, into the 1990s and her early nineties, she would spend a month or more in the Austrian Alps in the town of Lofer. I visited her there three or four times. Once I went with Nina after she retired. I also took Kathy there. Kathy and Elsa had developed a very close friendship and were able to share secrets. It was so nice to see this relationship not as grandmother and grandchild but as friends sharing confidences. Elsa loved Lofer, where she enjoyed many summers and was visited by family and friends. Henry and I bought a bench with her name placed on her favorite walk. Kathy was with me when we surprised her with the bench. There are lovely photos of Kathy and Elsa on that bench.

Now that I am ninety, I appreciate how well Elsa functioned. In Lofer, she climbed with us into her late eighties. A favorite climb was around 1,500 feet to a gorgeous Alp where there was a restaurant. Eerily, from there one could look across at Berchtesgaden, Hitler's mountain retreat. And Elsa kept her mental faculties and saw her friends until her death at the age of ninety-two in 1997. After having lunch with a friend on the West Side, she fell, fractured her skull, and went into a coma from which she never recovered. I had the sad duty as her health care proxy to direct the removal of the tubes that kept her breathing after checking with the doctors and Henry.

In 1993, there was another reapportionment based on the 1992 census. This time I found my district pushed farther north and into Riverdale. I liked representing this new area, which was quite different from the neighborhoods I had represented. I established myself quite well and worked with the numerous local organizations, which were very prevalent in Riverdale.

## AN ATTEMPT TO CLIMB THE MATTERHORN

After I visited Elsa in Lofer, I decided to go to Zermatt and see the Matterhorn in 1993. It had stayed in my memory since I was there with Henry and Hope in 1951. It was as stunning as I remembered it. I decided to try to climb it. I arranged for a guide. Two days before our planned hike, he took me in the morning on a practice climb with ropes to see if I could do it. It was the first time I climbed some steep rock pitches roped up.

Although I was in my early sixties, I felt fit and did well enough for the guide to say he thought I could do it. Maybe he was motivated by the $400 I was to pay him. He was German and told me he had been part of an expedition to Everest on which he had climbed to the top via the much harder northern route. He told me what equipment I needed to rent and to meet him the next evening at the Hörnlihütte, which is on the ridge of the Matterhorn, about ten thousand feet and the starting point of the climb.

Next day, I arranged for the equipment, which included boots, crampons to deal with the ice near the top, and a headlight, which I forgot but was able to get at the hut. I, maybe foolishly, in the afternoon visited the cemetery in Zermatt, where a number of the mountain's fatalities rest, including the four who died in the memorable first climb led by the British Edward Whymper in 1865. It is not considered a challenging Alpine climb for experienced mountaineers, but it does have its difficulties and dangers.

(I checked when writing this and learned that five hundred people have lost their lives on that mountain.)

In the late afternoon before my climb, I hiked up the Hörnlihütte. The walk up was fairly steep. But unlike an Adirondack climb, it was on a gravel path. The hut is quite large, and many people were there, as the next day was forecast to be a rare, beautiful climbing day. Shortly after I arrived, I heard someone being sick in the lavatory. Soon a helicopter swooped in and took down a young man who was suffering from altitude sickness. This may have begun to rattle me a bit. I had an early supper, where I spoke to an American father-and-son team who were making the climb without a guide. I was impressed. I met my guide, who had done a climb with a client that day and had just come down. We all bedded down early. The bed was on a big shelf with cushions shared by all the males sleeping in close proximity. We were given a blanket and a pillow. Lying together with so many bodies and the sound of heavy breathing and snoring, I could not sleep. So I took an Ambien sleeping pill. Big mistake. Only later did I remember being told that Ambien—and I assume other sleeping pills—are much more potent at high altitudes. Yet I barely slept.

Next morning, we were awakened around four. We were given a big breakfast, and off we went into the dark. We climbed by the light of our headlamp. Soon the lights of the other climbers receded far above as my guide and I, fastened as I was to him by rope, inched our way up. There were ladders and hand holds, but I still proceeded slowly. At one point, the guide had to come down to me and help me on a steep pitch. The sun rose on a spectacular view of mountains and glaciers. But then the Ambien kicked in. I became drowsier and drowsier and moved slowly and with difficulty. Finally, we reached a little hut to shelter people who might be caught in a storm or overcome by darkness. At this point, all I wanted to do was to sleep. I asked my guide if I could lie down in the shelter, which was very small. He said, "OK, but you must be roped up." I realized that on either side of the ridge we were climbing were precipitous drops, and if I rolled over, I would plunge down thousands of feet. After resting a while, my guide said, "We are not going to make the top and must go down." What height had I reached? Probably up to 11,500 of the 13,000-foot-high Matterhorn. It was just before one encountered ice and the need to use crampons.

Down we went. The descent was not made easier by my rented boots, which started to pain me greatly. Nor was it eased by my guide saying to be very careful at some places. At one point, he said a slip and fall there by some Japanese climbers caused their death. In case you are in suspense, let me assure you I got down safely. We reached the Hörnlihütte, which was serving drinks and food at outdoor tables on a beautiful day. I paid my guide, put my head on the table, and closed my eyes. When walking down, I saw a patch of grass on which to lie. I looked with awe at the mountain as I blissfully fell asleep. As at other times in my life, my enthusiasm exceeded my ability, in this case as a sixty-three-year-old. Nevertheless, it was a worthwhile adventure.

## MY BROTHER HENRY AND HIS FAMILY

I have not mentioned sufficiently my brother, Henry, and how important he was in my life. He was six and a half years older than me. After the death of my mother, he assumed almost maternal care of me. I didn't always appreciate this in my early years. We had many arguments, and he did beat me up a few times. Henry had a strong temper. I hope this is not a Leichter trait. He always tried to take care of me. I mentioned how he provided an allowance for me to attend the opera, had me join his Swarthmore friends for a summer, was the reason I was accepted at Swarthmore, paid for me to go to Europe in 1951, introduced me to the Riverside Democrats, and stepped aside for me as I advanced politically.

Henry and Hope were a close family with three sons, Fred, Willy, and Jamie. They lived close to us on the West Side. We socialized together often. They had bought an old farm in Elmore Vermont, near Stowe, and not far from Lake Champlain across from our Farm. It would take us one and a half hours to go there from our place. We visited each other. For many New Year's Eves, we visited them for an end-of-the-year ritual. After skiing, we would have a meal of ham, which we usually brought. Then we engaged in the old Viennese custom of melting lead to see what shapes could be shown on a screen. This was discontinued after I invited my friend Oliver Koppell to join us when he was nearby with his family. Oliver pointed out that inhaling lead was dangerous. After midnight, we would have Henry's pea soup and then go cross-country skiing around their fields. As Kathy and Josh got older, they wanted to be with their friends, and it was hard to get them to join us. Nina and I still went. We were there almost every year until the year's end 1994. Lovely memories.

## ANOTHER HALF-HEARTED ATTEMPT FOR CONGRESS

In 1992, I made my third inconclusive stab at a congressional seat. One day in September or maybe October, I was handing out leaflets and greeting voters at the downtown subway entrance at 110th and Broadway. I usually tried to get to voters in the morning and not in evening when people leaving the subways are tired and eager to get home. Someone told me that Ted Weiss, who had represented our congressional district since 1976, when I gave up on my best chance at Congress, had died. There was a vacancy that I thought might give me a chance to finally achieve my desire to be in Congress. However, the district created by the 1992 reapportionment was far different from what had been the Ryan district, centered on the West Side and later including all of northern Manhattan. This district stretched south from West Ninety-Sixth Street all the way to Coney Island. The joke was that this district ran from Nathan's (in Coney Island) to Zabar's (at West Eighty-Third Street and Broadway). This description caught the diversity of the district, which included a good part of the liberal West Side and Village but also the conservative areas of heavily Orthodox Jewish Borough Park in Brooklyn. I remember that after leaving the subway stop full of thoughts, I went to pick up my car at the maintenance garage on West Fifty-Seventh Street. Also there waiting for his car was Bill Moyers, who had been one of LBJ's main advisers and who later received great acclaim for his PBS programs. I knew him slightly. I asked whether it made sense for someone my age, then sixty-two, to go to Congress, where many years of service were required to get a position where you had legislative sway. While not discouraging me, he said it was somewhat late to start in Congress.

Without looking carefully at the political situation or other considerations, I decided just to go ahead. My decision was not really well thought out. It was propelled more by the disappointment that I had not, or could not, try for a congressional set in 1972, when Bill Ryan died, and again in 1976 when family and other reasons led me not to run. I could not let another chance, although slim, escape me. I proceeded, though I was cautioned by my friend Denny Farrell, who was the New York county leader, that the politics were not favorable. Jerry Nadler, who was an assemblyman from the West Side, saw that this was a perfect district for him. Even before Ted's death, he had made deals and locked up the votes to succeed. It was known that Ted was ailing. Nadler was really a perfect fit for the district. He had strong liberal credentials but was a practicing Jew and much better suited than I to deal with the Orthodox Jewish community in Brooklyn, whose rabbis controlled the votes of their congregations. These rabbis responded well to persons like Nadler, who had a Jewish religious background and whose political mendacity enabled him to deal with them. While I had developed a good relationship with the Orthodox community in northern Manhattan, this was mainly of German background and differed from the

Jewish communities of Borough Park. I would have been a fish out of water in Borough Park. This was not the right district for me.

As Ted Weiss's death occurred after the primary and before the general election, the candidate would be chosen not in a primary but by the party committee—the county committee of a few hundred—just as in 1972 when Bill Ryan died after his primary victory over Bella Abzug. There was a complication, as the district included a large part of Brooklyn, which would vote separately. But the outcome depended upon the votes of the Democratic Committee from Manhattan, consisting of about three hundred delegates. I threw myself into the race, maybe as much to satisfy myself that I had made an attempt to go to Congress after two previous chances in which I pulled back. It was as if I had to make up for those two times. Nina and I had already scheduled a trip to Israel. She had visited the Cornaros in Austria and then had gone to visit relatives of her mother in Bratislava. She was waiting for me in Vienna to join her. I called her to cancel the trip to Israel and have her return home.

I arranged a campaign that was just aimed at the three hundred or so county committee persons who would cast the votes. There was no time for mailings, so the outreach was by phone. Among the persons making calls were Josh and Dana, who came up from Washington to help. I also made calls to those who could vote at the meeting, which was a week or so away. Besides myself, there was another assemblyman and Ted's widow seeking the nomination. It was all fruitless, as Nadler had commitments from the district leaders who controlled the votes of the county committee persons who came from their club and district. He had the votes going into the meeting. I made a rousing speech, but it was all for naught. The result was preordained. I don't remember being greatly disappointed.

# A BIT ABOUT OUR CHILDREN

A word about our children and our parenting.

This period saw big changes in the family. Kathy graduated from Fieldston in 1984, a progressive private school in the Riverdale section of the Bronx, which Josh also then attended. Nina and I agreed as a graduation present to her traveling through Europe with her then best friend, Johanna. Was it wise to allow two eighteen-year-old girls to travel by themselves? Nina and I were supportive and not that apprehensive. The trip went well except a frantic call from Kathy in Paris telling us that she had lost her wallet with her passport. It all worked out.

Another somewhat similar incident with Kathy occurred when she spent her junior year in Paris. She had taken a train ride from the South of France and had met an older man from Morocco on the train who invited her to visit him and his family in Marrakesh. We were apprehensive but reluctant to be controlling parents, so we said OK. I am not sure our permission mattered to Kathy, who was then twenty. She went with a friend. I told her to keep us informed of her whereabouts. When for a week we did not hear from her while she was in Marrakesh, I became worried. What might have happened to two young women traveling by themselves in Morocco? I had the worst thoughts, being a natural worrier. On the day I decided to call my friend Steve Solarz, the congressman, to have him ask the US ambassador in Morocco to look for them, that very morning we received a call from Kathy. They were safely back in Spain.

Kathy started Cornell in fall 1984. Josh graduated from Fieldston in 1986 and attended Wesleyan. Nina and I drove both children to the start of their college life. I was pleased with what they had achieved and that they were attending such good colleges. It was sad though to have them leave and for Nina and I to become empty nesters. We visited both of them a number of times. A special event for me was twice going from Albany to visit Kathy in Cornell and attend classes with her. I also remember Nina and I attending one or more classes at Wesleyan with Josh on what was probably Parents' Day. I believe both Kathy and Josh had good college experiences and made lifelong friends there.

In Kathy's junior year, she took a semester overseas in Paris. Fortunately, she ended up with a lovely family, the Vadepieds, with whom she formed a lifelong relationship. Nina and I, at separate times, visited her and stayed with the Vadepieds. They had a big apartment like ours on Riverside Drive. On occasional trips to Paris, I continued to visit them. Some of the family stayed with us in New York and once at the Farm.

Josh spent one semester in London. Nina visited him there. During that overseas semester, I arranged for him to come to Vienna for the special daylong event honoring my mother and Sophie Scholl. After the event, Josh and I went skiing in Kitzbühel.

Josh graduated Wesleyan in 1990. After hanging around home for a few weeks, working as a bartender, he decided to go to Boulder, Colorado. We paid for him to take a bartender course. It still amuses me to consider that after four years at an elite college and paying the tuition so he would not come out burdened by debt, we now paid for him to work as a bartender. I can't say we were enthusiastic about his going west with no serious plans, but we interposed no objection. I think this was in line with our tolerant approach to parenting. Maybe Kathy and Josh don't consider that it was so tolerant. Growing up in New York City, we accepted their going out at night when they became teenagers. It was not without concern. I remember one night particularly when I couldn't sleep because Josh was out late. I think he came back at 5:00 a.m., to my relief. I did tell them that no matter where they were, after 11:00 p.m., we would pay for them to take a taxi to come home. New York City was not considered as safe as it is now in 2020.

I can't judge whether Nina and I as parents were too tolerant or not tolerant enough, whether we did or did not impose clear rules. But we were loving parents. Whatever we did right and whatever wrong in parenting, the fact is that Kathy and Josh grew up to be well-functioning persons, strong, with a deep moral code, social concerns, successful in their life endeavors, and with loving spouses. They did not grow up—particularly in their teen years—in a harmonious household, as Nina's condition became a factor and our emotional separation grew. But both Nina and I always sought to maintain a strong and active family life. That Kathy and Josh turned out to be such fine persons may have been as much luck as anything Nina and I did as parents. I do think our love for them was a factor. However, no matter the reason, I am so proud of and happy with both my children.

Josh had a good year in Boulder, working in a restaurant and doing a lot of skiing. I visited him twice. We went to Vail to ski. After a year, he decided to go to Washington, DC. I think I helped him get a job with the Capital newspaper, the *Roll Call*, which covered Congress. After a while, he got a job with the Congressional Budget Office (CBO). This is a prestigious organization that scores the effects of congressional legislation—what the financial impact of legislation will be. Josh worked there as an analyst. It showed his ambition and skill that he secured a job there.

In what I think must be 1992, he met Dana in Washington. From my perspective, their relationship moved very quickly. He brought her to New York to meet Nina and me. She and Josh came to our apartment late at night. We were already asleep, but I heard them and went to give a greeting. When I went back to bed, Nina awakened and asked me about Dana. I replied, "She is beautiful." We got to know Dana and saw that she and Josh were happy together. They came to New York to help me in my congressional attempt and came to the Farm. We visited them in Washington. We were surprised when in April 1993, Josh called to say they had gotten married in Virginia. The ostensible reason for doing this without advance notice or having a public wedding was to get Dana covered by Josh's health insurance, which he got through his job. Shortly afterward, Nina and I went to Washington to have a congratulatory dinner with them and see them as a married couple.

Nina and I were not happy with Josh marrying and how it was done. We had gotten to know Dana somewhat. While we found her pleasant, we did not think she was the right partner for Josh. I won't go into the doubts we had, but it was also the rushed nature of their marriage that made us apprehensive. Our—certainly my—unease was heightened when Josh gave up his job with the CBO. They traveled to Portland, Oregon, to relocate, though after a while, they came east and went to Hanover, New Hampshire. They seemed very unmoored. I think it reflected Dana's restlessness and Josh's desire to please her.

Sadly, our relationship with them, and particularly with Josh, deteriorated. He became estranged from us. This may have reflected Josh and Dana sensing that we disapproved of their marriage and moving around the country in what struck me as an aimless fashion. Our contacts became fewer and punctuated by argumentative phone calls and loveless letters. They separated from us. For almost two years, we did not see Josh. After New Year's 1995, when Nina and I were driving home from the Henry and Hope Leichters in Vermont, Nina said, as we drove by Hanover, "Let's visit them." I demurred, as I did not think we would be welcomed, nor did we know where they lived.

Josh did let me know, in what must have been 1994, that he had taken his LSAT test. He was admitted to both Duke and Michigan and asked for financial support, which we readily agreed to provide. He chose University of Michigan. Why did our relationship spiral out of control? It is now all in the past, and to examine it and dwell on it will only open old wounds and provide no conclusive answers. I think there are lessons we all learned from it. The important thing is that it did not destroy our family and that my relationship with Josh is so good and strong now.

# CHAPTER 14

# 1994-1997: NINA'S TRAGIC END AND A NEW LIFE

The year 1994 was hard. Nina's condition deteriorated. She more rapidly switched from being manic to becoming depressed. The stable periods became less frequent. She became involved—maybe already in 1993— with a group of people who had bipolar conditions. She was on its board of directors and, with her organizational skills, was very helpful. She went on a lobbying trip to the Legislature, wearing a button that said, "Kiss me. I am bipolar." This engagement was very satisfying for her. I was supportive, as she kept me informed of her activities. I joined her on social occasions with the people who led this group.

In the summer of 1994, Nina and I had the idea of having a party for neighbors and friends at the Farm to celebrate saving our barns. The barns were in ever-worse shape. The middle barn, which was actually the oldest, with beams that dated to the late eighteenth century, was in danger of collapsing. My initial reaction was just to tear it down, but both Nina and Kathy argued that we had a responsibility to save old barns, which were disappearing. We hired a local worker, who jacked up the barn and put in a new foundation and sidings. We spent a good amount, but it was worth it. About a year earlier, we had work done to save another barn, which is nearer the house. The work being finished, we decided to have a barn raising. This was the tradition in the past when barns were built (usually by neighbors joining together). When the barn construction was finished, there was a party. Nina made the arrangements, sent out clever invitations, and arranged for a fiddler band, food, and refreshments. We may have had as many as fifty to sixty people attend—friends, neighbors, even my Senate colleague who represented the area showed up. It was a grand party that Nina's skills, honed when she ran the UFT's annual luncheons, made successful.

But as the year went on, Nina's condition deteriorated. The pendulum swung more frequently between depression and mania. It became harder to take care of her. She did some unusual things, not dangerous as in 1974, but out of character. One example, which I find both amusing and annoying, is that on two occasions when our housekeeper made her once-a-week appearance to clean the apartment, she took her to lunch at the Palm Room in the Plaza.

As Nina's condition deteriorated and reached a very worrisome stage, I visited doctors with her. These were psychopharmacologists who mainly just dispensed medication. A prescription to tamper down her manic state could bring on depression, and dealing with depression could bring on a manic state. To find the right balance was difficult. At one time, Nina's mania became so strong that I took her to see one of the doctors who treated her. He recommended that she should be hospitalized in New York Psychiatric Hospital, which is part of Presbyterian Hospital located at West 168th Street. I urged Nina to do this. She realized she was sick and agreed; we had her admitted. There she was under very close supervision. When her mania continued high, her doctor and other professionals at the facility recommended that to get her out of her manic state, she should have electric shock treatment. This was a hard decision to accept. I, of course, discussed it with Nina, who was then not fully capable of making decisions and left it up to me. I arranged a conference call with Kathy and Josh. I don't remember where he was then, and while our relationship was strained, I wanted him to be part of the decision. We discussed it for quite some time. Kathy and I were in favor, as we felt something needed to be done and this was the recommendation of the professionals. Josh was more dubious and questioned how it would help and what the negative and unforeseen consequences were. I had extensive discussion with the doctor, who gave me assurances that the likelihood of harm was very small and that there seemed no other way to get Nina out of the grip of the mania. I finally agreed.

The treatment went off without any complications and did quiet the mania. However, it was not a long-term solution. I visited Nina every day at the hospital. It was quite a procedure since the patients were locked in, and to get in there was a bothersome admittance procedure. It was very sad for me to see Nina in this setting in her hospital gown. She did not seem particularly upset at being there, and we had fairly normal conversations. She realized that she needed help.

It was typical of Nina that she became the leader of the group she was hospitalized with. During the days, the group was in a social room and able to interact. She made friends with two people there. One was a Hispanic woman. After she was released, she and her husband came to our house for a social visit. The other, who became a lifelong friend of Kathy and me, was Billy Sternberg. Billy struggled with depression. He appears in Kathy's documentary about Nina: *Here One Day*. Billy seemed to dedicate his time to writing about his grandfather Maurice Bloch, who was a confidant of FDR when he became governor. He was a campaign manager, minority leader of the Democrats in the New York State Assembly, and may have played a role in the mysterious disappearance of Judge Joseph Crater. The latter's disappearance, now almost ninety years ago, has become part of folklore.

As leader and spokesperson of the group, Nina one day got into an argument with the staff on behalf of the group objecting to something. As a result, I was advised, she was put overnight into solitary confinement. After about a week, Nina was discharged. Her mania had quieted, but she clearly was not well.

I was very low during this time. I remember watching the Super Bowl, which in the past I had always enjoyed, with one of my staff who came to be with me, knowing I was alone. I felt miserable. What kept me going was my legislative work and running around to community meetings. By being engaged, I escaped brooding that Nina's condition would not improve. I had a sense of being trapped in a painful situation to which there was no answer. This may have also unleashed a feeling that overcomes me when my life is not going as I expect. At those times, I feel unfortunate and that the odds in life are against me. I realize intellectually that this is not true and that in fact I have been very fortunate. But the deeper, lingering sense of misfortune, which may come from the loss of my mother and disrupted childhood, is hard to dispel.

## THE GERMAN GOVERNMENT INVITES ME FOR A TOUR

When Nina came home from the psychiatric institute, it was evident that she could not be left alone for prolonged periods. This presented a problem, as I was invited by the German government to be part of a small group of US-elected officials from across the country to observe how Germany was dealing with its immigrant community, mainly from Turkey, who had come as guest workers. Many had settled in Germany but were not well assimilated. They had children born in Germany who were raised there and attended school, but because Germany based citizenship not on place of birth, as in the US, but on blood, they were not citizens. There had been some publicized assaults on Turks and arson by right-wing anti-immigration groups in Germany. The government, by inviting us, wanted to show that it was dealing with the problem and that it was not so serious. I very much wanted to go but could not without having someone stay with Nina. Fortunately, Atea Ring, our friend at the Farm with whom Nina was close, agreed to stay with her for a week.

The visit and tour of Germany was very interesting and got me away from the dispirited mood at home. We went to Frankfurt, Bonn, Dresden, and Berlin. I left before the tour ended in Hamburg because I did not want to be away more than a week. We met with government officials, legislators, community activists, and some members of the Turkish community. The latter were not well organized, and even though their lives were now in Germany, their ties to Turkey remained. They were not that interested in being Germans or part of the German community. One reason that existed at that time was that if they took German citizenship, they could not own land in Turkey, which many still had. How different the American immigration experience and attitude is. Here, assimilation is the norm. It was a most interesting trip, and I became quite friendly with one of the participants, Lois Pines, who was a state senator from Massachusetts. I had Lois come and watch the Senate in Albany and meet some of my colleagues. She arranged for me to observe the Massachusetts Legislature. Nina and I visited her and stayed in her house near Boston.

## NINA'S CONDITION DETERIORATES

I tried to carry on as before upon returning from Germany. Nina's state was uneven. Looking back, it was evident that she was deteriorating. The mania and depression kept cycling back and forth. We did spend the summer at the Farm, and it was then that we had the barn raising. Neither

Josh nor Kathy were there, and while we carried on and there were good social times with the Derecskeys, it was not a happy summer.

In the fall and winter of 1994, events also conspired against Nina. The separation from Josh hurt. Kathy was in Pittsburgh. She came to visit on at least one occasion. At the end of the weekend, I drove her to LaGuardia Airport for her flight back. I don't know whether she said it, but it was obvious she had found it hard to be at home. Then a lifelong friend in Belgium, Jacqueline, with whom we had stayed during our 1981 European tour, wrote Nina that she no longer wanted to have any communication with her. I don't know why. It may have been due to some emotional problems Jacqueline was having, or Nina sent her a letter that she found offensive. Toward the end of the year, Nina was removed from the Board of Directors of her bipolar support group to which she had devoted much time and which gave her such satisfaction. I don't know what the reason was. It may have been that the person who ran it, who was somewhat domineering, may have felt threatened by Nina's independence and activism.

There were numerous doctor visits and, I think, changes of doctors. But all they did was prescribe medicine that might overcome the present mania but then opened her to depression. It was a seesaw. I was more and more concerned about Nina and sought to help her. But, sadly, I could not bring forth the empathy she craved. Nina was aware of this and in one or more of her notes and/or tapes complained specifically about my lack of empathy. I believe one reason for the absence of the empathy that she longed for was due to my denial of her condition. As I had throughout, since her diagnosis in 1974, I held on to a belief that this condition could be overcome by the next doctor, some different medicine, and Nina pulling herself together. I had the experience of the years in the 1980s when the lithium mostly worked. My denial helped me to function in both my legal and legislative life. It was not hard for me to carry on with my active life. On the contrary,

I welcomed it as an escape from the concern about Nina and the absence of a good marital life. I was able to compartmentalize, but it was still a very lonely time. I felt I had no one to turn to. Elsa was on a trip. I did have a good relationship with Henry and some friends, but these were not based on, nor did it encompass, sharing personal and emotional issues. I found it hard to be emotionally open. Maybe my reluctance to discuss it with others was that I felt it was something I had to solve myself. I probably should have availed myself of some psychological help. My attitude was that the problem could be solved if only we could find the answer to overcoming her bipolar state. Yes, I was in denial.

## MY FIRST GRANDCHILD—MEMPHIS

In October 1994, while I was in Vienna on a business trip, Memphis, our first grandchild, was born. I had just come from Zürich. I stayed at the Bristol, one of Vienna's finer hotels situated just across from the opera. My client met me there. (When on business, I traveled first class and stayed in five-star hotels. Those days are over.) When checking in at the hotel, the person at the desk greeted me as "Grosspapa of Memphis." A message had been left for me about Memphis's arrival. I knew Dana was expecting, but the gender of the child to come was not known. I was very excited at the news but puzzled whether it was a boy or girl. The name "Memphis" gave me no clue. I rushed upstairs to my room and made frantic phone calls to find out not just the gender but to make sure all was well and to extend congratulations. I finally reached Dana's mother, who informed me it was indeed a girl. In something of a daze, I went downstairs to walk around to calm down. As I walked out of the Bristol, I was met with a large sign stating "Memphis." I thought I was hallucinating. A more careful look showed it was an advertisement for Memphis cigarettes, one of the popular brands in Austria then. On a subsequent trip to Vienna, I stole one of these poster advertisements and gave it to Josh and Dana.

# THE SAD END

At the end of the year, we went to the Farm. It was even more lonely. No children. None of the usual activities. I remember that officials of the local Grange came to give us a pin for the twenty-five years we had been members. I continued our membership from when we first joined. While the Grange took positions I was against—for instance, it was against abortions—I thought it important to support local farming. I have a photo of the occasion. We looked like a Grant Wood painting with our sad looks.

For New Year's, we went to Henry and Hope in Vermont for the usual festivities. I think I was able to do some skiing. Nina was manic and difficult. Henry said to me at the end of our stay that I was an "angel" in my care of and patience with Nina. I have some hesitation in recounting this because I don't think I was an angel. I mention it to show that Nina's condition was getting noticeably worse and showed. I was trying to take care of her. In January, she spent a weekend with Sally, who commented to me that Nina's condition was not good and that she was difficult.

Events continued to conspire. We made plans in January to see our first grandchild, visiting Josh in Ann Arbor, where he was attending Michigan Law School. Nina developed a cold. When I told Josh, he asked us to postpone the trip over concern for baby Memphis. This made sense. I don't know whether seeing Memphis, her grandchild, and Josh after a long separation would have made a difference in what later happened. Her condition worsened. She was sometimes manic but mostly depressed. Physically, she also did not seem well. I was becoming more and more concerned and thought maybe I could find a sanitarium where she would get needed treatment. I called Gerda Schulman, a therapist who was a close friend of Elsa's, for advice. She said nothing came to mind immediately, but she would look around. By now, it was the first week of February 1995. I went with Nina to a new psychotherapist at the end of January or beginning of February, who prescribed a new medication. But her condition did not improve.

Sunday evening, February 5, we had a nice dinner at home. I first mentioned to her that it would be helpful for her if we could find a sanatorium that would address both her emotional and physical states. I don't remember her response. I sometimes wonder whether, rather than comforting her with my care, I was scaring her. Did it affect the next day's happening? It may not have, as it seems that Nina had suicide in mind for at least a week.

Monday, February 6, 1995, I got up maybe around eight or so. I planned to go to Albany, as the Senate was in session that week. As usual, I first went to the bathroom, brushed my teeth, and so on. Would my getting up earlier and coming down the hall more quickly have made a difference? When I did come down to the dining room, I expected Nina to be there having breakfast. She was not there. I assumed she must be somewhere else in the apartment and went looking. I thought she had to be somewhere. I didn't believe she had gone out. When I looked everywhere and didn't see her, I was puzzled. Whether it was by some intuition or the open dining room window, I looked out the window. By leaning way out, I saw some clothes, and then it struck me it might be Nina. I called 911. The police came readily, as well as a doctor from the medical examiner's office. They confirmed that it was Nina and that she was dead. The doctor offered to give me a tranquilizer, which I refused. I believe I then saw the suicide note that was left on a bureau in our bedroom. It was a sweet, generous note. And there were notes for Kathy and Josh.

I was in a daze but pulled myself together to make the painful phone calls to the children, Henry, Sally, and Pat in my Albany office, to say what happened and that I naturally would not be going to Albany. I even called the last doctor she saw, who had probably overdosed her and, by combatting mania, brought on a deeper depression. Henry and Sally came and helped in making arrangements. Henry went to the medical examiner's office to identify Nina. The day was a blur of activity. Kathy came from Pittsburgh with a colleague. Josh and Dana came with baby Memphis. I had not seen Josh for more than a year. The phone rang incessantly. Arrangements for a funeral service and her cremation had to be made. In the evening, many people came to pay respect—staff, friends, law colleagues, and some of my Senate colleagues, including, as my memory serves me, a couple of Republicans.

It was a hectic week, but all the arrangements kept me so busy that it somewhat stalled my mourning. There was so much to do in preparing for the funeral, which we decided would be at Riverside Memorial Chapel. Announcements had to go out, and we placed an obituary in the *Times*. There was much family togetherness, which made it easier. I had my first view of baby Memphis. It was good being together with Josh. I still have this picture in my mind of Kathy sitting on the floor of what I still call Josh's room, with a number of her friends who came to comfort her, including Chris, a former boyfriend and a colleague from the time she worked in Pittsburgh. Elsa was away in Portugal. I reached her by phone with the sad news. I had help from family, friends, and my staff, but much of it still came down to me.

The funeral was held in the main chamber at Riverside. The room was packed with friends, school and union colleagues, and many of my political colleagues. We played a section of the Brahms *Requiem*, which Nina loved ever since she had participated on her cello at a performance with an amateur orchestra, which may have been connected with Columbia University. Kathy, Josh, and I spoke, as did Susan Derecskey. It was a very touching service. I was so proud of Kathy and Josh, how they held up and spoke so beautifully. Afterward, many people told me how touched they were by their comments and the service. There were some unusual moments for me. A former New York City police sergeant, with whom I had played tennis but hadn't seen for some years, showed up and took over directing people to their seats and deciding who could be let into the family room before the service. Among the attendees were two of my childhood friends, one from Cherry Lawn and the other from my days at the High School of Commerce, whom I had not seen in over forty years. Kennedy Jr., with whom we had gone rafting, came.

I think we gave Nina a rightful farewell. I spoke about her active life and achievements and not of her illness and tragic end. I remember saying that she had made the decision on how to end her life and that we needed to respect that.

After the funeral, we had a reception at home. All I remember is that David, the head of the bipolar group that Nina had been so active in, and who kicked her off the Board of Directors, was there to my annoyance, especially as he gorged himself on food. Josh and family returned to Michigan, where he was attending the law school, and Kathy went back to Pittsburgh. I was then left alone in what had been Nina's and my home for twenty years. The next Monday, I returned to Albany. I might have taken more time away, but my response to tragedies, miseries, and misfortune is to be active and engaged. It can be considered escapism, but this has enabled me to be the survivor that I think I have been.

What was my emotional response to Nina's death? It was multifaceted. I was sad, hurt, and felt somewhat abandoned, some self-pity in seeing my life as filled with tragedies, but also some relief. I recognize that the latter may seem unseemly, but it was an acknowledgment that living with and taking care of Nina had become so burdensome. I was also concerned about Kathy and Josh but was basically assured that they would be OK. I was proud of how they had reacted to their mom's death, but it left its pain. I have in mind the photo I took of Kathy, probably in the late spring or summer of that year when we went to the Farm and climbed Owls

Head, not the one off Route 73 but on the trail we often took from 9N between Elizabethtown and Keene. When the children were younger, we would stop at a waterfall for a picnic. In the photo, one can see the pain and hurt she still carried. I admire her for the documentary (*Here One* Day) she made about Nina and what a catharsis the film was for her. Josh, who I think keeps his emotion more hidden, had his family and baby Memphis and his law school work to occupy him and filter the sad thoughts.

I carried Nina's ashes up to Noonmark in early spring and scattered them from the summit. We had so many nice hikes there together and with friends. And that is where I would like my ashes to be dispersed.

Nina's death was a shock. I never foresaw that it would end that way. Even though the last years with her had been difficult, as more and more my activities and enjoyment were without her, her absence from my life left a void. We were still bound together in many ways. This was another big loss in my life.

As I had in the past when I had an emotional shock, I responded by burying my grief and loss in activity. I continued being busy with my legislative and legal life, probably more so, as this was a salve to my wound.

I responded to the many condolence messages and to acknowledge the many people who came to the funeral.

I had asked people who wanted to make a contribution in her memory to do so to the West Side Mood Disorder Group, which Nina had been so enthusiastically involved with. An amount of about $6,500 was raised. There were numerous suggestions for a proper memorial. We decided on the Mount Sinai Psychiatric Department facility. Eventually, we provided for a special television set for multipurpose in a communal room in one of the buildings used by the Psychiatric Department. But it was not until December 2000, after working out an agreement with Mount Sinai, that I turned over about $8,000 (I added to the amount contributed). We had a ceremony in the room named in Nina's memory. The entire family, including Sally and Lester, and Josh with his children, were there.

## MELODY AND I COME TOGETHER

The biggest change in my life came as I sought out Melody. We renewed our relationship. I needed life with love and laughter after what had been unsatisfactory and difficult years in my marital life. I was fortunate to renew our relationship. Melody had retained a love for me. She had just broken off another relationship. Maybe it was too soon after Nina's death to have another relationship. Melody was living in Brooklyn, where she and someone she had been engaged to had purchased a brownstone. They had broken up. In the fall, Melody and I went on a tour of Greece, Crete, Santorini, and Istanbul. To the latter, it was the first of many trips there. It was escapism for me and to be free of constant worry and feeling I was not living fully. Melody was twenty-one years younger than I was and vivacious. Part of my attraction was her youth and that we were physically attracted to each other. She was funny, smart, and at times crazy.

Melody decided to move to Manhattan. She sold the brownstone. If she had held on a few more years, she would have received multiples from what she sold it for. She then bought a condominium on East Seventy-Second Street. I helped her financially. I visited her there frequently but continued to live at 448 Riverside until 1997. Kathy was then living there with me. She had decided to leave Pittsburgh, among other reasons to be with me and also Elsa.

## MY GRANDCHILD ETHAN ARRIVES,
## AND ELSA PASSES ON

On March 19, 1997, Ethan, Josh and Dana's second child, was born. I think it was in the middle of the week. Kathy and I had Elsa over for dinner on Saturday of that week. It was a very joyous time, and Elsa, who was already ninety-one years old, was in a great mood and was functioning so well. She still lived alone and planned to continue to spend the summer in the Austrian Alps.

The next day, I flew to Detroit and drove to Ann Arbor, where Josh and family then lived, as he was finishing his third year at Michigan Law School. I saw my new grandson. As Dana and Josh busied themselves with the new baby, I played with Memphis. Not significant, but it is in my memory, I spent most of the time washing what seemed like a week's worth of accumulated dishes. I was there only for the day and returned that night to New York, as the next day, Monday, I had to be in Albany for the legislative session.

Next day, when I arrived at my office in Albany, I was told to call Kathy, or maybe Henry. Elsa had a bad fall and was in a hospital. I promptly returned to New York and met in the hospital Henry, Kathy, Hope, and Gerda Schulman, Elsa's closest friend. Elsa had fractured her skull in the fall and was in a coma. Her condition was serious. She never came out of the coma. The prognosis, I was told, was very bad. Elsa lingered in that state for ten or more days. The doctor's advised us that there was no prospect for recovery. She was being kept alive only by the machines she was attached to. After ten days or so, we finally had to make the decision to end her life. This primarily fell to me, as I had her health proxy. I shared this responsibility with Henry and other family members. The decision was made collectively. I was the one who gave the instructions to the doctors to disconnect her from the machines.

The next day, which was a Saturday, I had my annual West Side Conference. As I was leaving home to attend the conference, where I was to make the opening remarks, I received a call from her doctor saying she had died. It was very difficult for me to carry on in the conference, as my thoughts were of Elsa, and I needed to mourn. But I did my part in the conference and oversaw it as in previous years. It went off well. I think once again my survivor instincts and history of burying pain through activity carried me through.

I have missed Elsa in the years that have passed. Even now, more than twenty years later, I wish I could draw on her wisdom and love.

Kathy met Andrew in, I think, 1997. They quickly became a couple. I met him for the first time after one of the West Side Community Conferences. I immediately liked him. Their romance blossomed, and before long, Andrew moved into the family apartment at 448 Riverside.

Around this time, Melody and I decided to live together. It made sense to leave the eight-room apartment at 448 Riverside and let it be Kathy and Andrew's home. I didn't want to live there with Melody. Because of rent laws, I was able to pass this spacious apartment, which Columbia wanted for a senior faculty member, to Kathy. It gave me satisfaction and happiness for Andrew and Kathy to live there and to ease their life. They are a strong twosome.

Melody and I decided to get a home on the East Side, which she preferred. We found a two-bedroom condominium at 216 East Forty-Seventh Street, near the UN, not far from the Broadway theaters, next to a Y with a passable gym and centrally located near Grand Central. I provided the money for the purchase, as Melody had limited funds. She rented a professional office at East Seventy-Second Street, where she practiced as a psychologist. Her practice was decent. I think she was able to establish close relationships with her patients, and one in particular was so attached to Melody that she moved into a building down the street to be close to her. Our time together was good and satisfying. It became the third leg of my tripod—the Senate, my legal practice, and home life.

# CHAPTER 15

# 1997–2000: END OF MY LEGISLATIVE SERVICE

Until 1998, I continued active as a senator, both in Albany and in my district. I focused more than before on campaign finance reform and issued a number of reports showing questionable campaign contributions and how these raised issues of undue influence. One of my broadsides was over an illegal campaign contribution of $150,000 by Donald Trump to the Senate Republicans. He sought to hide it as a contribution by his wife. I called for an investigation by the State Election Commission. This got some publicity and, as expected, resulted in a public attack on me by Trump, who called me a sexist and then, his most common pejorative, "a loser." Nothing ever came of the investigation.

I took on the issue of what is called *pay for play*, political contributions, mainly by law firms, to get business from the state, primarily on bond issues. This became a major issue and has resulted in some restrictions on this practice. For instance, the state comptroller, who controls the bond issues, now won't hire law firms who made a campaign contribution to him.

I also took on another state subsidy program that allowed localities to issue bonds for supposed economic development. However, as with so many of these economic development programs, it was ineffective, costly, and often ended by putting local stores out of business through loans to, for example, large grocery chains, among others.

## MARIO CUOMO—A DIFFICULT GOVERNOR

The biggest change in the Legislature was that Mario Cuomo had been defeated in trying for a fourth term by George Pataki. I never had a good relationship with Cuomo. I found him a great orator but a non-achiever as a governor. He was a difficult person to get along with. He had a distrust of people and a streak of meanness. Our relationship was at best strained. Once on the Senate floor when we were waiting in vain for him to act on some matter important to the city, in frustration I said, "Does New York still have a governor?" Within a few minutes, Pat, my secretary, came to get me, saying the governor was on the phone. I went back to my office to take his call. He obviously had been listening to the Senate debate. I thought, *Doesn't he have something better to do?* Anyhow, he kept me on the phone for twenty minutes justifying himself. What a waste of time for him and me. My colleagues and others complained how difficult it was to reach the governor. When I heard these complaints, I would point out I had no difficulty in getting to the governor. I said, "All I have to do is say something negative about him, and he will call."

As an example of his lack of leadership, I issued a report on how New York was near the bottom of the states' funding higher public education. Both the city university (CUNY) and the state university system (SUNY) were declining in academic standing at the same time that there was increased enrollment and a need for a well-educated workforce. This is just another example of how I became engaged in myriad issues that caught my attention.

One of my gripes with Cuomo was that he did nothing to help the Senate Democrats. In all my time in the Senate, as we fought to gain the majority, he was either of no help or undermined our efforts. It was the lack of help from a Democratic governor, who is the head of the party, and gerrymandered districts, which kept the Republicans in the Senate in the majority. An example of Cuomo's disengagement, if not outright disdain, for the Senate Democrats was when he agreed to a reapportion map that not only disregarded the Senate Democrats but also hurt the Democratic members of Congress. He easily could have secured a fairer, favorable—or at least not unfavorable—congressional map. But he did nothing. I challenged him on reapportionment when he attended one of the Democratic caucuses. He gave an evasive, incomprehensible answer. The result was that the Democrats lost congressional seats, and my friend Steve Solarz effectively had his old district dismembered. His was now a very different district from the one that included most of southern Brooklyn. The district he was forced to run in had been created as a majority Hispanic district. He lost in a primary. A real loss for Congress. He was not the only senior Democrat who, as a result of this reapportionment, lost their seat or retired. I can never forgive Mario Cuomo for, as I have said many times, being the only governor in the fifty states who did not try to protect congressional members of his party.

## CHALLENGING A NEW GOVERNOR— GEORGE PATAKI

Pataki, elected in 1994 as governor, had been a colleague of mine in the Senate. We were not close. I don't think he was close to anyone, but he clearly showed his ambition. It was an uphill battle for him to take down Cuomo. But 1994 was a Republican year, and Cuomo ran a lousy campaign. So, for the first time since 1975, I had to deal with a Republican governor.

I took on Pataki and his administration on a number of issues. His was a right-of-center administration and nothing like the rabid conservatism of today's Republican Party and the Trump presidency (this is written in January 2018). For example, Pataki supported abortion rights. His vulnerability was questionable ethical standards and ineffective financial policies. I made news by pointing out ethically questionable fundraising. This did result in some limitations on fundraising from entities and persons who had financial dealings with the government. But as I see the currently shameful fundraising of Governor Andrew Cuomo and Mayor Bill de Blasio, we have a long way to go keep money from special interests influencing government policies.

My main effort was to oppose subsidies and grants to businesses that did not create jobs or better economic conditions. I, and others, called this corporate welfare. I issued reports that showed how little or no benefits had flowed from these subsidies. My argument was that it made more sense to take the money spent on corporate welfare and use it to improve general business conditions, for example, reduce utility costs, provide education and job training, among others. My criticism was not just of Pataki but also of Rudy Giuliani, New York's mayor from 1993 to 2001. Thus, I opposed tax breaks to NBC and World News, which was the usual way these subsidies were given out. As I was quoted in the *Daily News*, "Rupert Murdoch is the last person in the world who needs a handout from the city." The *Economist*, the prominent journal, criticizing corporate welfare in an article titled "Come and Get It," quoted me in calling for bank incentives to be scrapped. The sad result of all these gifts to business is that much less was left for the government to spend on traditional services and effective job creation.

I also took on Giuliani's proposal to move Yankee Stadium from the Bronx to Manhattan's West Side. I arranged a hearing at which I had experts on sports stadiums testify how little economic benefit these brought, though governments spent billions to attract sports teams. As with so much of the corporate welfare that the city gave out, it was prompted by threats to move to another state, usually New Jersey. Mostly these were idle threats to squeeze money out of the city and/or state. I said if the Yankees want to move to New Jersey, they will be called the Secaucus Yankees. Fortunately, this never happened. But in 2001–2, Michael Bloomberg, then New York's mayor, wanted to build a stadium for the New York Jets on the Hudson waterfront as part of a proposal to bring the Olympics to New York City. By then, I was out of the Legislature but still involved in creating the Hudson River Park, and a big stadium on the waterfront would have been devastating. I did what I could to oppose it. Fortunately, this failed to be realized.

My attacks on corporate welfare received a fair amount of coverage, as did some of my other reports. I actively opposed some bank mergers for failing to serve minority or poorer communities. I continued to hold press conferences, and my debates on the Senate floor were occasionally covered. I was still an active legislator.

I was greatly helped in my legislative work by an excellent staff. Over the years, I had managed to hire really gifted and talented, young people who did so much of the work in gathering the many reports I issued. Also, during my years in Albany, I had such a devoted assistant, Pat Gioia. She was much more than my secretary. She managed the Albany office. While in New York, I could dictate to her over the phones the numerous letters I wrote to constituents, fellow legislators, state officials, and so on. My friend Steve Solarz, in a candid admission by a public official, once said, "Franz, we are no better than our staff and hopefully as good as they are." Very true. One of the pleasures I have is that I have remained friends with many of my former staffers. We still have periodic lunches.

## SPONSORING COMMUNITY CONFERENCES

Starting in 1974, I sponsored an annual public issue discussion, called the West Side Conference. This had been started by Ryan. I held these conferences annually through 1998. They were held in his memory. It was a lot of work organizing the conferences. There was a plenary session where I had one or two main speakers. This was followed by panel discussions of four panelists and a moderator. I had to make numerous contacts to try to get participants. It was particularly hard to get top-name plenary speakers. Over the years, I had some luminaries—among others, Senator Patrick Moynihan, Secretary of HEW Donna Shalala, Rudy Giuliani when he was the much acclaimed US attorney for the Southern District of New York, Chuck Schumer, then a congressman. I had a brochure printed that I mailed and distributed.

On the day of one of the conferences, I had Josh, then maybe twelve or thirteen, hand out the brochures on Broadway to attract an audience. He was harassed by Larouche supporters (a crazy political cult that also annoyed me in northern Manhattan). They screamed at him, "Leichter is a drug dealer." Josh held his ground. They tried to disrupt one or more conferences and usually attacked me for my bill legalizing marijuana, which I first introduced in 1970 or 1971. Now, I must point out, many states have legalized marijuana use under state restrictions (which my bill also provided), and New York has now followed. After the conference, I hosted a party. Initially, these were at my home. The conferences were attended by 250–300 people. It was a lot of work, but I was assisted by my staff and volunteers.

In the meantime, I was appointed to the Hudson Greenway Commission, which was to create, as far as possible, a public passageway from the tip of Manhattan to Troy along the Hudson River. Through some foul-up with the Dinkins administration, Manhattan was left out of the legislation creating the Greenway. I managed to get this legislatively rectified. I was quite active in the commission. I explored ways to have a trail along the Bronx shore. This was difficult, as the railroad tracks ran at some points right to the river. I organized walking tours to explore how this might be done. Nothing came of it, and the Greenway has pretty much faded away.

## LEGISLATIVE SERVICE LOSES ITS ALLURE

But my heart wasn't in it anymore. Much of the excitement and satisfaction were gone. The quality of the Senate members had deteriorated. Partisanship had become more extreme. Governor George Pataki was a Republican and pursued policies such as the death penalty, which I strongly opposed. With a Republican Senate and a Democratic Assembly, little was accomplished in those years. The annual budget, which under the Constitution had to be enacted by April 1, became mired in disagreements and was not passed in one year until late summer. This meant that the session continued far into the year. Decisions were made by what was referred to as the "three men in a room"—that is the governor, Assembly speaker, and Senate majority leader, with very limited member involvement. I continued with my reports, press releases, debates in the Senate, and community activities and visibility. I was involved but not really engaged. For some time, I had been seeking something else in public service. I began to pursue a position with the Clinton administration. The time had come to leave.

It seemed with every Senate colleague of either party who left, was replaced by someone less able. On the Republican side, this resulted in former Assembly members taking these seats, as they were eager to move on to the Senate and leave the minority status they had. These Republicans came from the Assembly, dominated by the Democrats, where they were largely marginalized. Now that they were in the majority, they wanted to apply the same marginalization they endured on the Senate Democratic minority. I called them hawks. This also represented the political divisiveness that was becoming prevalent not only in Albany but in Washington and throughout the country. Any Republican proposal or bill that came to the Senate floor for a vote had to be passed because party unity and control was more important than merit or public good. In one debate, being frustrated as Republicans were about to pass a bill, which some Republican members admitted to me privately was flawed, I said, "If a Republican bill came on the floor providing that all Republican senators were to be shot at dawn, the Republicans would nevertheless vote for and pass that bill rather than enduring in their view the ignominy of having a Republican bill defeated." My remarks drew some chuckles, but the flawed bill passed anyway.

Another factor that made my Senate experience less and less appealing was that dysfunction had set in. Throughout my legislative years, except for my six years in the Assembly, New York state government was divided. In my first twenty years in the Senate, there was a Democratic governor, and the Assembly had a large Democratic majority. In the last four, there was a Republican governor, a Republican Senate majority, and a Democratic majority in the Assembly. Governor Hugh Carey, in his first term, managed to find common ground. But under Governor Cuomo, who I found inept in getting agreement with the Legislature, and then under Governor Pataki, divineness increased. Compromise was seen as weakness, and on many issues there was a stalemate. An example was the late passage of the state budget, which under the Constitution has to be enacted by April 1. In many years, it took until the summer, and sometimes into the fall, until agreement was finally reached on a budget.

I also became evermore dismayed by the role of money in influencing election and public policy. Until we end financing campaigns through large, mainly unregulated contributions, our democracy is in peril. I saw in the Legislature the pernicious effect of the need to have a large campaign chest. If an elected official showed he or she had a big treasury, that certainly discouraged challengers. I saw votes determined and legislation passed due to who made campaign contributions. The claim by elected public officials that they are not influenced by their contributors is laughable. I saw a chart showing that, over an extended period, the largest contributor to New York legislators was Donald Trump. Almost all of this went to the Senate Republicans. He certainly understood how to influence public officials. The situation has been made so much worse by the decision of the majority conservatives on the Supreme Court in *Citizens United* that allowed corporations and unions to make unlimited campaign contributions and opened up more loopholes making it possible to keep certain campaign contributions secret.

I too had to raise money. I had an annual fundraiser. But I was lousy at it and hated doing it. My campaign treasury was always small and among the lowest in the Legislature. Fortunately, I was so safe in my district that I had no need for a robust campaign chest. If I had credible challengers, what would I have done? As I said in a previous chapter, one of the reasons I dropped out of the city comptroller race in 1985 was that I felt uneasy about how and from whom I would need to raise the hundreds of thousands (more likely now, millions). It was a suspect contribution from Trump that finally made me decide that if I stayed in the campaign, I would end being compromised by campaign fundraising. And as a senator, I did return to Trump a $1,000 contribution he sent me.

Being in the Legislature had become less and less attractive and more burdensome. There were two main factors in addition to fatigue as I was approaching my thirtieth year in Albany. When I entered the Senate, it had many highly competent members of both parties who saw their purpose as not solely political advancement or betterment for their party. That is not to say that politics were absent or that it did not play a significant role in how policy was formed and executed; nor were members not conscious of their constituents' wishes and views. In my early years, I had the impression that when matters of real public urgency required action, a way could be found for the two parties and the governor to come together. Compromise was not a dirty word. The best example of that is saving New York City from bankruptcy in 1975–6 and possibly averting a worldwide financial calamity. The higher level of ability also meant that the debates were more substantive and interesting. As I mentioned before, throughout my Senate tenure, I was frequently on my feet debating bills—probably much more than any other member—and enjoyed the repartee.

In the spring of 1998, I decided I had finally had enough. I would not run for another term. I had served thirty years in the Legislature. Past time to leave. In April or May, I informed my staff that I would not continue after the end of my term on December 31, 1998. I issued a release. The *New York Times* ran a nice story about me.

## CREATING THE HUDSON RIVER PARK

Before I left, I worked for and accomplished one of my major achievements: the creation of the Hudson River Park. Together with my Assembly colleague Richard Gottfried, we drafted a bill in 1994 to save the Hudson waterfront from commercial development. It had some support from the environmental community, but there was little interest from the Cuomo administration. Cuomo had set up two commissions to recommend what was to be done with the waterfront. This was now state property, as the state had purchased a narrow strip from the bulkhead to the highway in anticipation of building Westway. This was to have been a superhighway along the Hudson in New York City, with a park on top. It generated strong opposition, especially on the West Side and throughout my district. I was very actively involved in the effort to stop Westway. When Westway was abandoned after a court found its construction would adversely affect fish in the Hudson, the Cuomo commissions recommended a park on the stretch of state land that extended from southern Manhattan to West Fifty-Seventh Street. The very sketchy proposals allowed for some commercial development to pay for the park's upkeep. But Cuomo was indecisive and failed to provide direction. I spoke to him once about our bill. I said to him, "Governor, if that park is built under your leadership and administration, a hundred years from now, that is what you will be remembered for, just as are the mayors who built Central Park." Cuomo hemmed and hawed and said I didn't have full community support for the bill. While true, there was no proposal, even manna from heaven, which could ever get unanimous support from this opinionated community I represented. If manna from heaven came, some would protest that it was not gluten-free. So the Gotfried-Leichter bill didn't move. Cuomo then lost his election in 1994 for a fourth term to George Pataki, who, growing up near the Hudson, had a much friendlier attitude for such a park.

I continued working on establishing a waterfront park. The need became more pressing as the old commercial piers were deteriorating and falling into the river. This entire stretch of the waterfront was dilapidated, dangerous, and inaccessible. What made it even more unattractive, but also opened up the possibility of a park and access to the waterfront, was that an elevated highway that had existed along this stretch had collapsed some years before. The State now had to build a replacement ground-level highway. In building support for the Gottfried-Leichter bill, we succeeded in getting the major environmental groups to now actively support our bill. This bill prohibited any commercial buildings. It provided that three very large, mainly intact piers could have limited commercial usage in order to provide revenue for the maintenance of the park. To build the park, the state and the city would each provide $200 million. There was one obstacle. Opposition came from the most surprising group.

In the fight against Westway, the main mover and organizer had been Marcie Bienstock. I worked closely with her, and we had a good relationship.

But her interest had been primarily with preventing landfill in the river for the super highway and its effect on marine life. Marcie now saw herself as the chief protector of the Hudson River and was against any work along the Hudson and irrationally against our bill, which would preserve the waterfront from commercial development and did not provide for any landfill. On the contrary, we provided in our bill for the creation of an estuary. Nevertheless, she waged a campaign of disinformation against our park proposal, and she had credibility because of her fight against Westway. She managed to gather some opposition to our bill. Marcie also controlled the local chapter of the Sierra Club, which at one time was a most influential environmental group. The local chapter included just ten members under Marcie's thumb. She and the club ran a most deceptive opposition. One leaflet it put out accused me of wanting to turn the waterfront over to Donald Trump and that my bill would commercialize the waterfront. Our bill did just the opposite. I think opposition also came from some of the residents of the West Village who saw the waterfront as their backyard and were fearful of their neighborhood being overrun by visitors to the park.

I attended many meetings, met with groups, and worked with prominent environmental groups that rallied in support of our bill. I held rallies and press conferences, pointing out how dangerous the decaying piers were and how these would be rebuilt as part of the park. It was a grueling fight and in some respects the most disturbing I faced while in the Legislature. Yes, I was involved in fights over abortion and the death penalty, among the more divisive issues. But much as I disagreed with opponents to these measures and policies, I could understand the basis for their position. But opposition to the park, by the very people who should have been our main supporters, and their false claims and arguments really bothered me.

In 1998, we made a much more concerted effort to have the bill passed. The major environmental groups were more involved and played a significant role. The biggest difference from previous years was that Governor George Pataki had concern for the Hudson and was more environmentally inclined than Cuomo. The bill began to move. On the last night of the 1998 session, which was in December at a special session, I negotiated the final aspect with one of the governor's counsel. The bill now had the governor's active backing. On the last day of the session and my last day as a legislator, the bill came to the floor of both houses and was passed. In speaking for the bill, I quoted JFK, who had said, "Victory has a thousand fathers, but defeat is an orphan." I said this bill had a thousand fathers. It passed unanimously. A great ending to my legislative career.

As my legislative career ended, I was honored by a number of the community groups I had worked with and supported. These included community boards, environmental organizations, waterfront advocates, and others. There was a large party for me of people I had worked with at a room at Presbyterian Hospital. Kathy made a video of people who spoke about our association. I was invited to be the guest on an ABC Sunday talk show on New York state issues. ABC had me as a commentator on the 1998 election that November. I was asked to join a number of boards, including the Fund for Modern Courts, Dorot (a senior service organization), the local chapter of the Environmental Legal Defense Fund, and Common Cause. I also served on a committee of the New York City Bar Association.

## A FULL-TIME LAWYER REBUILDING MY PRACTICE

Out of the Legislature, starting in 1999, I was now a full-time lawyer. For a couple years in the late mid-nineties, my practice—that is legal matters I brought to the firm, which I usually handled myself—diminished. My take from the firm, based on a percentage of the business I brought in, became negligible, and the firm, which was then run by an aggressive manager, eliminated the basic pay I was to receive. The decline in my practice was partly due to the firm's banking practice leaving to join another firm. I had to give up representing an American government fund to help the economies of nations that had been part of the southern Soviet Union (referred to as the Stan nations), of which my friend Steve Solarz had been appointed chairman by Bill Clinton. That was a consolation prize after Clinton had nominated Steve as ambassador to India and then withdrew the nomination because of some alleged improper immigration help he sought to give to a reputed Hong Kong mob boss. Steve told me the whole story, and I think it was a bum rap, though he may have been a bit careless. And Steve and I were already planning my visit to the US embassy in New Delhi. Steve made me the counsel for the fund, which I had the banking section of the firm handle. When they left, since it had handled the matter and I was unfamiliar with the work, I lost that business.

I had to rebuild my legal practice after the fallow years I developed some interesting matters. My main client became the Mexican Government Development Bank, Nafinsa. My work included the bankruptcy of the Mexican government-owned airline, Aeromexico. I had some trips to Mexico City. But then fortune partly reversed itself. The counsel, with whom I had such a good relationship, lost his position when a new government came to power. He ended up as counsel to the Mexican embassy in Washington, which he had me represent in a minor case.

But then Lady Luck shined on me again. At a funeral, I sat next to a judge with whom I had a friendly relationship. We chatted and remembered our political ties. A few days later, he appointed me as receiver for a major foreclosure by a Japanese bank of a large Park Avenue office building. Under New York law, when a mortgage holder forecloses for default in paying, the foreclosure has to be approved by the courts, which appoints a receiver to manage the building and collect rent until the foreclosure (which at times is contested) is finalized and the creditor takes possession of the building. This was a very lucrative appointment. As receiver, I was entitled to up to 5 percent of the total rentals collected, which, as I recollect, was well over a million dollars a month. For getting the full commission, I had my firm agree to do the work on leases, which for such a building can be quite complicated. The receivership lasted only six or seven months and, besides bringing me good income, was also very interesting. I hired a major real estate management firm, Cushman & Wakefield, as manager and had weekly meetings with that firm, reviewed financial statements, talked and negotiated with prospective tenants, and spent some time inspecting my prize building.

I then had an issue with my firm, which wanted to go back to my original agreement of paying me a basic salary (about $60,000) plus a percentage of business I brought in. I took the position that since the firm had abrogated our agreement by cutting my basic salary I demanded a larger share of the total commission that came to the firm from the receivership. We settled amicably.

## LIFE WITH MELODY

Melody and I traveled a lot. We went to London a few times for long weekends. We would leave Thursday or sometimes Friday and stay until Monday or Tuesday. We went to the theater every day and once went to a matinee and evening performance on the same day. We also visited Cambridge and Oxford. Another trip was to Vienna and then Paris. Either in 1999 or 2000, Steve Solarz invited us and our friends Lorraine and Oliver Koppell on a cruise in a yacht a Turkish oligarch had made available to him. We sailed what is called the Blue Sea for five days in great comfort and beauty. Among our stops was a beautiful Greek island where we experienced a full eclipse of the moon.

My relationship with Melody grew in these years. We were physically attracted to each other and enjoyed going out to dinner, movies, and the theater. Melody had an enjoyment for life, which I wanted to be part of then and needed. She was fun to be with, but she could also be difficult, obstinate, and easily angered. We argued a lot. She liked to drink, smoke, and was fond of marijuana. She was also smart, opinionated, and loved the theater. At times, she seemed to me unhinged. She was a therapist and seemed very good in her work. After we were together, she got a PhD from Yeshiva as a psychotherapist. I believe at that time she was very much in love with me. My feeling for her was more nuanced—an appreciation, enjoyment but also wariness of her instability.

## RESTLESS—TRYING TO GET BACK INTO PUBLIC LIFE IN THE CLINTON ADMINISTRATION

Life was good again. Yet I was not satisfied with just being a practicing lawyer. I missed the public policy issues I dealt with as a legislator. Maybe there was also a sense, probably instilled in me from the example of my parents, that one should be engaged in public life and one's community. As I ended my legislative career in 1998, I did not want to give up public life and just devote myself to my legal practice. Starting in 1997, I tried to get a position in the Clinton administration as he began his second term. What I sought was the American ambassadorship to Austria. What an achievement that would be. I had friends in the Jewish community and in Congress who pitched in on my behalf. Overtures on my behalf were made to the Administration Personnel Office, which handled political appointments. It soon became obvious that this was a vain quest. The Austrian ambassadorship had traditionally gone to big contributors. My seventy-five-dollar contribution to the Clinton campaign did not put me into play against contributors in the hundreds of thousands. This was made clear to me when I met with the Personnel Office in Washington. I was told that if I had my heart set on an ambassadorship, there might be a possibility of an insignificant African country. Even that was just thrown out as a gesture.

However, because I managed to get so many public officials to urge the administration to find something for me, the Personnel Office felt it had to find a position for me. I worked at it. I got every Democratic member of the New York congressional delegation, even Senator Moynahan, except one (Nidya Vasquez, who had defeated my friend Steve) to write a letter of support to the Personnel Office. This had some effect. At one time, it suggested an appointment to a commission preserving Jewish cemeteries in Europe. Then came an offer to become a representative in Vienna for the Organization for Security and Cooperation in Europe (OSCE). This would provide me with an apartment and driver in Vienna. I went for an interview at the Pentagon. If a firm offer had come through, I might have taken it, so desperate was I to find something to stay in public life. But what about my marriage to Melody and her practice in New York and my family here? Fortunately, before I had to make a decision, I received a call from the Personnel Office, with whom I was in constant contact and pestered. I was told that a position as one of the Democratic directors of the FHFB, a position that once had been mentioned to me as a possibility if a position opened up, had become vacant. This appealed to me, as it was an area I was interested in—housing development.

The FHFB was constituted, as were a number of these congressionally created supervisory boards, with two members of each party, with the fifth member from the president's party. For the FHFB, it was the secretary of housing and urban renewal. The position required Senate confirmation. One holdup in my getting this post was that it was held by a Democrat who, while nominally confirmed for one of the Democratic seats, had gotten the position through the Republican senator from New York, Alphonse D'Amato, when the Republicans held the Senate majority and he was chairman of the Banking Committee. His six-year term had expired, and the Democratic chairman of FHFB wanted to get rid of him. While his term had expired, there was a legal issue whether he could be removed until a successor was chosen and confirmed. (Coincidentally, I knew this person, Larry Costiglio, quite well because he had been a bank lobbyist in Albany, and I had gone out to dinner with him and his co-lobbyist a few times.) Yes, particularly in my early days in the Legislature, I would have dinner with or attend events sponsored by lobbyists. It was common then, but it would have been better not to do this and is now prohibited. Finally, the White House removed him. He sued, which further delayed my appointment.

My nomination by Clinton finally came through in 1999. However, the Senate would not take up my confirmation. It was stuck with numerous other Clinton nominations. I urged the Personnel Office to give me a recess appointment (a power the president has to fill a vacant position, which requires Senate confirmation, but which he/she may fill when the Senate is out of session for holidays or other reasons). But the appointment is valid only for the year in which it is made and the succeeding year. I had my Washington friends lobby on my behalf for such an appointment, but Clinton was wary of making recess appointments, which always draw the ire of the Senate. I was a small fish—a tadpole—in the political maneuvering over confirmations. It reached a point where I told the Personnel Office I might have to withdraw, as the uncertainty hindered me from taking on clients or legal matters. If, as I hoped, I would soon have this position, I would then be precluded from any outside legal work.

# KATHY AND ANDREW GET MARRIED

In 1999, I had the joy of Kathy and Andrew's wedding. The ceremony was on a dock on Saranac Lake where the camp that Andrew attended was situated. In the evening, we had a party at the Farm. A large tent was set up for the more than one hundred guests. Food was provided by a caterer from Vermont, and a band performed. The weather, which had been cold the week leading up to the wedding, cooperated. It was a beautiful event. When Kathy and Andrew said they wanted to have the marriage at our Farm, I said that would be fine but that not many people would come to such a faraway place. I was wrong. So many of both their and my friends came. Cousins showed up from Austin, Texas, and some came from far distances, including my friends the Solarzes, from Washington. Kathy scoured the countryside to find accommodations in hotels, B&Bs, and motels. We had a joyous, full weekend of celebrating a wonderful couple. Their marriage has given them happiness and me great satisfaction to see them in such a good, strong, supportive relationship. Also, it gave me two more loving grandchildren.

# CHAPTER 16

# 2000-2006: THE WASHINGTON GIG

As I entered the new millennium, my desire to leave my law practice and be confirmed as a director of the FHFB heightened. Meantime, I continued to practice law with Walter, Conston, Alexander & Green. I did have an interesting new case for my Mexican client, the bank Nacional Financiera, which again took me to Mexico City.

As I missed being involved in public policy, I sought to continue my quest to reform the Legislature. I thought if I got a bipartisan group of retired senators to agree to some basic reforms, it would have some impact. I did manage to pull such a statement together. But it was ignored. I soon became aware that I was a has-been. Once out of office, your influence is nil. My friend Steve Solarz told me that once in O'Hare Airport, he was stopped by a woman who said, "You look familiar. Didn't you used to be someone?"

I pestered the Office of Personnel Management to get Bill Clinton to give me a recess appointment for the position he had nominated me for, director of the FHFB. I continued to get support from my congressional friends and others. Importantly, I reached out to an old acquaintance, Harold Ickes, who was close to Clinton and had served as his deputy chief of staff.

Finally, in July 2000, I was included in a list of recess appointees. What made this happen was that the Republicans in the Senate were holding up Clinton's judicial nominees. He became so exasperated that he made a number of recess appointments in July 2000, which fortunately included me. I took it and resigned from my law firm, Walter, Conston, Alexander & Green, even though, as I explained, a recess appointment is good only for the year in which it is made and the following year. As I saw it, I took a chance that a new president after the 2000 election might not reappoint me to a full term of six years.

Before starting my position, I went to the Farm. For my seventieth birthday, I asked Kathy and Andrew to join me for a trip to the White Mountains. I wanted to celebrate entering my eighth decade by climbing Mount Washington. I succeeded in reaching the summit without too much difficulty. We went up Tuckerman Ravine and down Boott Spur, a lengthier route. I mention what seems like a minor detail in the hope that children, grandchildren, and maybe other descendants will have the pleasure of climbing there and that this will have meaning for them. It makes me happy that my love of hiking has been passed along to my children and grandchildren. I know they will, in the future, experience the same joy as I had in numerous hikes there (and elsewhere), starting in 1943. It has been a significant part of my life.

It was exciting to have this new experience as a federal financial regulator. I liked the status and the challenge of being a director of the FHFB. It consisted of five members. Two had to be Democrats, and two Republicans. The fifth member was the secretary of housing and urban development so that the president's party always has the dominant say. The FHFB regulated twelve regional home loan banks. These banks were like a cooperative to which banks in their region could join by buying stock. This would entitle them to borrow money to lend to their customers for housing mortgages.

The Home Loan Bank system was known as a GSE (government-supported enterprise), as were our larger and more prominent sister companies, Fannie Mae and Freddie Mac. In the housing and financial crash of 2008, the federal government had to bail these two out with many billions of dollars and in effect nationalize them. I take no, or almost no, credit for the Home Loan Bank system not requiring a bailout. As a cooperative, the Home Loan Banks had more capital, and the collateral it required a local member bank to put up to get a loan was under our supervision and proved much better than the dodgy collateral that many commercial and investment banks took, which were chock-full of questionable subprime mortgages. The major contribution I made was to get the Home Loan Banks to avoid predatory lending by its member local banks by refusing to accept as collateral unaffordable mortgages, which had been pushed on people who didn't understand the risk.

My position as director was interesting and at times challenging. I had a full-time secretary and an assistant. As with my legislative staff, I fortunately picked good people and am still in contact and friendly with the people I hired. I also developed a friendship with the other Democratic board member, Allan Mendelowitz. He is in Washington, yet we speak regularly, and whenever I go to Washington, I meet with him and some of the people I worked with.

My duties as a board member were not arduous. There was a monthly meeting. I attended some meetings of the local Home Loan Banks. Each of these had their own board, and choosing members for these boards, which was one of our responsibilities, created much lobbying and contention when George W. Bush became president and the Republicans were now in the majority. The board meetings of the twelve Home Loan Banks were either in their home city or often at very nice resorts and were very pleasant visits. I was also invited to the conventions and events of trade groups who were engaged with the system, such as the National Association of

Home Builders, a major economic and political power. The latter held its conventions in Las Vegas or Orlando. Every February, I was invited to a conference in Park City, which allowed time for skiing. Twice I took Josh with me. Through these conferences and meetings, I met some bankers and mortgage lenders who bore significant responsibility for the collapse of the housing market and the subsequent Great Recession. All of this required quite a bit of traveling, which I enjoyed.

I would go to Washington every Monday and usually return late Wednesday. I rarely stayed until Thursday. I liked Washington. I stayed in a local hotel, but on numerous nights, I would stay with my friends Steve and Nina Solarz, who lived in Washington's suburb of McLean, Virginia. They were so welcoming and generous. How fortunate I was to have them as friends ever since Steve and I entered the Legislature together in 1969. Nina often said, "Franz is the best thing that happened to Steve in politics." This is quite an exaggeration. But certainly my friendship with Steve and Nina was one of the major rewards of my political life. At many of these evenings at the Solarzes', there were present friends and contacts from his very active congressional tenure devoted to foreign affairs. Steve had welcomed to his congressional office exiles from a number of Asian and Middle Eastern countries while these were under some form of dictatorship. As these countries became more democratic, these exiles returned and became leaders of their countries, including South Korea, the Philippines, and Pakistan. They remembered Steve and would be invited to dinner when in Washington, as were some other important politicians from these countries or other guests. I attended a number of these dinners. The stay with the Solarzes provided not only interest but also comfort and the pleasure of good friendships.

When not visiting Steve and Nina, I would frequently go to performances at the John F. Kennedy Center for the Performing Arts and local theaters. I also had in Washington a friend of my early years in politics, Cora

Rubenstein, who with her husband, Marty, lived near us on Riverside Drive and whose son was one of Josh's best friends in their early years. They had moved to Washington in the 1970s. Marty had died. On occasion, I stayed with Cora. All in all, not a bad life.

As I had only a recess appointment, I became worried that if George W. Bush won the presidency, I would not be nominated to a full term when my recess appointment expired on December 31, 2001. While my seat had to be filled by a Democrat, Bush could nominate a Democrat who had supported him. As the campaign between Bush and Gore was close, I became more concerned that I would lose this position and had doubts whether I could get back into my law practice. I was in Vienna when I learned that the Supreme Court decided for Bush over Gore. I became quite anxious. In fact, so much so that I had trouble sleeping and became sleep deprived for two or three months. I had some tough days in Washington with very little sleep.

What I didn't realize was that the Democrats in the Senate, who were in the majority, would insist on choosing the Democratic members of FHFB. I made sure, enlisting my former Albany roommate Chuck Schumer, now a senator from New York, that I was the Democrat the Senate would put forward in negotiating these and other appointments with the Bush White House. I ended up being part of a package of nominees, which included my friend Allan Mendelowitz as the two Democratic members of FHFB. I was thus one of the few people who received nominations from both Clinton and Bush. Even then, it took some time until all the politicking in the Senate over confirmations was resolved. I think it was not until November 2001 that I was confirmed after a hearing of the Senate Housing and Urban Affairs Committee. I now had a full six-year term. I was definitely sleeping better, though uneven sleep has bothered me many times until today. I always seem to find something to be anxious about.

At the same time that I was confirmed, so was a Republican appointee to FHFB, John Korsmo, who was then designated chairman. As such, he had authority over FHFB and had the votes (his, the other Republican Board member, and the secretary of Housing and Urban Development). So after thirty years in the minority in Legislature, I again was being outvoted. Korsmo was a diehard Republican from North Dakota. He brought in as his chief of staff a very aggressive Republican, Tom Casey. Instead of being collegial, they were determined to minimize Mendelowitz's and my role. They brought partisanship to FHFB. Conflict soon broke into the open.

I was not going to allow Korsmo and Casey to marginalize me and my colleague Allan Mendelowitz just because we were Democrats. I knew we had to assert ourselves to have our standing recognized. I had proven in many years in the Legislature that I knew how to assert myself, often by putting out press releases and getting media coverage. When I found a plan Korsmo and Casey were hatching to give the latter a position in the office that marketed our bonds to raise funds and give him an excessive pay, I was able to bring this out publicly. Their plan collapsed.

So once again, I found myself having to deal with a majority I frequently disagreed with. Not only I, but the presidents of the twelve Home Loan Banks, had trouble with Korsmo. Not infrequently, they complained to me. There was a nice denouement. Korsmo was investigated by the FBI for using his office and government equipment, such as a computer, for partisan political work. Then he was charged with lying to the FBI. He was forced to resign and had to plead guilty to criminal charges. A victory. His successor was nicer but inept. The administration soon replaced her with Ronnie Rosenstein, a wealthy Clevelander who made big contributions to George W. Bush and with whom I had a good relationship.

# MY LIFE WITH MELODY

During these years, Melody and I continued living together at 216 East Forty-Seventh Street in a two-bedroom condominium. We enjoyed furnishing our home. We went antique searching on Atlantic Avenue in Brooklyn (almost all gone as the area gentrified), and in Hudson, New York. Melody had an office at East Seventy-Ninth Street and First Avenue. Her practice seemed to be going well. Our building was what is known as a sliver building, which means it was very narrow, with only two apartments per floor. The neighboring apartment, a large one-bedroom, was occupied, we were told, by the daughter of the Hong Kong billionaire who developed our building. She seemed never to be there. We had asked the staff to let us know when she would come, as we wanted to explore buying her apartment. When she made one of her infrequent visits to the building, we made our move. Melody handled her very shrewdly. She invited her for tea and gave her a present. This is an appreciated Chinese custom. She finally agreed to sell us her apartment. When we acquired it, Melody used the living room as her office and to see clients. We hired an architect friend of Melody's, who combined the two apartments. We now had a very comfortable and workable setup.

The building had its advantages, mainly location near Grand Central, but also complications. Shortly after I moved in, I was asked to join the Board of Directors at the condominium. The president belonged to a prominent New York real estate family, the Kaufmans, who owned a number of commercial buildings. He was old, ill-tempered, and hated dogs (or his wife did). He tried to run the building as if it was his private domain. Melody was determined to get a dog. The building's lease did have a no-pet provision. I secured the consent of the other board members to have a dog. I thought I had Kaufman's consent by telling him we would not take the dog in the elevator but use the stairs to our apartment on the fourth floor. We got a wonderful dog, whom Melody shrewdly chose among available canines at a shelter in Long Island. Andie, as the dog was named, was a survivor dog, a mix of Rottweiler and Australian sheepherding dog. She was smart, lovely, and a great pet. I miss her. She must be in dog heaven with Cocoa, the golden retriever we got for Kathy and Josh. She, too, gave me pleasure for ten years.

Some months after we got Andie, Kaufman, probably egged on by his wife, became very hostile and unpleasant. He sued the building agent for not preventing us from bringing a dog into the building. At the next annual meeting, he sought to have me removed from the Board of Directors. I really had no interest in continuing in what was a somewhat burdensome post and responsibility. Kaufman put up a candidate against me. There were now six people running for the five positions. I wasn't going to let Kaufman drive me off, and I felt I had better stay on the Board to protect our having Andie. Not being a stranger to campaigns, and having only forty-three condominium owners to solicit, I was not only reelected, but Kaufman was kicked off the Board. As he had been the president, the other board members insisted I assume the presidency. I couldn't refuse, as no one else was willing to assume the position.

So for the next five or six years, I served in this thankless post and had to deal with all the building's issues, staff, and occupants' complaints. Among the problems I had to deal with, the worst was when the cooling unit for the air-conditioning failed as summer approached. We had to buy a new cooling unit and hire a crane company to raise it to the roof some forty stories high after getting the city's permission to close off our street on a Saturday. The cost was significant, and I had to levy an assessment on each unit, which of course met with complaints. Fortunately, I had a good superintendent and then an efficient managing agent whom I hired. And every annual election, I had to beat back Kaufman wanting to return to the Board and oust me. This all added unnecessary burden to my life.

Melody's and my early years were satisfying. We enjoyed each other. We got on well and had a strong physical relationship. Melody, as I wrote before, was smart, fun-loving, stubborn, and given to irascibility. She would easily take offense. We had a lot of fights, mainly over minor matters. She could be very determined and at other times lackadaisical. She showed determination by writing her thesis to finally get her PhD in social work from Yeshiva University. I urged her on and supported her financially to get this done. She had a difficult childhood. Her mother and father divorced early in her childhood. She had a strained relationship with her mother. I think she was partly determined to get a PhD because her mother had acquired one. But when her mother needed to get assisted-living care and then a nursing home, she took charge. She had a half-brother with whom she had an on-and-off relationship. Her real affection was for her father. He was something of a con man but could be fun to be with when he wasn't putting his arm on you. I think she was always after his love, which she didn't have as a child. Early in our relationship, I saw her instability. But on balance, I did not see it as a serious drawback.

Melody had been pressing me to get married. I wasn't eager to get married again. Yet I appreciated her devotion to me and that, as a much younger woman—twenty-one years younger—she could have easily found someone her age. I was in my seventieth year, and it was evident to me that I would predecease her. I don't know whether I fully loved her, but I was happy with her and didn't want the relationship to end. I don't think she would have left me if I had continued to resist marriage. Finally, my decision to give in and marry her was based mainly on a feeling I owed it to her and was satisfied with our being together for the few years I thought I had left—so why not do it? In August 2000, my friend Judge Edward Lehner married us in a simple ceremony in our home with just two friends as witnesses.

We spent our honeymoon first in Paris and then visited Steve and Nina Solarz in a beautiful house they had built on the Mediterranean coast in Turkey, in a small village called Kalkan. Steve had many contacts in Turkey and decided to have a vacation home there. He asked me if I wanted to go fifty-fifty with him when he planned the house. I said I could not see myself using such a house that took almost twenty-four hours to get there. It was not like going to Fire Island or even the five-hour drive from New York City to the Farm. I also did not have the resources to be a partner in the big and expensive house he and Nina built, which has been featured in architectural magazines. They have maintained a live-in couple as caretakers and cook. While not a part owner, I have had the pleasure of visiting them almost every summer since 2001. They have been the most generous of hosts and the best of friends. In 2013, I took all of Kathy's family and Memphis there for a grand week. In June 2018, I took Ethan there since he was the only grandchild who had not been there.

About my marriage, I did something stupid, with good but flawed intentions. Kathy was pregnant with Otto when I married. I thought she might be upset by my marriage. I didn't want to give her what she might take as unwelcome news, which might impact her pregnancy. So I kept it secret from my children and brother, Henry, until after Kathy gave birth. The upshot was that when I finally told my family about the marriage, they were all angry with me for keeping it secret. However, it caused no real rift. I don't really know how they felt about Melody, but they were friendly and accepting. They were supportive.

## MY GRANDCHILDREN ENRICH MY LIFE

I was so pleased when Kathy, while pregnant, told me she would name the child, if he was a boy, Otto, after my father. Otto came into our lives in July 2001. He was born in the Allen Pavilion of Presbyterian Hospital that I had some role in having built. I took him home with mother and father in my Volvo. I was too nervous to drive and left it to Andrew. My third grandchild has given me great pleasure. Unlike with Memphis and Ethan, who were in Massachusetts, I could easily visit Otto. And I did very often. When Kathy was pregnant with Theo, I took Otto out frequently. I have such good memories of wheeling him around in his stroller while I told him a story I made up about a family of dinosaurs. Three years later, Theo was born, and he too added joy to my life. When he attended preschool, I would often pick him up and take him to the School at Columbia to pick up Otto, who was there in kindergarten. Later, as both boys moved up through elementary school, I would go to the School at Columbia on numerous occasions to bring them home.

While distance kept me from the same close contact with my older two grandchildren, I did visit them for birthdays, holidays, and special events, such as when Memphis was part of her piano teacher's student recital. Over the years as I saw my grandchildren grow up, our relationships changed and accommodated itself to their different stages. They have added much richness to my life. The joy they brought me was tempered at times by my worry about some aspect or issue in their lives. I am a big worrier. That they loom so large in my hope for them and desire for their well-being and success is evidence of how important they are in my life.

## TRAVELING

Melody and I traveled a great deal. We went to London for long weekends. We traveled a number of times to Amsterdam, took a cruise in the Baltic from Copenhagen to Stockholm, stopping in the Baltic nations and Saint Petersburg. We went to Alaska, going to Denali Park, and then took a cruise down the coast to Vancouver. We traveled to Paris and Vienna. We visited my friend Elizabeth Clark in the Virgin Islands and twice went to Bermuda, where Melody attended conferences. My travel lust continued strong. While I no longer had my overseas business trips, I scheduled at least two major trips each year.

In 2000, I was asked to join a small group headed by my friend Steve Solarz to visit Russia and meet with government officials. It was a fascinating trip. I arrived in Moscow earlier than the rest of the group and hired a local Muscovite to take me around. She had a sad and interesting history. Her father was a leading Bolshevik who was murdered in one of Stalin's purges. She and her mother lived in danger and poverty. I took an overnight trip to St. Petersburg.

This beautiful city showed years of neglect. I did get to see a wonderful performance of *Swan Lake* at the Mariinsky Theater and to visit the Hermitage Museum with its wonderful Rembrandt paintings and my favorite work of Matisse. Back in Moscow, we had meetings with top Russian officials but only with Putin's staff. He had not yet become president.

In 2003, I took the family to Austria to spend some days in the little Alpine village of Lofer, where Elsa had spent numerous summers. From there, we went to Vienna, where there was a book party celebrating the publishing of a book about my father's disappointing return to Vienna in 1947–8.

In 2007, I took Kathy and Josh to the Ravensbrück memorial of the concentration camp. This is where my mother was held from 1939 to 1942 before she was taken to be murdered in March of that year when the Nazis decided to make the camp Judenfrei—empty of Jews. We were there when the annual celebration of the camp occurred together with a few Austrian survivors of the camp. When we arrived, we were assigned rooms in what had been the dormitory for the Gestapo guards. My initial reaction was that I could not possibly stay there and began to make arrangements to stay in the neighboring town. But then I thought, *Let the Nazi guards turn over in their graves, thinking a Jew is staying there.* I remained and had a good night's sleep. Kathy had brought a film crew and did a lot of filming of the camp and interviews with the survivors. They had arranged a remembrance service for my mother. They brought from Vienna an actress who read the poem "Brother," which my mother wrote while imprisoned. Of course, the poem could not be written down, but it was remembered by some of her fellow inmates and was transcribed when they were freed and returned to Vienna. Present at the ceremony for my mother was a survivor from Germany who was in the camp with my mother and actually remembered the title and some words from another poem she wrote, "Blutige Hände" ("Bloody Hands"), which referred to the work detail she was assigned to, unloading bricks without gloves. This was the hardest work detail to which they assigned political Jewish prisoners. This poem sadly has not been remembered. Through arrangements made by inmates, probably her close friend Rosa Jochmann, my mother was transferred to sewing uniforms. As Rosa told me, my mother didn't know how to sew, so other women made sure to fill her quota while she lectured on European history.

It was a very moving and emotional visit. I am so satisfied that I was able to take my children there and to have them understand something of her life. In the camp, there is a memorial museum where the survivors of each country have their own memorial in one of the cells in what was the punishment block. The Austrian exhibit features my mother. I visited the camp on two other occasions, including the big commemoration on the fiftieth anniversary of its liberation in 1995, a very moving experience where I marched with the Austrian survivors to the nearby lake where the Nazis threw the ashes of their victims. Two events stand out from the visit with my children. One was Josh saying that he couldn't believe he could have lasted more than a few days as a prisoner there. The other was on our second and last night. The survivors had dinner and then sang old socialist and Viennese songs. Some I knew and was able to join in. Then they ended by singing some Beatles songs. What amazing people.

I hope my grandchildren and other descendants will visit Ravensbrück and be reminded of their very brave and honored ancestor.

In about 2004, I went on a tour of the Normandy beaches, which Steve Solarz arranged. He invited numerous friends, including the English ambassador to France. I had visited these beaches once before. How moving to see the area where such an important battle took place, which helped to determine the outcome of World War II. In the following year, Steve arranged another trip, this time to Gallipoli, an important battle during World War I. Again, Steve gathered another interesting group, which included Paul Wolfowitz, a key instigator of the Iraq War but a very pleasant person to travel with.

The year 2006 started well. In January, I went on a trip with Steve and Nina Solarz to New Zealand and Australia. The initiative for the trip was tickets I was able to get to the Australian Tennis Open in Melbourne in January of that year. We decided to make it the fulcrum of a journey to what is called Down Under. Steve, who had a wanderlust that even exceeded mine and the skill of a seasoned travel agent, did the planning and arrangements. We first flew to Auckland in New Zealand from San Francisco, where I had stayed to visit Kathy and family during their two years there while Andrew had a fellowship at the University of San Francisco Medical School. In Auckland, we stayed in a resort on a nearby island. Next came Christchurch and a trip to Mount Cook. From there, we went to Queenstown. On the way, we stayed overnight with Dick Allen, who had been Reagan's national security adviser. I mention this detail only as an example of the large network Steve had acquired. These tended to be very interesting, though quite a few were foreign policy hawks (called neocons) with whose views I differed but who were impressive and whose positions demanded attention if not agreement. Next we flew to Sydney for a few days, and then to Hobart in Tasmania. We toured this island in the southern Pacific. We went on to a luxurious resort on Great Lizard Island in the Great Barrier Reef, which afforded amazing snorkeling. We ended in Melbourne and spent two days at the Australian Open. For Steve and me, it was the fourth of the tennis Grand Slams we had seen together. In addition to Australia, we had gone to Wimbledon in London, Roland Garros in Paris, and, of course, the US Open in Flushing Meadow. What a great trip.

## END OF MY POSITION AS DIRECTOR OF THE FHFB. WHAT TO DO NEXT?

I came back from Australia via San Francisco at the end of January 2006 and stayed with Kathy and family for a couple of days. Arriving back in NYC, I was in a good mood. Next morning, while having a leisurely breakfast and reading the *Times*, I received a call from Ronny Rosenstein, the FHFB's chair and a Republican,. He gave me ominous news. He told me I had better call Senator Schumer, as he had heard the Democrats might replace me. My six-year term was expiring at the beginning of July. I had been fairly confident that the Democrats would see to it that I was renominated for another six-year term and confirmed.

The next few months, I was nervous. I tried to call Schumer, but he was not taking my calls. Still, I somehow could not believe I would be spurned by Schumer. He had been a political friend. When he first served in the State Assembly, we shared an apartment. He then was elected to Congress, and in 1998, when running for senator from New York, I supported him in a tough primary for this position. He was helpful in my getting the position at the FHFB. I couldn't believe he would not protect me. Finally, he agreed to see me. The news he gave me was not positive. He made it pretty clear that the decision had been made to nominate someone else in my place. At one time, I remember him saying, "The horse is out of the barn." I stupidly tried to show the good work I was doing and policies I was getting the FHFB to pursue, such as against predatory lending. Good work and smart policy initiatives were insignificant against the political winds. Schumer said he would get me back on the FHFB next year by replacing my friend Allan Mendelowitz, whose term was expiring in early 2007. I told him I would not accept this offer, as Allan was my friend.

I should just have accepted my fate, for on reflection, it is clear the decision had been made. But that is not my way. I tried to enlist support. Ronny Rosenstein tried to help me. We had become friends, and he wanted me to stay on the FHFB. He even flew up to New York for a luncheon with a big Democratic Hillary Clinton financial supporter, with whom he was friendly, to get him to enlist the help of Hillary, then the junior New York senator. I wrote a letter to Hillary, which he said he would get into her hands. Did he? I don't know. It didn't matter. The decision had been made by the majority leader, Harry Reid, as Schumer had all but told me. Later, I found out that the Senate Democrats took my position to satisfy a big contributor from Texas who was asking for a place in the government for someone he was close to. I didn't believe this could happen, even as I really knew it would.

My successor was nominated and swiftly confirmed. My position at the FHFB was finished. I was at the Farm for July Fourth weekend and from there flew to Washington to pack up and say my goodbyes. I met my successor and made sure he retained my secretary with whom I had developed a real friendship. As a very nice gesture, Ronnie Rosenstein arranged a few weeks after I left to have my service recognized in a formal Board resolution and threw a farewell party for me. He invited Melody to join me and had the FHFB pick up the expenses. Many employees came to say they were pleased to work with me. I had built a good reputation and made friends. It had been a good six years. I wish it had continued. Even if I had been nominated and confirmed for a second six-year term, it would not have lasted long. The FHFB was abolished in 2008, as all three government-supported enterprises, Fannie Mae, Freddie Mac, and the FHFB, were placed into a new regulatory structure as a consequence of the meltdown in housing and the mortgage frenzy that led to the Great Recession.

On my last day at the FHFB, July 6, 2006, I received a call from my dear friend Steve Solarz. I thought he was in Turkey and that he was calling to wish me good luck, as he knew I was leaving the FHFB. I was shocked when he told me he had been diagnosed with esophageal cancer. On the train ride back to New York that evening, my mind alternated between concern over Steve and what was I going to do next.

As I lost my position, I became depressed. But it did not last long. I was now almost seventy-six, but I felt well and energetic and did not want to retire. But what to do. I made a half-hearted effort to return to legal practice with my old firm, which shortly after I left in 2000 had been acquired and merged into a large Atlanta law firm. But I really had no desire to go back to the practice, and more significantly, I had no clients. I explored becoming a board member of one of the smaller savings banks that were part of the New York Home Loan Bank. But there was no interest. I sought to join a fairly large financial firm that dealt with the Home Loan Bank system, among other interests. I talked to a lawyer with a prominent Washington law firm about helping with an effort he was involved in regarding changes to the Home Loan system. I would have been a lobbyist. Not really a good fit for me. But it shows my desire to find some engagement and to make some money. Nothing came of this either. My real interest was to do some writing, especially about how the government responded to New York's fiscal crisis in 1975. My aim was to show how government could work and how during this period there was sufficient bipartisanship to have the Legislature with a Republican majority in the Senate and a Democratic governor work together constructively and successfully to create a solution. I pitched my plan for the book to one of the main participants, a financial advisor to Governor Hugh Carey. He was not interested. I could have proceeded alone. But I thought I needed some help financially to hire a researcher. I also was not sure of getting a publisher, and I didn't want to spend two or more years writing this and then not have it published. So I dropped the idea. A few years later, one of my Senate colleagues who had an academic background and the backing of Wagner College wrote a book on this period as a testament to Carey, in whose name he had established an archive. He had gotten Carey to donate his papers to the college. He had not been in the Senate during the financial crisis period, and his book was not very good. However, Wagner published it. I regret that I did not have the resources or the confidence to write this book.

Despite my efforts, I really had no full-time career activity after July 2006. I did have some work and modest financial returns from two receiverships and a guardianship that I received through my friend Ed Lehner, who was a New York State Supreme Court justice. The guardianship was for an elderly German refugee living in Washington Heights who had Alzheimer's. Under New York law, if a person is declared incompetent by a court, and if there is no near relative, the court then appoints someone to be the guardian of the person and her finances. I took this on partly to be of help but also for what income it would provide. Actually, she had little money—and the commissions one is entitled to as a guardian depend upon the assets of the person declared incompetent. I did take care of her. I hired a full-time aid and visited her about once a week.

The two conservatorships were more interesting and remunerative. The first involved the publisher of *Hustler* magazine, Larry Flynt (a somewhat pornographic magazine which sought to be more sexually revealing than

*Playboy*). It was quite successful for a while, and Flynt had a big mansion on the East Side. But as porn became available on the internet, it folded. Flynt was being sued by a Texas company that had loaned him money and had a judgment against him. It sought to collect this through a New York court, where Flynt and his company were. Under New York law, this required the appointment of a receiver to collect the judgment. I worked fairly extensively and did recover some money. But it ended fairly soon.

The other receivership was more substantial. This was for a high-rise residential building located on West Seventy-Fifth Street, just off Amsterdam Avenue. It was in the Lincoln Center area and valuable, but only if it could change its use. It had been and was still primarily an SRO—that is a single-room occupancy building—with many small rooms, many of them sharing a bathroom and kitchen. There had been quite a few such buildings on the West Side that provided cheap housing for mainly single, older, and occasionally disabled persons. But because the building was in an area that had become affluent, if a developer could change the occupancy and create apartments, the value of the building would greatly increase.

One such developer had acquired the building and, based on his plans to convert the building, got a substantial mortgage from Merrill Lynch. When the latter came under financial stress and was acquired by Bank of America, it unloaded whole portfolios of mortgages. One such portfolio was acquired by GE Capital, which included hundreds or possibly thousands of mortgages. GE Capital was part of GE and for some years had been a bigger revenue creator, then its industrial divisions. This gave me an insight into the madness of the nation's financial system leading to the Great Recession of 2008. First, why did Merrill Lynch write a mortgage for a building that could not readily, if at all, be converted from a SRO into multiple apartments? The residents of the SRO were protected by the rent laws and could not be evicted. And why did GE buy this big portfolio of mortgages from Merrill Lynch without carefully checking the properties included?

What happened was inevitable. The developer could not evict the tenants, though it dangled money for those willing to move. It also used some hard tactics like bringing questionable eviction proceedings and not providing services. This raised the wrath of local public officials, who sought to protect the tenants. The developer went belly-up and defaulted on its mortgage. GE moved in court to foreclose. In such a proceeding, a receiver is appointed, who has full authority to manage the building, that is collect the rent, pay the staff, see that services are provided, as if he/she were the owner, while the foreclosure proceeding went slowly on. I was appointed the receiver.

This proved to be interesting, required a fair amount of work, and was somewhat remunerative, but not as much as it would have been if I could have charged on an hourly basis. But it gave me a sense that I was still engaged in some work that was important. I visited the building at least once a week and met with the managing agent I hired. There were some staff and occasional tenant issues. My main aim, consistent with my legal obligation, was to protect the SRO tenants and to keep the building from being converted to a Class A building. I worked closely with the local council member who had sought to protect the tenants. The irony was that she then screwed me by not reappointing me to the Board of Directors of the Hudson River Park Trust (HRPT) when she became borough president of Manhattan, who, under the legislation for the park I had negotiated, had the appointing power for the three community representatives. When you no longer have a public position, you have no leverage. You are naked. Loyalty in the competitive world of politics is a weak reed to rely on.

There were interesting aspects to the receivership. When GE decided to liquidate GE Capital, it sought to sell off many of its assets, some at firehouse sale. When it sought to sell the mortgage on the building, I brought a proceeding in court to stop it unless I approved of the financial viability of the purchaser. By this time, the cost of operating the building exceeded the rents, and I had required GE to make up the shortfall. I wanted to be certain that any purchaser/successor to GE had the financial means to put money into the building as required. This worked out well, as GE found a purchaser who did have the means. I established a good relationship with GE's successor, and he enabled me to cover operating expenses. Just to note how money is made in New York City real estate. The purchaser from GE paid $18 million for a mortgage that with accrued interest approached, as I best remember, amounted to $40 million. Two years later, the successor to GE sold the building, which by then he had acquired title to through the foreclosure, for $48 million. Later I heard a rumor that the latest purchaser put the building up for sale for $90 million. Crazy.

## GETTING THE HUDSON RIVER PARK BUILT

From 1999 until December 2014, I served as a director of the HRPT, the act that I had been instrumental in getting passed as my last legislative accomplishment in 1998. The act provided that on the Board of the HRPT there would be three community representatives appointed by the Manhattan borough president. I had negotiated this last piece late at night on the next-to-last day of the session in 1998 with the representative of the governor. Initially the governor wanted no community representatives on the Board, which was to be composed of five gubernatorial and five mayoral appointees. Under the compromise I worked out, there would be three community representatives who between them would have two votes.

FRANZ LEICHTER

In 1999 when the Board of the HRPT was constituted, I was named as one of the three community representatives.

I was very involved as a director in the construction of the Hudson River Park. The Board met monthly to pass on contracts and make policy. There were many issues, complications, fights for funding, and fending off the opposition of a few people who continued to oppose the park. I attended numerous meetings and reviewed contracts and memoranda. It was important for me to still be engaged in public policy, and it was satisfying to be part of the Board charged with creating the Park.

The work in developing the park proceeded but not always easily. It is hard to develop any public work in New York without some opposition and combat. The trust proceeded by first reconstructing as parkland a number of piers that were falling into the river. These stretched out into the river, providing contact with the river and providing a great view of the harbor. An esplanade, walkway, and bicycle path were built. It is now possible to bike almost the entire length of the Manhattan shore. Recreational space was provided, as well as food stands and restaurants. Sites were created for access to the river for boating. A center for environmental study of the river is being built and more. There are three very large, enclosed piers, one of which has become a sports complex; a second will have a large food market, park, and offices for Google. The third remains an issue, but a ball field that was created as a temporary measure has become a fixture, as has a large parking facility, which does provide revenue for the park. Already, as I write this, the park has transformed the waterfront and has been an incentive for residential and commercial development across the highway that runs along the park. Much remains to be done, but what has been built attracts thousands of people on good weather weekends.

I have seen many waterfront parks in Hong Kong, Sydney, Rio, Buenos Aires, San Francisco, and Baltimore but none that are as large and have as many outdoor and indoor facilities as the Hudson River Park. It has given me great satisfaction to have been instrumental in the creation of this park and to have been so engaged in the construction process. I consider it my main public achievement.

My directorship ended when I resigned in December 2014 because the newly elected Manhattan borough president would not commit to reappointing me and did not work with me and the other Board members. I was disappointed to leave the Board and more so because the borough president was a political ally whom I had supported. There was political skullduggery behind this, which I won't go into. That is life in politics.

# CHAPTER 17

# 2006-2010: A GOOD LIFE BUT SOME SAD LOSSES

These were years of contrast. My life changed, as I no longer held any public position, nor had any law practice outside of the receiverships I mentioned in the previous chapter. As I was now free from obligations, I spent more time with my family. Family had always been important to me, but my life with two jobs—as senator and practicing lawyer—did not give me as much time as I now had. Having Kathy and her family in New York made it possible to stay in close contact. I also took some trips to see Josh and his children and saw them grow, but not as often as I wanted to. The year 2010 was one of fascinating trips balanced by deaths of people very close to me.

Kathy and Andrew, with their two sons, Otto and Theo, live in the large apartment at 448 Riverside Drive, with its wonderful view of the Hudson. Nina, Kathy, Josh, and I had moved there in 1975. I moved out in 1997. Fortunately, Kathy and her family were allowed to stay there under the rent laws. About once a week, I would have dinner with them, especially after 2010. I spent as much time as possible with Otto and Theo.

After a time in New Haven and in Pittsburgh, Kathy had become a full-time documentary maker. Kathy has directed and produced two major documentaries: *A Day's Work a Day's Pay* and *Here One Day*. The first, which she did with a colleague from Cornell, was first shown in 2004 to a full house in a large auditorium. *Here One Day* was finished around 2012. It is the story of Nina and how she developed bipolar disorder and dealt with it before committing suicide and how her children and I responded during her illness and after her death. I so admire Kathy for having the courage to deal with the tragic death of her mother and tell her story. I believe making this film and facing her pain directly has been therapeutic for her. She uses both films as a teaching and advocacy tool. She has held numerous screenings, especially of *Here One Day*. Both films received much critical praise and were shown at numerous festivals. She also did a documentary on Elsa, *Passing On*, based on an oral interview she filmed of Elsa at my suggestion.

Josh and his children lived for many years in Wellesley, Massachusetts. He had acquired a position as an associate at a prominent Boston law firm, after graduating from Michigan Law School. I had visited him in Ann Arbor and now went to visit him, Dana, Memphis, and Ethan, first in Sudbury and then, when they moved, in Wellesley. I wanted to have my grandchildren in my life and as close a relationship as physical separation allowed.

Through my visits to Ann Arbor and in Massachusetts, Josh and I overcame our hurts over the separation that had occurred. We had some talks, though I don't remember any very open, emotional discussions. I think neither Josh nor I find it that easy to be emotionally open about our feelings. It might have been counterproductive for us to express whatever resentments we had that may have led to our separation. I believe our burying the past was more due to our getting together and showing how much we cared and loved each other. We both wanted to end our alienation and did not need a cathartic moment.

## AND MORE TRAVELING

I continued my travels during this period. I took a trip to Budapest, Kraków, and Berlin. I took a sleeper from Budapest to Kraków and kept on being awakened by loud shouts of "Passport!" as we crossed and recrossed various frontiers. This brought to mind the fright of refugees as they heard these shouts when fleeing from persecution.

I find it more illuminating to explore cities that are new to me by walking, sometimes even aimlessly. I find pleasure and interest also walking in cities that are familiar. Even walking through New York City, where I have lived now for eighty years, has an element of adventure. On this trip, I did much walking in Budapest, Kraków, and Berlin.

Kraków is near Auschwitz, and it is from there that people make the pilgrimage to that infamous place of barbarity. I didn't go, as I did not feel emotionally capable of being there. I have been to other concentration camps, which after an initial sense of horror and fright I was able to view without running away, though it left an indelible memory. I regret now that in effect I chickened out from visiting Auschwitz. During my stay in Kraków, I did visit sites where Jews were mistreated, including a former synagogue that had become a museum. There I saw a video that the Nazis had shot in the Warsaw Ghetto. One scene showed a mother with a young child who had such a look of misery. It so impressed me that I can clearly recollect it now. I walked out thinking, *How can one go on living a comfortable and good life knowing that such horrors occurred?* But that evening, I went to a Jewish-style restaurant with a klezmer band and enjoyed myself. To survive and handle the downsides in life, we have, and need, the ability to rebalance as if we are seeking to steady ourselves on a seesaw. It was satisfying to see some Jewish life return to Kraków.

From Kraków, I went to Berlin and met my friend Franz Mueller. We stayed with a friend of his. The three of us visited Ravensbrück. It was my second visit there. On the way back to Berlin, we visited one of the palaces of the former German emperors. What a contrast.

In October 2007, I participated in a WQXR (the New York City classical music station) tour of China. It was excellent. We started in Hong Kong, where our previous Chinese neighbor, from whom we had bought the adjoining apartment, made her car and chauffeur available. One night, I left the group to visit the island gambling mecca Macau. The tour then visited numerous Chinese cities, including Beijing, Shanghai, and Xian, and cruised for three days on the Yangtze going through the Three Gorges Dam. Fascinating. I was greatly impressed by how China was modernizing. Much of its infrastructure surpasses conditions in the US, and in the eleven years since my visit, I assume the US infrastructure— trains, roads, subways, and other—compares even more poorly.

Not quite eighty, in 2009 I visited London. From there, I went to Edinburgh for its annual cultural festival. Then I took a cruise of the Norwegian fjords and on return to London met up with Josh, who was there on a business trip.

Later that year, Henry and I were awarded the Medal of the City of Vienna in a lovely ceremony in the Rathaus (Vienna's city hall). Henry was accompanied by Hope, Freddy, and Jamie. Sadly, he was not well and had to use a wheelchair. However, his spirits were good, and he told his jokes with usual gusto at the numerous dinners we were invited to. At the end of the visit, he became ill and had to be hospitalized. The medals and the ceremony were arranged by our good family friend, Renata Brauner, who at that time was the vice mayor of Vienna. Renata, in her official capacity, was the Viennese dignitary who represented the city at the Vienna Opera Ball in New York. She always invited Hope and me to attend as her guests. These were elaborate and pretentious affairs. Everyone attended in tuxedos, except for one person—me. I had struggled too often with putting on a tuxedo for numerous events, and my tuxedo didn't fit anymore. To hell with formal dress and pretense.

## MELODY DEVELOPS A DETERIORATING DISEASE AND DIES

As these years went on, the joy I had with Melody diminished. Partly this may have been due to the fact that we never established a deeper relationship. Our coming and being together was based more on our mutual enjoyment and seeking pleasure. Was this due to my not being able to establish closer emotional relationships with women after the loss of my mother? If I had ever said this to Melody, she would have told me, as she did on other occasions when I analyzed myself or others, "This is psychobabble." But there was another reason. Melody was beginning to be affected by a disease of the brain. Strangely enough, it is named after an Czech physician who had the same name as my mother's maiden name, Pick, and who first discovered this disease. The symptoms before 2008 were not that visible. She was somewhat more irritable and less interested in going out. She was spending more time watching movies on TV. She spent less time with friends. Her practice began to decline.

Around 2006, she became friendly with a person who was something of a con man—like her father. They enjoyed smoking marijuana together. I sold him my car and also lent him some money, which he never repaid. I was sort of relieved that she had this friendship that satisfied her. It also freed me from providing some of the companionship. Nevertheless, I tried to continue as before and was not particularly worried or upset. I was in some denial, as I had been initially with Nina. At times, she functioned well. She arranged for her mother to move to assisted living and sold her apartment. Together we visited her mother. Her relationship with her half-brother improved, and we went a few times to visit him in Long Island. Thus, there was no dramatic change in our relationship or life together until 2008.

By 2008, it became more apparent that she was not well. She actually took the initiative and saw a neurologist at NYU. A brain scan showed a possible spot on her brain. It was inconclusive, and there was no follow-up. As the symptoms became more pronounced and evident, not only to me but to two of her close friends, we became concerned. It may have been late in 2008 or early in 2009 that I arranged for her to see a specialist at Columbia Presbyterian. Her friend Leora came along. The doctor made the tentative diagnosis that she may have Pick's disease, which attacks the frontal lobes of the brain. There didn't seem to be anything that could be done to arrest or hopefully reverse the deterioration.

Melody became more nonfunctional. She would spend all day in bed with our dog, Andie, watching old movies, especially of Betty Davis, and listening to Bob Dylan. It then became necessary to hire a caretaker for her. Fortunately, I had bought long-term care insurance, so some of the cost was covered. As her condition deteriorated, she became calmer and even seemed happy. I realized this was a chronic condition and could go on for years. How was I to cover the expenses of twenty-four-hour home care? I decided to sell the larger of our two condos and to move nearby to a rental apartment. The one bedroom we had acquired from its Chinese owner and joined to our initial two bedroom apartment could not have reasonably accommodated us both. Selling what had been the two-bedroom unit would provide a financial cushion for what may be many years of care for Melody. This became complicated and bothersome because Melody had given a power of attorney to her friend Leora. I think this was coerced while Melody was not competent. I had a lot of trouble with Leora—the messy details I won't go into. I found a new apartment nearby on East

Forty-Fourth Street, with the idea that this would enable me to stay close to Melody and see her daily and be involved in her care.

I moved into my new apartment and asked Kathy to help me get settled. It was on Sunday, January 10, 2010, that she came with her two boys to help. After a day of unpacking and moving furniture around, I took them to dinner at a restaurant I liked on East Forty-Second Street. At some point as we parted, I looked at my cell phone and saw that Stephanie, who was Melody's main caretaker, had tried to reach me, leaving a message that there was an emergency.

I rushed back. When I came to my apartment building, I saw the flashing lights of an ambulance. I feared the worst. When I entered the apartment, Stephanie, the aide, met me. She said Melody had died. As she described it, she and Melody were in the living room. She started taking her back to bed when Melody began wobbling. Stephanie had to hold her up and just managed to get her to the bed, on which she collapsed. Stephanie called 911 when she noticed that Melody was not breathing. She called me and then Leora when she couldn't reach me. Leora was there when I came. I was stunned and remember sitting in a chair, not believing what had just happened. The emergency workers removed Melody. That was the end.

Leora had taken over. She called Melody's doctor and arranged for a death certificate. I said we needed an autopsy, but Leora very strenuously objected. I often wonder why. It still puzzles me that the doctor agreed to a death certificates solely on Leora's word. Leora and I discussed funeral arrangements. It struck me as surreal. Was this really happening?

I finally went back to my new apartment, taking Andie, our dog, with me. I was shocked by the suddenness and sorrowful that this beautiful, at one time so vivacious woman, so much younger than I was, and my partner for thirteen years, had met this early death. But I was also relieved that I would not have the burden of taking care of her and that she would not suffer years of lingering in a diminishing state. Yes, I was relieved that I would not have to see and spend time with the shadow of the woman I had married.

The funeral for Melody was at Frank E. Campbell—the Funeral Chapel on Madison Avenue. That was where she had arranged her father's funeral a few years previously and generally where WASP East Siders have their funerals. That is what she would have wanted. I gave one of the eulogies. Kathy, Otto, Henry, and Hope came, as did my friends Steve and Nina Solarz, who came from the Washington area. The burial was in Staten Island near the grave of her father, whose love she so pined over.

As I look back on these days and recollect all the difficulties, I was not depressed though low at times. But my interest in life and being active were undiminished. I think my emotional response was that misfortune was characteristic of my life, and I could deal with it. However, Melody's decline and death were not what I expected. But I did not fall into despair or lament about how this could happen to me. I accepted her death as if it was in the nature of my life that I would suffer misfortunes— deprived of my mother in my early years and two marriages that ended tragically. It was sad, but that was my fate. I believe that having suffered through the separation of my mother and dealing with it emotionally has hardened me and enabled me to cope with Nina's and Melody's tragedies. I was both weakened and strengthened by these misfortunes—weakened by a perpetual pessimism and strengthened by acquiring the emotional toughness to go on and pursue life actively. My many trips in 2010 were my way to continue to connect to a life of interest and enjoyment.

## AND STILL MORE TRAVELING

In late January into February, as I sought to put Melody's death behind me, I went to Santiago, Chile, and then took a stunning trip by boat through lakes framed by volcanoes to the Argentine border. After a day in Bariloche, a resort town, I flew to Buenos Aires. It was my third trip to this city, which I greatly enjoy. As usual, I did a lot of walking. The night before joining my Antarctica tour, I managed to reach a distant cousin, Pedro Leichter, and had dinner with him and his wife. I had visited his parents, one of whom was a first cousin of my father, some years before on my first trip to Buenos Aires.

The tour flew us to Uchida, on the very southern tip of South America. There we boarded our cruise ship for the crossing of the Drake passage to the northern tip of a peninsula attached to Antarctica. Although this passage is considered to have some of the most turbulent seas, we crossed fairly smoothly. On the return trip, we did experience rough seas. For six days, we cruised along the Antarctica coast. The scenery was stunning, just glaciers and no human habitation, except for two research stations we visited. Every day, we went ashore in rubber rafts and walked among penguins, seals, sea lions, and birds of all descriptions. I also saw firsthand the effects of global warming. We cruised among enormous ice floes, as large as a city block, which had fallen off the glaciers. Another world and another great trip.

In March 2010, I took Josh, Ethan, and Memphis skiing in Park City, Utah. Skiing had become one of my great enjoyments, since Nina and I first went in 1960. I had been to Park City numerous times. While on the FHFB, there were annual conferences in Park City, which permitted ample time for skiing. In April, Kathy and I went to Austin, Texas, for a reunion of the Schmidt family, relatives of Nina's mother with whom we were quite close. In September 2010, I took a train trip across Canada, starting in Toronto. First I visited my army buddy Carmen Seminara in Niagara Falls. The train was mainly for tourists. I had a comfortable train compartment. I was able to get off at Banff and visit Lake Louise. I did some great hiking, though I had to wait at the trail heads to connect with a group of hikers. There was a sign warning of grizzly bears and a $5,000 fine if you hiked alone. I was more afraid of the fine than the bears. The Canadian Rockies are so beautiful. I cherish mountains so much. After three lovely days at Lake Louise, I got back to the train and took it to its terminus in Vancouver.

In August 2010, I had a special visit to Nina and Steve's beautiful home in Kalkan, Turkey. Steve invited some of the participants in the study group we had formed in Albany when in the Assembly. Steve placed great emphasis upon keeping current relationships with his friends—more so than anyone I ever knew. In 2004, he had the thirtieth reunion of the study group at his house in Virginia. Oliver and his wife, Lorraine, came to Kalkan, as did Eric Hirschhorn with his wife, Leah. Eric had been our counsel and sole staff member of our Assembly study group. I brought along Steve Gottlieb, a member of our study group who declined to challenge me in 1972 when our districts were joined through reapportionment. Sadly, he was not in good shape, and I had to act as guardian when he and I stopped off in Istanbul for a couple of days. Steve and Nina held a birthday party for me, as it was near my eightieth birthday. Instead of a birthday cake, or maybe in addition, they hired a belly dancer. But sadly, Steve was not well and had terrible coughing and swallowing episodes. It was so painful to see him endure these. But nevertheless, he was joyous, and he and Nina were their usual great hosts. What dear friends. Since my first visit with Melody in 2001, I have visited them almost every summer. At first it was for about a week, but more recently, since Steve's death, I have stayed there for longer periods.

As I write this in July 2019, I have just come back from spending three weeks there. The routine has been almost the same. A delicious and late Turkish breakfast, after which we are driven to the dock, where the Solarzes always charter Captain Erdan's boat. We take this to one of the inlets along the shore of the big bay. There we relax, swim, read, talk, and sleep. The captain serves a very good and bountiful lunch, followed by more of the same relaxation. Around five, we return to the harbor and are driven back to the house. I usually read by the infinity pool and sometimes take a dip from where it feels as if you are going to swim into Kalkan's Bay about a thousand feet below. Steve is usually busy with his emails, while I wait for access to the computer. We gather around 7:00 p.m. at a place called the Philosophers' Corner for drinks and discussion. Dinner, at about 8:00 p.m., is a usually delicious, traditional Turkish meal cooked by the wife of the caretaker couple.

After my visit with Steve and Nina in 2010, I flew to Tel Aviv. My former staffer and friend Erwin Rose was there with his family. His wife, who served in the Foreign Service, held an important position in the US embassy. I spent a few days there. One day I visited Jerusalem. It was my second time in a city I find fascinating. I enjoy that city for its interesting, though not always good, history and its diversity and beauty. After a few days' good stay, Erwin and I flew on my eightieth birthday, August 19, to the Red Sea and took a taxi to Petra in Jordan. This is one of the magnificent sites of antiquity with stunning architecture. We arrived in late afternoon but were still able to hire guides, who took us on horseback to a hilly site to look down on Petra. Next day, we walked through Petra. We then flew back to the Red Sea, where we went snorkeling.

Next day, I flew from Eilat to Luxor, the ancient capital of the Pharos, via Amman and Cairo. Luxor was fascinating. I had excellent tour guides. I was taken to excavated tombs, temples, and palaces four thousand years old. So interesting to see the magnificence of this important historical society. I also had a boat ride in a traditional skiff on the Nile. I was allowed to briefly steer. I was left with the impression of an interesting civilization with its architecture, displays, and organization.

From Luxor, I flew to Cairo and spent four interesting days there. I had tour guides from the same company as in Luxor. These were Christians, and they complained bitterly to me about the discrimination they faced. Hosni Mubarak was at that time still the president-autocrat. I believe the Christians are treated even worse today. They took me to their church— very attractive—of which they were very proud. The highlight was a tour of the great pyramids and riding a camel around the great pyramid and the famous sphinx. The camel was a foul animal that tried to throw me off when its handler tried to climb in behind me to avoid the long walk back. I was charmed by the Museum of Egyptian Antiquities, which gave me further appreciation of the life of the ancient Egyptian kingdoms. I did a lot of walking and felt safe and at ease, except when crossing the streets, which was a life-risking experience.

I was there during Ramadan, and I enjoyed seeing the Muslim families relishing breaking the daily fast with meals at outdoor restaurants. One of the walks I took was through what is known as the Islamist neighborhood. On reflection, this walk I took may have been somewhat foolish and certainly would not be safe now for an obvious Westerner in a neighborhood with no other tourists, taxis, or any easy exit. The streets were just narrow alleyways that twisted and turned. I pride myself on my sense of direction but soon became lost. I was heading to a well-known mosque, and a number of times I had to ask directions, which didn't seem to be given in a friendly or understandable way. Finally, I came upon someone who spoke English. He was an engineer but told me he could not get a job and was working as a carpenter. He said he would take me to the mosque I was looking for. On the way, he asked if I wanted to see his mosque. I thought it best to acquiesce. He then asked me if I believed in

God. I was becoming a bit apprehensive and assured him I did. Once there, he insisted I meet the Iman, which prudence again dictated I agreed to. It turned out this was just a ruse for getting me to make a big contribution. Again, prudence led me to say yes. I thought it best to give, though not the big amounts he expected. He then left me to find the mosque I was looking for on my own, which I finally did. This little episode is not an isolated case of my adventurism and also a certain fearlessness. Most of these types of adventures—like trying to climb the Matterhorn when I was in my sixties—reflected an ignorance and disregard of risk. This turned out to be one of the many rewarding trips I was able to take in my seventies and eighties. But in truth, fearlessness requires that you understand the risk. Now, I think any foreigner today who did what I did in Egypt would be grabbed as a hostage. I do hope that a change will occur in Egypt and that my descendants will have the chance to visit this fascinating city and country to connect with its historical splendor and significance.

The year that started with Melody's death ended with the death of two people so important in my life.

## STEVE SOLARZ DIES

Steve Solarz, since the time of my visit to his Turkish home in August 2010, continued to fail. I visited him in the fall at his home in McLean, Virginia. I was pained to see how he was declining. Toward the end of November, he was hospitalized. Nina called me and indicated he may be nearing the end. It was evident to me that I had better come to see him. I immediately left for Washington. The entire family had gathered. I spent some days at the hospital to be with him. I was staying at their home with Nina and considered part of the family. I would read Steve the *Times* and tried to cheer him up by reminding him of some of our pranks in Albany. He was calm, completely accepting what was coming.

A couple of years before, while we were at the US Open, he received a call about the result of a recent test that was not that reassuring. He seemed resigned for what might happen and said, "Well, I have had a good life." And that was his attitude as he was on his deathbed. One afternoon, I joined Nina and her son Randy to look at a cemetery, knowing the end was near. Nina, as usual, was clear-eyed, pragmatic, and strong. On our drive there, she received a call that Steve was near death. I seem to recollect that by the time we got back to the hospital, he had died.

The funeral was well attended by members of Congress, senators, and many of his wide circle of friends, including from his childhood. I was honored that Nina asked me to give one of the eulogies. I worked on it the night before. The words came easily. It was one of the few speeches of the hundreds I made that I didn't afterward think or regret that I hadn't made a particular point, left something out, or dwelled on an irrelevancy.

Steve was one of my best friends. We bonded when we both came to Albany as freshmen and kept in close contact from then on. I must give special credit for this to Steve, for whom friendships were very important and who worked to see that they were maintained. He took care of his friends. As I mentioned before, when Marcos was overthrown in the Philippines, he took me along with a congressional delegation to Manila in 1986. I saw him develop, from what I considered a diamond in the rough, who put some of his colleagues off by seeming self-centered and too aggressive, into a very effective and well-regarded legislator. It is interesting to see how age and the knocks of life sometimes help us to develop and bring out better characteristics. It may be because we found our place and are less focused on our achievements and open to more aspects of life. Nina was so helpful and key in that change in Steve. As I said in my eulogy, Steve would not have become what he became without Nina. Steve played an important role in numerous international matters. Cory Aquino, who took over as president of the Philippines, called him the "Lafayette of the Philippines" for his opposition to Marcos. He befriended many foreign leaders, some of whom he got to know as refugees from their country's dictatorship, who, when the dictatorships were overthrown for more democratic governance, became the leaders of their country. It was his idea that prompted UN action to end the genocide in Cambodia.

I sometimes kidded Steve that he knew more international leaders than he knew Democratic district leaders in his congressional district. This hurt him when the 1992 redistricting occurred and his district was essentially eliminated. He lost a primary in 1992 in a district that was now majority Latino. His years until his death were very productive. He used his foreign contacts to develop a remunerative consulting business. His main achievement was joining with a former US ambassador to create the International Crisis Group, which has developed into a prestigious, worldwide non-governmental organization pinpointing crisis spots and offering recommendations for avoiding conflict. Yes, he did lead a good life. It was productive, and he made an impact. I miss him greatly but am thankful that through him I have developed such a close friendship with Nina. She often says somewhat hyperbolically that I was the best thing that happened to Steve in politics. The reverse is certainly true for me.

## MY BROTHER, HENRY, DIES

During these years, I became more concerned about Henry. Starting maybe in 2005 or 2006, he began to have physical issues affecting his mobility. And a couple of years later, he exhibited some dementia. As his condition worsened, I became alarmed and urged Hope and his children to have him undergo a full examination at a well-respected geriatric service at Mount Sinai Hospital. I am not sure that this was ever done. I am not certain what his diagnosis was, and his family may not have been willing to share it with me. Possibly it was some form of Parkinson's. As his mobility declined, arrangements were made for him to have an aide. He was hospitalized for a time at St. Luke's Hospital and then stayed at the Amsterdam nursing home on West 112th Street. On my visits, I would bring him an *appfelstrudel* with *schlag* from the Hungarian pastry shop, which he ate with his usual gusto. Toward the end of 2010, he was taken by his family to their vacation home in Lake Elmore in Vermont. As he became sicker, Henry entered a nursing home nearby. I kept in touch about his condition with Hope. His aide, Charles, was there to help take care of him. Charles told me this story, which shows Henry had not lost his fighting spirit. The nursing home provided entertainment by a choir group one day. After the songs were finished, the emcee said there would now be a sermon by a minister—or was it that he said, "Let us pray"? Whatever, Henry yelled out, "Oh shit."

Around December 16 or 17, Hope called to tell me that Henry had taken a turn for the worse. The problem seemed to be an infection. I flew to Burlington and rented a car to drive to the family home in Lake Elmore, Vermont. I visited Henry the next couple of days, but he was in and out of a coma, and there was no chance to speak to him. On the night of December 19, I had already gone to the hotel where I was staying and was asleep when the minister from the nursing home came to tell me Henry was failing. When I arrived at the nursing home, Henry was already dead. Sadly, I never had a chance to say goodbye. I would have told him how much I loved him and thanked him for all he had done for me. I stayed another day with the family before returning to New York.

Henry was more than a brother to me. He tried to fill in for my mother. At times, I was grateful for his care, but at other times, I chaffed that he was assuming what I considered overbearing, older brotherly control. Throughout our lives, Henry was a very supportive and loving brother. He had genuine concern and interest in my welfare. I think of his many generous acts, among which were these: including me in the summer of

1947, after my junior year in high school, to live with his Swarthmore classmates, all veterans, in a house they rented for that summer; giving me $2.50 a month in 1947–8 to attend cultural events even though he was scraping by financially on the GI Bill; paying for me in the summer of 1951 to come to Europe and travel with Hope and him. These are only a few examples that showed his care for me and exceeded what one expects an older brother to do for his sibling. The greatest benefit he gave me was to introduce and bring me into his political world when I graduated Harvard Law School in 1957. This enabled my career of public service. But it resulted in my pushing Henry aside as I assumed ever more significant positions in our political club and eventually entered the Legislature. Henry, after a while, gave up his political activities and any desires he may have had for public office. Henry never showed any resentment at his pushy younger brother. On the contrary, he was unfailingly supportive. I often thought with remorse and guilt that my political career came at the expense of his. In these early years, I was so intoxicated with a political life that it was not until later that I appreciated that my political career was eclipsing Henry. In mitigation, my becoming active in the Morningside and West Side community was also due to Nina. She lived in that community and was active in the Riverside Democrats. And as we fell in love, we both decided to make our home there.

Except for rare flare-ups (Henry had the Leichter temper), our relationship was strong, good, and enjoyable. Henry was good company to be with. He was more joyous and fun loving than I was. He took life easier, and his palette was of brighter colors. We had many good laughs and enjoyable times together. I miss him. I am so grateful for what he did for me. He was so important in my life.

# CHAPTER 18

# 2011–2020: CONTINUING
# TO ENJOY LIFE

As I entered my eighties, my life continued to be active and fulsome. It had its customary ups and downs but more of the former, though at times I only appreciated them afterward.

Fortunately, my health has remained good, allowing me to continue doing so many of the things that appeal to and are meaningful to me. Instead of following a chronological treatment, as most of the previous chapters did, I will seek to focus on aspects of my life as they occurred in these years.

## TRANSLATING MY PARENTS' WRITINGS AND FURTHERING THEIR REMEMBRANCE

One of the more satisfying activities I engaged in was bringing attention to my mother and father's work and reputation. My mother's life, though short, was full of accomplishments. She is recognized in Austria for her pioneering studies and publications as a sociologist, her political activism, and her martyrdom at the hands of the Nazis.

My first project was to complete the translation of her memoir and letters my father wrote to her in 1938–9, while in Paris. The translations had been started by Henry, but a number of chapters of my mother's memoir had not been translated. At the same time, I wanted a translation of my father's letters to my mother, which he wrote while exiled in Paris. He could not send these to her at that time, as she was imprisoned in Vienna and then in the Ravensbrück. He knew they would probably never reach her and would only direct the Gestapo to her and him. They constitute a diary of his days in Paris. They are full of love and show the difficulties he had as a refugee, assuming the parental care for Henry and me while everything he cared for and had worked for in Europe and much of the world was being destroyed.

These letters have quite an odyssey. When we fled Paris in May 1940, as the German armies approached, we left everything in our apartment, including the letters. When Henry, then a US soldier, went to the apartment in 1944, much of our furniture and books were still there and had not been disturbed by the people who took over our apartment. But the letters were not there. Surprisingly, they were found in Moscow in the late 1990s by Austrian historians who were writing a book about my father's disappointing experience when he returned to Austria in 1947. How did they get to Moscow? My theory is that the people who took over our apartment found the letters. As these were in German, they were fearful and turned them in to the police. The latter gave them to the Gestapo, which transferred them to Berlin. When the Russians came to Berlin, they swooped up all the Gestapo files and took them to Moscow. Typical of both the Nazi and Communist regimes, who gave such attention to surveilling their citizens and suspected opponents, they were not only kept but properly catalogued.

When the Austrian historians inquired of the Moscow archive whether there was any file on Otto Leichter, the letters showed up. Also included were a couple of newsletters I wrote as a child in Paris. These had such exclamations as "Phooey the Nazis" and "The workers will win." My father's letters have been published in Austria in a book titled *Briefe ohne Antwort (Letters Without an Answer)*.

I thought it important that my mother's and father's grandchildren and future descendants have these in a language they could read. Getting a translator was neither easy nor inexpensive. I went through two before connecting with a good translator in Vienna. It took about three years to get the translations finished, which I then sent to my parents' grandchildren. I hope that in their busy lives, they will find the time to get to know their grandparents through these works.

Both my mother's memoir and my father's letters (diary) are so interesting and illuminate their lives. My mother's memoir was written while she was imprisoned in Vienna, waiting to be tried on the charge of treason. Unfortunately, she finished only the chapters up to attending the University of Vienna. There are piercing analyses of her father, mother, and sister Vally. She recounts how growing up in a comfortable middle-class family, she became aware of the misery of the underprivileged, the beginning of her life work to overcome inequality and oppression. Her descriptions are so open and honest. Before she could finish, she was taken by the Gestapo after being acquitted of treason and convicted only of the seemingly minor charge of having smuggled letters out of the jail. She was sent to Ravensbrück, the concentration camp outside of Berlin, where with the other Jewish prisoners she was killed in or about February 1942. She did learn that her husband and children, whom she lovingly referred to as "meine drei Buben" (my three boys), were safely out of Europe in America.

I got the idea of doing a documentary of my mother when Kathy started on her family documentary, which initially was to be about the effect on a family of a loss of two mothers, Käthe and Nina. Kathy shot quite a lot of footage regarding my mother in Vienna and Ravensbrück. But then her documentary ended up being solely Nina's story, which she so effectively told in *Here One Day*. The editor of her film once said to me that there was this unused footage about my mother that could be the basis of a documentary. This gave me the idea that maybe a documentary about my mother could be made.

In 2013, when I was in Vienna with Kathy, Andrew, Memphis, Otto, and Theo, I decided to explore making a documentary about my mother. I met with the director of the Arbeiterkammer (Chamber for Workers), a semipublic agency that represents the interests of working people. It is a hybrid between our Department of Labor and unemployment offices. I pitched the idea of the documentary to its director and the administrator of the women's division, who knew all about my mother. My mother had been the founder of the women's division of the Chamber in about 1926. Some years before 2013, the Chamber had put up a memorial to my mother on the building where the Chamber was located when she worked there in the 1920s. I asked the Chamber to put up the seed money for the documentary. The meeting went well, and the director seemed inclined to help.

Then good fortune stepped in. Kathy knew a prominent Austrian documentary filmmaker, Helene Maimann. We had breakfast with her and pitched the documentary. She said she was involved in some other projects. When one of these collapsed, she agreed to do the documentary. She went to the Chamber and inquired about its commitment to the documentary. When they saw we had a well-known Austrian filmmaker as director, this gave the project credibility. The Chamber committed to 50,000 euros in seed money. I was ready to raise the additional $150,000 that would be needed. But it turned out that Helene worked closely with a successful producer, Kurt Stocker. He arranged for all the financing through the Austrian public television network, ORF, and some German TV outlets. I was not called on to raise any money.

Helene Maimann made it clear that this was her documentary. She didn't want any interference. Her focus was on my mother's work and significance and not on her tragic death. I brought her in touch with Jill Lewis, who is English and was then a professor at Swansea University in Wales. Jill had contacted me about two years earlier to let me know she was working on a biography of my mother. Jill knew a great deal about my mother's early professional career and wrote some papers and gave talks about her at historical conferences. I got together with Jill a few times in Vienna and in England, and we became friends. Unfortunately, she has not been well, and the biography will never be finished.

Helene's aim was to finish the documentary in time for it to be shown on International Women's Day in March 2016. In April 2014, I went to Vienna for her to shoot scenes with me. These barely ended up in the documentary. Helene met her self-imposed deadline. On March 6, 2016, the film was shown to a large audience at a festive event. A number of family and friends attended. Kathy, Josh, Fred, and Jennifer and Henry's widow, Hope, came. I was there with my friend Sylvia. I joined Helene Maimann, the director, after the showing for a Q&A. The entire week was joyous. I met with my young Austrian friends (more about them later), there was a formal lunch in City Hall hosted by the chairman of the city council, and even time for some museum visits—a must for me when I am in Vienna. And it ended on our departure eve with a Shabbat dinner given by the director of the Jewish Museum and her husband whom I had befriended. On December 8, the film was shown on Austrian television.

I then set about to show the film in New York. I had good relations with the Austrian Cultural Forum in New York. When I suggested it show the documentary, the director readily agreed to make it part of a week's events acknowledging the fiftieth anniversary of Austrian refugees in New York. Helene and Kurt took care of the English subtitles so the film was viewable by an English-speaking audience. The documentary was shown at the Austrian Cultural Forum on June 7, 2017. Almost the entire family—mine and Henry's—were there. Beforehand, I arranged for us all to have a private dinner in a Viennese restaurant. From there, I took everyone in a hired bus to the screening. It so happened that Heinz Fischer and his wife, Margit, were in town and attended. Fischer had just ended his very successful two terms as president of Austria (a mainly ceremonial post but not without some impact). The Fischers knew my father and had become good friends of Henry and Hope, as their son stayed with them in New York for six months. Heinz Fischer, Helene Maimann, and I did the Q&A after the film. This was followed by a reception. A great event, family reunion, and homage to my mother.

In 2017, I received an email from the Portrait Theater in Vienna. It informed me that it was planning to do a theatrical piece about my mother and a contemporary sociologist. As I found out the Portrait Theater was really Anita Zieher, its founder, playwright, and main performer. It does plays about prominent women, always doing a pair. It had a successful play about Marie Curie and another physicist, which was performed not only in Austria but also in the US. I was, of course, pleased to have a play about my mother, which I gathered would focus on her work as a sociologist. She would be paired with Marie Jahoda. Marie was another sociologist who had made a pioneering study of unemployment in Marienthal, a midsized Austrian industrial town. She was a leftist socialist like my mother. She survived the Holocaust, fortunately being expelled from Austria in 1937 after being imprisoned. She had a successful career after the war teaching in England and for a while at NYU. It turned out her daughter, then Lotte Lazarsfeld (her father, Paul, was a famous sociologist who taught at Columbia University), also attended Swarthmore while Henry and I were there. She was a year ahead of me. Unfortunately, we had no contact despite the connection of our mothers.

I provided some information to Anita Zieher and got her in touch with Lotte. The play was scheduled to be performed in Vienna on February 13. I decided to attend. I had a lovely week in Vienna. On the day I arrived, I was asked to tape my reminiscences about my mother and Rosa Jochmann at the archive of the Socialist Party (SPO). I saw my young Austrian friends, met with people at the Arbeiterkammer, and saw some other friends. The highlight of course was the play. Obviously, it was in German. I understood maybe 50 percent. It was given in the auditorium of the Arbeiterkammer and was well attended. I found the play somewhat static and not that dramatic. It was essentially about two women speaking of their very interesting and productive work and the challenges they faced as Austria became a fascist country and then succumbed to the Nazis. But it lacked action, except for the move of some props. The play received favorable reviews in a number of Viennese newspapers. The play has since been performed throughout Austria and in Berlin.

I thought it important to have it read by the family and arranged to have it translated into English. This also prompted both Anita and me to see if it could be produced in the US. Anita pursued the Austrian Foreign Ministry to financially support a US tour. The ministry would only give its support if there were enough venues found in the US for its performance. I sent the translation to Lotte and asked if she could get a performance space at MIT, where she had taught for many years. She got a venue. I pitched the play to my friends at the Austrian Cultural Forum in New York (ACFNY). Disappointingly, they were not that supportive initially. My friends explained that the leadership was having its four-year turnover, and they didn't want to make a commitment for the new administration. I began to doubt whether there would be a US tour. I became more dubious as Anita was pressing us to get the potential venues to provide some financing. Both Lotte and I told her that it was hard enough to get venues at sites like MIT and that these would not provide any financing. I visited Lotte in June 2018 in Cambridge to discuss how we could get the play performed in the US and to make the connection we failed to make while at Swarthmore sixty-eight years earlier.

Anita was more determined and hopeful than I was. She arranged for a performance in Washington, DC, at the Austrian Cultural Forum and in Los Angeles and Atlanta. Then, to my pleasant surprise, the ACFNY said it would sponsor a performance and provide some financial help. This may have been furthered by the previous head of the Austrian Cultural Forum, who coincidentally was in Vienna for the February 13 performance and told me she liked it. The play was first performed at MIT on April 1, 2019. Memphis, Dana, and Fred and Jennifer's son Alex attended. After a performance at Emory University in Atlanta, it was produced at the Austrian Cultural Forum in New York, where Kathy's family and numerous friends were able to see it. I did a Q&A with Lotte and the two actresses. Next was Washington, where I went and took Nina Solarz and her two children. I did a Q&A there too. Then it was performed in Los Angeles where Henry's three children and Hope attended with Josh. How wonderful that my family was able to see this play. I received numerous highly favorable comments about the play and how moved people were by the performance. At the Q&A in New York, Lotte said that when she read the play, it seemed lacking in dramatic content. Now that she saw it produced on stage, she found it effective. So, out of my uncertain effort to get this performed in the US, my doubt that we would find venues and financing, and then concern that the audience would find it boring to have two women talk about their lives, it turned out so well.

# REUNION WITH MY CHILDHOOD FRIEND HELMUT, WHOSE IDENTITY WAS USED TO SMUGGLE ME OUT OF AUSTRIA AND GETTING YAD VASHEM TO DESIGNATE IRMA TURNSEK, WHO TOOK ME OUT THROUGH NAZI GERMANY, AS A RIGHTEOUS AMONG THE NATIONS

In 2014, I received an email from Yad Vashem, the Holocaust Museum in Jerusalem. It asked me to confirm that Irma Turnsek had smuggled me safely out of Austria in 1938. An application had been made by her son, Helmut, to have her recognized by Yad Vashem as a Righteous Among the Nations—the designation and list the museum compiles of non-Jews who risked their lives by safeguarding and helping Jews escape extermination. I immediately affirmed that this was true. My father and I had lost contact with Irma, whom we knew was in London and had been reunited with her son, Helmut, my childhood playmate whose identity was used to smuggle me out of Austria. I asked the museum to give me Helmut's contact information. After a while, I did receive this and sent an email to Helmut. I got no answer for some weeks. I assumed he wanted nothing to do with me, having used his identity to get out of Nazi Austria, where he then had eight miserable years separated from his mother. I knew that Irma, his mother, was unable to return to Austria from England to pick him up, after she had taken me safely to Belgium, and that he spent the entire war years in Austria. But after some weeks, I received a very welcoming response from Helmut. He had been unable to reply earlier because he was hospitalized with lung cancer. He said it was wonderful to be back in contact and hoped we might see each other.

Knowing he had a serious medical condition, I decided to promptly visit him in London. In April 2015, we had a moving get-together at his home in London with his family present. Sylvia Smoller, my companion at that time, joined me. Lovingly, Kathy and Josh arranged for our reunion to be taped by a video crew. Helmut and I spent time recounting our lives in the fifty-seven years since we had last seen each other. His life during the war had been hard until 1946 or 1947 when Irma was finally able to go get him and bring him to England. Like me, he had become an attorney. For many years, he worked as an attorney for what is called the Royal Estates, the properties of the royals. He and his wife, Doreen, proudly showed me a certificate they had received from Queen Elizabeth on their sixtieth wedding anniversary.

Among other matters we discussed was why his mother did not bring him out of Austria until after the war's end. I surmised to him that the outbreak of the World War in September 1939 made this impossible. No, that was not the reason, he said. As I recounted in a previous chapter, the plan hatched by my mother was for his mother, after depositing me in Belgium and getting settled in England, where she had secured a position as a domestic, to return to Austria and bring Helmut back to England. The reason she did not return before the war to bring him to England, Helmut explained, was that Irma was informed that the Gestapo knew she had smuggled me out of Austria and that she would be arrested if she showed up in Austria. It was not possible for her to return to Austria.

It then occurred to me how the Gestapo knew that she had smuggled me out of Austria. I explained to him that, in all probability, my mother had confided this, as well as her planned departure from Vienna with Henry, to Hans Pav, a close family friend and former colleague of my father at the *Arbeiter-Zeitung* before the 1934 fascist coup banned the paper. Sadly, he had become an informer for the Gestapo and betrayed my mother to the Gestapo (among many others) as she planned to leave Austria. It was clear to me, I told Helmut, that my mother must have told Pav that Irma smuggled me out of Austria. Pav then informed the Gestapo. How Irma was informed of the danger she faced in Austria was not clear, except that it became known fairly quickly that Pav was a Gestapo operative. My mother, once imprisoned, quickly figured out that it was Pav who had betrayed her. She probably got the word out.

It was evident at our meeting that Helmut's health was very bad. One week after our meeting, he died. I think he held out until we could have our reunion.

In my discussion with Helmut and his family, they mentioned how important it was to have Irma be designated by Yad Vashem as a Righteous Among the Nations. I promised to do all I could to help this along. I got in touch with Irena Steinfeldt at Yad Vashem, who oversaw these designations. I was informed what was holding this up was that Yad Vashem questioned why Irma did not go back to Austria before the outbreak of the war to be reunited with Helmut. I did not understand why this mattered. Her bravery was in taking a Jewish boy through Nazi Germany with a false identity and passport. But for Yad Vashem, the suspicion that she was not interested in getting Helmut had stymied the designation. I was now able to answer this. Fortunately, we had the video where Helmut and I discussed why Irma was prevented from returning to Austria. And my friend Sylvia, who had videotaped part of our reunion, had also just managed to capture this discussion. I sent these video clips together with a description of Pav's betrayal. His betrayal of my mother is covered in Herbert Steiner's biography of my mother, which I also sent to Yad Vashem. I was able to supply confirmation in Henry's recounting in his book, *Eine Kinderheit*, of how he challenged Pav in jail when he visited Vienna as a GI in 1945. This helped to establish why the information that my mother likely gave to Pav made it impossible for Irma to return to Austria. Then, and it may have been decisive, I got a former colleague in the Legislature, who was now in Congress and had a reputation as a strong friend and supporter of Israel, to write a supporting letter, which I drafted, setting out the whole story. This explanation satisfied Yad Vashem, and I was shortly informed that Irma Turnsek would be honored by being listed as a Righteous Among the Nations. This meant so much to the Turnsek family and to me. My help had paid back in a small measure what she had done for me and the miserable years Helmut had growing up without his mother in Austria until 1947.

In November 2015, a ceremony was held at the Israeli embassy in London, formally recognizing Irma's designation by giving a medal to her family. It was a wonderful event attended not just by Irma's family but a number of diplomats, including the Austrian ambassador to England, whom I had gotten to know when he was stationed in Washington. I spoke at the ceremony of how I owed my life to Irma's bravery. Kathy, Josh, Kyra, Memphis, and Otto came to London for the ceremony, as did my friend Sylvia.

## PROMPTING HEIDELBERG UNIVERSITY TO RESTORE MY MOTHER'S DOCTORATE, WHICH THE NAZIS HAD CANCELLED

On a visit to Vienna in 2013, I was advised that my mother's doctorate from Heidelberg, which the Nazis had cancelled, had never been restored. The Nazis had cancelled the doctorates of all Jews. These were restored after the war. But it seemed my mother's was not. Why? Apparently because she was deemed a criminal, having been sent to a concentration camp. I even have a copy of a letter from the Gestapo delivered to my mother while she was Ravensbrück, instructing her that she was not to use the title "Doktor," as her doctorate had been cancelled. This shows the meanness and pettiness of the Nazis that they would go to these lengths to humiliate her, as if being in a concentration camp was not sufficient oppression. I have no idea how I came across this letter. Someone in Vienna must have found it and given it to me.

I wrote to the *rektor* (the chancellor) of Heidelberg University to point out this injustice. In return, I received from him and the chairman of the social science department a lengthy mea culpa letter. Both not only apologized but wrote how painful it was that the university had committed this outrage during the Nazi period. They also took responsibility for not informing all the Jews whose doctorates had been cancelled that this action had been done. Finally, they invited me to visit the university if I was in Europe.

In late October 2014, the opportunity came to visit Heidelberg. I had planned a trip to Vienna with Sylvia, and we were also going to Paris, where Sylvia had a conference. After a few days in Vienna, we flew to Munich and on to Heidelberg. The university treated us royally, putting us up in the best hotel and covering our expenses. Helene Maimann came with a video crew to film for the documentary on my mother. Jill Lewis came too. All the filming Helene Maimann did there ended up on the cutting room floor and is not in the documentary.

Heidelberg University arranged a special event where my mother's diploma was re-awarded. I was given a copy. The rektor and numerous university officials attended. I made a speech expressing both my pain and pride in being in Heidelberg and what it meant to have this recognition of my mother. Afterward, the rektor took us to dinner. The University arranged a gathering of some university professors who were specialists in the work of Max Weber, the famous sociologist with whom my mother had studied. The gathering was in Weber's former home. It was so special for me to sit in what had been Weber's living room, where he met with my mother and other students as they sought to convince him (unsuccessfully) to express his opposition to Germany's continued participation in World War I.

I had time to walk through Heidelberg. Fortunately, the university and town were not bombed and survived War II intact. How meaningful to be in Heidelberg, which had been an important part of my mother's life.

I should explain how my mother had come to study in Heidelberg. She had enrolled in economics and sociology studies in the University of Vienna. But the University at that time would not grant diplomas in these disciplines to women. She thus had to finish her studies in Heidelberg. She enrolled there in 1917. Soon she became active in antiwar protests and I suspect was a leader among student groups opposing the war. As a consequence, the army expelled her from Germany before she could take the final oral exam for her doctorate. Possibly because of connections her father had, or maybe Max Weber intervened on her behalf, she was allowed back into Germany but only for some three weeks to finish her work and take the oral exam for her doctorate, which was awarded to her.

## MY FRIEND SYLVIA SMOLLER

Toward the end of 2010, through Andrew Moran's parents and another couple, I was introduced to Sylvia Smoller. Sylvia's husband had died early in 2010, around the same time Melody died. It was her third marriage that ended with the death of her husband. She told me that all three of her marriages were loving and gratifying. Sylvia had a very successful career as an epidemiologist. She was a professor for many years at the Albert Einstein College of Medicine in the Bronx. She was responsible for getting major grants from the National Institute of Health for the University and Montefiore Hospital, to which Albert Einstein is connected, to participate in nationwide studies on women's and Hispanic health. She retired in 2013 and is now an emeritus professor.

Sylvia came to this country, like me, as a refugee. Her parents managed to get visas for the three of them from the Japanese consul in Lithuania. He gave thousands of visas to Jews fleeing the Nazis after they had overrun Poland against the wishes of the Japanese government. With the visas to Japan as a transit point, they crossed Russia to Vladivostok and took a boat to Japan. Eventually, they were able to get passage to the US. She grew up in New York, attending Hunter High School.

Sylvia is very accomplished and interested in many of the same things as I am. She is highly intelligent and leads an active life centered on her extensive family and friends. Our conversations were usually lively. They tended to be often on current events and usually serious. I think this was more reflective of my approach. Sylvia could be vivacious and very enthusiastic when she liked something. Some of our values differed, but these were minor, as there are with any couple.

Together we went to the theater, movies, lectures, and other events. In three winters, we spent a month in Sarasota, Florida. We took three ocean cruises and two river cruises. We traveled to London, Vienna, Paris, Sicily, Rome, and Tokyo. I often had dinner at her home. She had me meet her many friends and family. I similarly invited her to meet my friends and to participate in my family events. For instance, she invited me to join her for a family bat mitzvah in Phoenix. And I had her join me in Hawaii for Josh and Kyra's wedding. My friends and family all liked Sylvia. We were a couple.

For many years, until 2017, our relationship went fairly well. In many ways, we matched so well—background, intellectual interests, culture, and more. But it was not a perfect fit. Early on in our becoming a couple, I noticed the difference in our expectations and said to Sylvia, "You want a lover. I want a companion." Sylvia wanted the emotional and physical closeness that she had with her husbands. I came off marriages that were more difficult. I just had been through Melody's illness and was not ready for, or available to give, the emotional attachment Sylvia looked for, nor was I interested in the physical intimacy she wanted.

I did not make some of the accommodations that would have shown her more of a commitment to our relationship and avoided giving her the feeling that I was fitting her into my life only when it was convenient for me. I continued to spend the summers at the Farm, and while she did visit me there for a week or so, from her viewpoint, I was not available, not only as a lover but as a companion. She was bothered by my visits to Nina Solarz in Turkey. Actually, these tended to be for no more than a week or ten days. But it gave her not only a sense that I was not including her in my life but possibly led her to question what my attachment was to Nina. I might have invited Sylvia to join me in Turkey, and I am sure Nina would have been welcoming. But I thought it an imposition to ask Nina to have another guest. I may have also been influenced by believing Sylvia would not fit in and change my enjoyment with Nina and our discussions, which were based on our common political experiences. Nina and I are very good friends. She has been so supportive and generous. But there were never any romantic aspects. As I think of it now, it was selfish of me to be so wedded to my customary summer plans without including her. It was a sore point for her.

Sylvia never stated what she wanted for a satisfying relationship. We never had a meaningful discussion of what we each desired in the relationship and what accommodations we could make. I tried a few times to open a discussion, but it never resulted in her opening up and engaging in a discussion to see how we could accommodate our differences.

Sylvia had a friend, John, whom she had known for many years. He was English and lived in London. I didn't pay that much attention to it, but it was evident that John was a special friend. How it came about, whether in

November 2015 when we went together to London for the ceremony for Irma Turnsek, Sylvia and John became lovers. He wanted to marry her. She told me about this sometime in 2016. I was accepting and not particularly bothered, and this may reflect the depth of my emotional attachment. I accepted that John made sense for her, as she wanted a partner who gave her the emotional support and intimacy she was used to from her marriages. I told her that as long as her visits to London and his to New York were limited, we could otherwise continue with our relationship. And, indeed in the winter 2016–7, we took a cruise to the Caribbean and stayed in West Palm Beach for a few days. Toward the end of 2017, she told me that John would be coming to New York for more prolonged periods. I said this was for me the end of our being, as I understood it, a couple and continuing with the relationship we had for these years. It no longer worked for me. We are still good friends. I do cherish the time I had with her, and my appreciation of her is undiminished. She was an important part of my life. We are in occasional contact and go out to dinner and to some events.

My life in these years was mainly filled with family, travels, theater, music, and the cultural richness of New York, in addition to the time and work I did to make my mother and father better known not only to my family but also to a wider audience.

## AND THE TRAVELING CONTINUES

I had some more great trips during these years. I won't go into details on most. One I will describe in greater length as an example and also because it was so varied and interesting is a trip with Sylvia that started in Vienna in October 2014. There were multiple events I was invited to. I was asked to speak to the graduating class of the Socialist Party school for upcoming leaders. They had chosen my mother as the past socialist leader whom that class would honor. This is a tradition for each year's class. The speech went well. Afterward, they took Sylvia and me to dinner. The next day, or maybe two days later, there was a commemorative event in the Central Cemetery where I was asked to speak at the memorial of the founders and leaders of the Socialist Party: Victor Adler, his son Fritz Adler, and Otto Bauer. Afterward, the leaders of the class marched to the memorial to my father and mother and laid a wreath. Throughout our stay, we were taken care of and transported by one of the leaders of the group, Reinhard Leitner. He has become a friend, along with two others from the group, I am in contact with and see when in Vienna. In Vienna, Reinhard drives me around, and he does so also for members of my family on their visits. Reinhard came with a number of Viennese socialists to New York in 2016. I arranged a tour of a charter school and a discussion with some members of the New York City Council.

After Vienna, Sylvia and I went to Heidelberg for the ceremony restoring my mother's doctorate. I have written about this event above. From there, we went to Paris by a TGF,—high-speed train. Sylvia had a conference there. Meanwhile, I enjoyed this city that is so dear to me. One of the highlights was seeing the Louis Vuitton Museum designed by Frank Gehry. It is an architectural masterpiece. What a great trip.

And my eighties saw many exciting and enjoyable trips, which I will try to recall and list without too much detail, as I don't want to make this into a travelogue.

I continued my annual summer visit to the Solarz's beautiful and spacious villa in Turkey. It is perched on a hill overlooking a bay of the Mediterranean. They have a couple taking care of their house. The wife is a wonderful cook, and we have delicious Turkish meals. Often while I was there, and especially when Steve was alive, there were interesting guests:

American ambassadors to Turkey, the head of the International Red Cross, Ronald Reagan's arms control adviser, and more.

In April 2011, I was in London and Paris with Josh, Memphis, and Ethan. We had very full days in London and then went by the Chunnel train to Paris to show Memphis and Ethan my beloved Paris. Unfortunately, I ate and drank carelessly and failed to take my diuretic. I had an episode of fluid in the lungs and fell sick in the middle of the night. Josh managed to call for an ambulance. As the EMS personnel spoke no English, he managed to reach Kathy by phone to translate. I was rushed to a hospital, where I received excellent care. No waiting in an emergency room. A senior doctor promptly made a diagnosis that I did not have a heart attack and pumped me full of a diuretic to clear my lungs. I was there, as I remember, one night in a large, private room. After being drained of all the water that I had accumulated, I was discharged. There was no charge. Yes, universal health care, which France provides, apparently even to foreigners who ate and drank carelessly, is a right that makes sense. As Josh and family had to return to the States, I stayed two days in Paris with Willy and Helene Leichter, where Willy's job had taken him for a year. I took Willy and his daughter Caroline to see the apartment we had occupied in 1938–40 in Issy-les-Moulineaux. It was my first time back.

In September 2011, after visiting Nina in Kalkan, I flew to Bucharest. I went to a former synagogue turned into a museum for signs of my great-grandfather. At one time, he had been a very rich banker and traveled in winter by train in a private compartment to the Côte d'Azur in France, stopping in Vienna. The opening sentences of my mother's memoir describe how as a little girl she was lifted up by her Romanian grandfather staying in the fancy hotel Metropole. Ironically, this became the headquarters of the Gestapo, where my mother was taken when she was arrested. Strange world. There was a photo in the museum taken sometime before World War I of Jewish bankers. I assume one of these was my great-grandfather.

Family history tells how he lost his fortune in unwise investments in the US stock market, possibly in the crash of 1907.

In October 2011, I flew to South Africa. An interesting trip starting with a visit to Victoria Falls, a safari in Kruger National Park, and visits to Johannesburg and Cape Town. At Victoria Falls, I arrived at a very nice Victorian-style hotel in the late afternoon after having traveled all night from New York via Johannesburg. I was told that in half an hour, access to the falls would be closed, as evening was approaching. I decided to get a quick glimpse of the falls, as they were just a ten-minute walk away and one could hear them. On the path out of the hotel's enclosure, I was alone. I saw these large clumps of poop and assumed they must be from oxen ferrying carts of visitors. Then it dawned on me that this might come from elephants. Next I noticed some wild boars with evil-looking tusks munching on grass. A native came by selling local handiworks. He spoke decent English and told me that a bull elephant just a couple of weeks ago killed a guide near where I was. Realizing my lonely sojourn was not wise, I overpaid him in buying one of his wares and hurried back to the hotel.

My South African trip was arranged through a travel agency that provided me with good guides. I saw much. The next day, I visited these amazing falls and took a boat ride on the river, watching crocodiles and hippopotamus. The safari was particularly exciting. I stayed in a very comfortable—almost luxurious—camp. Every day, we would get up at 5:30 for the first day's tour and then go out again in the late afternoon. These are the times the animals are active. We traveled through the bush in a Land Rover that accommodated twelve people sitting in elevated seats. I saw what are called the main five animals—wild dogs (rarely seen, I was told), leopards, lions, elephants, and rhinos—and many more. The animals were used to these vehicles and paid them no attention. You could get quite close to them. This was one of the numerous trips I was fortunate to take, each of which qualified as a trip of a lifetime.

In June 2012, I went on a land tour to the Dalmatian Coast in Croatia. We started in Zagreb and then flew to Dubrovnik and motored up the coast to Venice. Beautiful scenery and historic sites as we went along the Adriatic.

In August 2012, after visiting Nina in Kalkan, I went to Ephesus and Pergamum, the latter a once great antiquity site that the Germans looted and whose works can now be seen in Berlin. I was particularly enchanted by the remnants of one of the world's first hospitals, founded by the famous Doctor Galen. Its motto was that no one dies here. The reason was it would not take in very sick people. This approach has guided American health care insurers.

Continuing my wanderlust, October–November 2012 saw me off to Southeast Asia. I flew to Singapore. A somewhat surreal city of Victorian structures and monuments, modern high rises with parks on top, beautiful gardens, a shopping mecca, which turned in the last thirty years from an impoverished backwater into a highly successful economic powerhouse, with strict social control but a good social safety net.

From there, I flew to Hanoi in Vietnam. Through my old lefty acquaintance, the one who arranged my Cuba trip, I had breakfast with a former ambassador to the US and the chair of the Parliamentary Committee on Foreign Affairs. They pleaded for the US to do more for the victims of the Agent Orange bombings by the US during the Vietnam War. They obviously were misinformed about my importance. It is a disgrace that the many people suffering from cancer and other ailments as a result of the unconstrained use of this defoliate chemical are not receiving compensation. I also saw the result of the use of Agent Orange driving through what had been a native forest that was leveled by bombing replaced with invasive weeds. Agent Orange was used to defoliate these forests so as to deny coverage to the Vietcong fighters. The US pretty much washed its hands of what could be considered a form of chemical warfare.

The Vietnam trip was arranged by a travel agency that provided excellent guides. They took us through the country, including a stunning boat tour of a seascape, the Mekong Delta, and Saigon, as it used to be called in colonial days, now renamed Ho Chi Minh City. Interestingly, one of my guides badmouthed the communist regime for its corruption. When I asked him if he was not risking imprisonment, he said that would happen only if he said this on social media. One highlight of the trip was that I watched the reelection of Obama on November 6. I was then in Da Nang, which had been the main base during the Vietnam War, with a major air base, port, and entry place for the more than five hundred thousand US troops that participated in that calamitous war. How unreal to be there to watch an American election in a very comfortable hotel room. What joy when I saw Obama win. My impression of Vietnam was of hardworking people, a very young population, for whom the war is the past and who bear no grudge against Americans.

Next came Cambodia, where I visited the great temples of Angkor Wat. Impressive and stunning. I did well walking up the steep steps of the temples as I waved off our guide, who was nervous about my falling off.

The final stop in Southeast Asia was Bangkok in Thailand. There I had no arranged tour or guides. I stayed at a five-star hotel. The morning after arriving, I noticed a lot of activity and Americans with sniffing dogs on a leash. None of the staff would respond to my question of what was going on. But I finally realized that Obama was coming and would be staying at the same hotel. I knew he was to attend a conference of Southeast Asian leaders. I was told by a talkative American that he would arrive soon. I placed myself on a balcony overlooking the entrance, ready to shout, "Four more years." I waited an hour before realizing he was probably being brought in by a back entrance. At least I can say that Obama and I slept under the same roof.

It was eye-opening to see the security that enveloped the hotel. To leave and enter, one had to go through screening. Another talkative American who was monitoring the screening told me that all the equipment, vehicles, and paraphernalia came a day earlier on another military jumbo jet. It's satisfying that our presidents receive such protection but dismaying how necessary this is in our present world.

I enjoyed Bangkok, visiting some of its stunning temples, a boat ride on the big Phraya River, which bisects the city, and walking to take in the sights and smells of an Asian city.

Fortunately, my return flight coincided with Kathy showing her documentary, *Here One Day*, at a prestigious film festival in Amsterdam. My flight back had a stop in Frankfurt, where I was able to catch a flight to Amsterdam. Kathy and Josh, with Kyra, were already in Amsterdam and had rented a house. Unfortunately, Memphis and Ethan, who had planned to come with Josh, didn't make it, as Ethan's passport didn't have the necessary six months before renewal. Memphis, the good sister, decided to stay back with him. It was so exciting to see Kathy's documentary at the festival.

As always, I loved being in Amsterdam, a city I have visited often, by myself, with my family, and at least twice with Melody. I enjoy walking along the canals and going to its great museums. Kathy's film was well received. We had good times together. On Thanksgiving, I took the family and Kathy's editor, Paula, and Luke, a Dutch native and friend who had once stayed with us in New York, to dinner. Instead of turkey, we had a good Dutch meal. The next day, for another screening of the documentary, the Vadepied family, with whom Kathy had stayed during her college year abroad, came from Paris. How lovely of them. I had to leave the luncheon early to catch my flight back to New York City. What a fabulous experience and such a great trip to Southeast Asia.

In March 2013, I joined a tour of Cuba. It was organized and led by what I call an old lefty (someone politically way left)—the same old lefty who had arranged my meeting in Vietnam—and included some hedge fund and Wall Street investors. We met with some government ministers. I was charmed by Havana and the Cuban people, other than the government types. The effect of the US embargo was visible in the worn look of buildings and the taxis that were 1950s American cars. What I saw of the countryside was beautiful. An American who married a prominent Cuban artist, summed up the Castro revolution and regime well, saying it gave the people "dignity." But, sadly now, and because of US policy and the regime's inflexible authoritarianism, it is mired in poverty.

In April–May 2013, Sylvia and I joined another couple, friends of Sylvia, for a tour of Sicily. I had been there previously with Melody. Afterward, we visited Rome for a few days.

In June 2013, I took Kathy's family and Memphis to Vienna and then to Nina's villa in Kalkan. Staying at Nina's lovely home and meeting some of her family was a treat for my family and a joy for me that I could give them this pleasure. When they returned to the States, I went to Israel. There I connected with what I call my Israeli family. They were not blood relatives, but a great-uncle had married my grandmother's sister. They escaped the Holocaust through Denmark and settled in Israel after the war. They took me to the kibbutz, right under the Golan Heights, where they first settled and endured bombings in the 1967 War. The family seems very well off and nice.

In October 2013, Sylvia and I joined a couple, longtime friends of Sylvia (they had been with them on a tour of Sicily), for a cruise down the Rhône River in France from Lyon to Marseille. We first visited Nice on the Côte d'Azur, where Nina and I had been in 1963. My visit to Marseille was the first since going there with Papa and Henry to get our visa to the US.

Being big on nostalgia, I sought out the US consulate from where we got our visas, but it had moved since 1940. From there, we traveled to Paris by TGV. What a swift, pleasant ride, unlike Amtrak.

In August–September 2014, I joined a tour of Iceland. Very interesting and enjoyable. The island is an ecological wonder, sitting where two tectonic plates meet and the earth's crust is thin—volcanoes, glaciers, many scenic waterfalls, hot water pools (one of which I went into while it was quite cold in the air), lovely green pastures. From there, I flew to Kalkan to visit Nina.

July 2015 was a very special trip to Hawaii for Josh and Kyra's wedding. Sylvia accompanied me. We spent a week there enjoying the families and friends gathered for such a happy event. Sylvia and I flew back via San Francisco, where we had a nice few days visiting with my first staffer and friend, Elizabeth Clark, and Sylvia's cousins.

In December 2015, Sylvia and I spent a long weekend in Tokyo. This came about because Sylvia was invited to attend the premiere of a film about the Japanese consul Chiune Sugihara, who had saved thousands of Jews after the Nazis' conquest of Poland by giving them visas to Japan. Sylvia's family secured these precious visas. She was about to decline the invitation when I told her to say she would come with a friend but had to travel business class. The Japanese agreed. We had a full three days being treated exceptionally well and put up in suites in one of the city's best luxury hotels, the Peninsula, which overlooks the royal palaces. What a difference for me to be in the Ginza, where the hotel was located, from my days in 1955, hanging out there as an American soldier and staying in a barrack on an American base. During the day, we had a guide and car at our disposal. It was my first time back in Japan since my army days in 1955. How much had changed—not only in the city but in my life.

In March 2016, I was in Vienna with family members for the showing of the Käthe Leichter documentary, which I mentioned above.

In May 2016, I returned to Portugal for the first time since leaving from Lisbon for the States in September 1940. I made it a point to visit the railroad station where we arrived on a late August night and said, "This is the most beautiful city," because unlike the cities I had left, there was no blackout. What took me there was a river cruise Sylvia and her friends with whom we had cruised down the Rhône planned on the Douro in northern Portugal, known as the River of Gold. Unfortunately, the river was flooded, and the boat couldn't leave the dock. We were limited to daily bus trips.

In June of that year, I met Memphis and Ethan in Vienna. They had been in Germany with their mother. Unfortunately, Ethan was sick part of the time, but he recovered the last two days and joined us in showing them my favorite places in Vienna, including a visit to the street and housing project named after my mother and to our home in Mauer.

The year 2017 started with a cruise with Sylvia in the West Indies. In June, I visited Nina's in Kalkan. There were a few trips in the US, including the joyous graduation of Memphis from The College of Wooster and a sad trip to San Francisco in November for a memorial service for my friend and first staff hire, Elizabeth Clark. She died too young. I miss her.

February 2018 took me to Vienna to see the Leichter/Jahoda play. Shortly after returning from Vienna, I went on a trip with Road Scholar to Costa Rica, a country I had wanted to visit for many years. I aborted the trip after a few days, as I had trouble sleeping, I had signed up for a trip that lasted too long, and also had left my Kindle on a plane and was upset not to have anything to read. I regretted that I sort of panicked and decided to leave. I did get to see the side on the Atlantic and found the wildlife and vegetation very interesting.

In May–June 2018, I took Ethan to Kalkan, as he was the only grandchild who had not been there. I wanted to spend a couple of days in Istanbul to show him this city I find so interesting, but safety concerns led me to take him straight through to Kalkan. To go there directly from New York requires almost an entire day. At Nina's invitation, I returned in September. In October, I celebrated Josh's fiftieth birthday party at the beautiful home he and Kyra have created, situated among many acres of lush greenery. I was there again at the end of the year with Kathy's family. I enjoy my visits there.

In March 2019, I went with my friend Barbara Sawiztki on a tour of the Galapagos. It was grand—beautiful, enjoyable, and special to walk among sea lions, turtles, iguanas, and numerous species of birds who have no fear of or interest in humans.

And the travels have continued. In June 2019, I spent three weeks in Kalkan and from there went to Vienna for a week. I returned to Nina's Turkey villa in September. I know my travels must soon come to an end, but hopefully there are still a few left in me.

Why have I described all these trips, which may, as there are so many, make for tedious reading? In part, it was the pleasure I took in remembering these voyages. But mainly to let you know what was important to me. Wanderlust was—and still is—a part of me. But what did it represent, and why was it so significant to me? It reflected my interest in the world, places, people, nature, and events. Even after my many years in New York and familiarity with a neighborhood, I will seek an out-of-the-way street I have not walked for a while to get to my destination, instead of a more direct and usual route, to see how it has changed and for a different experience.

# THE WALKING GROUP

Shortly after I left FHFB, I organized a group of friends to visit New York City neighborhoods. It started with my desire to see Williamsburg. I asked a friend if he would like to join me. Together we walked the streets of this changing neighborhood and through its Hassidic community. Out of this grew many more walks by a group of six friends. Since then, we have probably walked through forty or more neighborhoods in the city. We also went to Newark, Jersey City, Hoboken, and the Franklin D. Roosevelt Presidential Library in Hyde Park. Our walks were usually monthly but with time were less frequent.

We would walk, sometimes aimlessly through streets, observing the buildings, at times entering a real estate office to find out about the neighborhood's economic vitality, and ending up at a local restaurant for lunch. In winter, we would visit museums. With the passage of years, some of the group developed mobility issues. So after some years and many tours getting to see the diversity of our city, our group walked less and less. Eventually, after some years, we just met for lunch.

# CONTINUING TO FIND WAYS TO ENJOY AND FILL MY DAYS

Another pleasure that has filled my life is reading. While in the Legislature, and having in effect two occupations, I had little time for leisurely reading. Especially in the past decade, I have been able to enjoy many books. In the main, these were nonfiction—histories, biographies, current economic analysis—and an occasional novel. How enriching. My reading is mainly at bedtime, as during the day, readings are filled with the *New York Times*, *Washington Post* (since the advent of Trump), the *Economist*, and the *New Yorker*.

In about 2018, I was invited to join a writers' group. This consists of seven people whose writing differs. One, for instance, writes only poetry. Another may present a writing on a scientific topic, and another writes about personal experiences. Much of the writing is good and interesting. Usually three people will read a piece, which has been sent around beforehand so members have a chance to become acquainted with the work and prepare their comments. After each reading, we have a discussion with friendly criticism, comments, and suggestions. I started with reading chapters from this memoir. I received some valuable feedback. Lately, I have presented fiction stories based on my legislative and political experience. We meet twice a month in one of the participants' apartments. Afterward, we go for dinner in a local restaurant. Since the pandemic, we have continued through Zoom.

My days since leaving the FHFB in 2006 are filled, in addition to family gatherings, with meals with friends, theater, concerts, opera, and an occasional lecture. How fortunate to live in New York with its bountiful resources.

Time-consuming for me are the technology changes of the past twenty years. The computer, internet, cell phones, and even streaming on TV I find often challenging and take too much of my time. I am a technology klutz. But could I have written these reminiscences in this form and with the convenience of making additions, changes, and deletions without a computer? I could not have managed to get it published for family and friends without the help of my grandchildren, Memphis and Theo.

I find the world and people so interesting at the same time that I am mainly pessimistic about society and life generally. Travel was a way of broadening and embracing life. It also represented a restlessness, escapism, and never being fully satisfied—a continuous search for something different and new. My father, who understood me so well, asked me at one time, "Are you never satisfied?" The answer is no. Sylvia once asked at a family gathering for us to say if we were satisfied with what we had. Theo, my youngest grandson, answered, "Yes, but I want more." That expresses my sentiment.

I feel guilty at times about devoting so much of my life to the pleasure of travel and what New York offers culturally. Since I left FHFB in 2016, I have not done some meaningful social service. Shouldn't I have gotten involved in some pro bono work? For example, I could have found organizations that mentor young people. I never made a serious effort to find a way to be useful. Was it that I feared I would not be satisfied with a role that was not significant and had some visibility? Why is mentoring a young student not significant? I think this pressure I feel to be actively engaged in some societally significant endeavor comes from the model of my parents. Am I competing with them or trying to live up to their activism and standard? Of course, I did not expect to live that long after being diagnosed in 1997 with congestive heart failure and wanted to see as much of the world as what I thought my imminent mortality would permit.

Yes, my life for the past decade has been good, focused on my family and enjoyment of culture and travel. I have kept my interest in world events. I worry about my country in the time of Trump. I miss not being fully involved politically, as I was for so many years. I am often reminded of Steve Solarz's experience in O'Hare Airport, after leaving Congress, when someone stopped him and asked, "Didn't you use to be somebody?" Sometimes I feel as if I used to be someone. I, too, often have to remind myself of how fortunate I have been to overcome a sense of being nonproductive and not having achieved what I might have.

I am so happy with my children, their spouses, and grandchildren. I am proud of my daughter and son. I am fortunate to have this family and that we have strong and loving relationships. They are all leading good and purposeful lives, What joy they have given me. When I was diagnosed with congestive heart failure in 1997, and understanding my mortality, I just wanted to see my grandchildren grow up some. And I have. I was at the college graduations of Memphis and Ethan and have seen Otto and Theo doing well in high school. That is not to say I don't worry about them. I am a perpetual worrier. I never had such persistent concerns about my children as I have for my grandchildren. It was a different time, and with age, my anxiety has heightened. I have been an anxious person, not surprising considering my childhood trauma. Yet my anxiety and penchant for worrying have not hindered my activities or kept me from engaging in some risky adventures.

Yes, I have been fortunate. I survived the Holocaust due to my mother's care and my father's strength, perseverance, and foresight. I had the example of my parents' concern and fight for those less fortunate and their political interest and activism. I was blessed with supportive family members and valuable friends. I was scarred by the tragic, early loss of my mother. My two marriages ended tragically. But here I am now ninety years old and managing with the support of my family in the time of the pandemic.

I will leave any summing up to those who knew and cared for me.

# ADDENDUM

# FRANZ AND DONALD TRUMP

During my years in the Legislature, I had a number of contacts with Donald Trump. I thought for family lore it is worth describing them as a footnote to my memoir.

In 1971, with my colleague Oliver Koppell, I introduced a bill in the Legislature requiring the Port Authority to sell the World Trade Center. At the time, the bill had no chance of passage, though it garnered a little publicity. I should mention that the port authority did finally sell the World Trade Center shortly before the Twin Towers were destroyed on September 11, 2001.

The bill we introduced garnered some minor publicity. One day, my secretary in my law office told me there was a Donald Trump on the phone who wanted to speak to me. I didn't know who that was, but I knew the name Trump because of his father's project in Coney Island. I took the call, and after introducing himself, Trump started by saying how smart I must be to put in such a brilliant bill. He went on in this vein before saying that he had a buyer for the World Trade Center. He told me that he had talked to Prudential Insurance and it was interested. After a while, it became clear to me that he was just looking for a broker's commission. He did not understand that my bill had no chance of passage, and if it had, it would have still required action by the New Jersey Legislature and the governors of New York and New Jersey. I thanked him for his interest and told him of the hurdles to getting the Twin Towers on the market.

In the 1980s, my district ran along the Hudson River from northern Manhattan to West Twenty-Third Street. Between West Seventieth and Sixtieth Streets, there were old, unused rail tracks that had been used when freight from and to New Jersey was carried by ferries. Trump had bought this property either from the railroads or an intermediate buyer. Give him credit for seeing the potential of this property. He then announced plans for a gigantic development. My constituents were in an uproar over his proposal, as it would be out of scale, block views of the waterfront, and cast large shadows on Lincoln Center and up to Central Park.

I don't know how it was arranged, but I had at least two meetings with him in his office in Trump Tower. In one, he told me that he wanted to build the world's tallest building, or perhaps it was the tallest residential building. I told him we would never agree to that. He said, "Franz, if I can't build that, I might as well retire to Palm Beach and play polo." I told him my constituents would be pleased if he did. I continued to oppose his development.

In the late 1980s (I don't remember the exact year), I received a check for $1,000 from Donald Trump for a fundraiser I was having. I returned the check after calling Trump. I said, "Thanks for the contribution, but I don't think it would be helpful to you or me." He answered, "Thanks, I need it." I certainly did the right thing. Now I regret that I did not make a photocopy of the check.

In 1985, I announced I would run in a primary against Jay Goldin, who was then the incumbent city comptroller. This is a citywide position and would require raising much more money than I had ever raised before.

Goldin already had a war chest of over one million. At a time when I was struggling financially in my campaign, I was approached by a former state senator and CBS correspondent with whom I had been friendly for some years. He said he had a $3,000 check for my campaign from some person in Chicago. He wanted me to know this came through Donald Trump. There was then, and probably still is now, a practice of giving larger amounts to the candidate you expected to win. This was known as A money. But to cover your bet, you gave a smaller amount to the dark horse candidate. So I received the B money, as I am sure he gave much more to Goldin. At that time, I was weighing whether to continue my campaign. This helped me to reach a decision not to go on. There wasn't anything overtly illegal in my accepting this contribution, but campaign finance laws required you disclose who contributed to your campaign. Was this Trump's money that he was concealing? This would be illegal. If it was a contribution he solicited, that would be legal. I felt sufficiently uncomfortable not to accept the contribution, and it helped me to decide to quit the race.

In 1990, an agreement was reached with Trump by the mayoral administration of David Dinkins. The negotiation was initiated by a very active and good West Side urban conservationist group that I worked with over the years, which sought to scale down the size of the buildings Trump planned to build. The agreement also provided that he would build a park connecting Riverside Park, which then ended at West Seventy-Second Street, and the hoped-for Hudson River Park, which was not authorized until 1998 under my bill. He was also supposed to make improvements to the Seventy-Second Street subway at Broadway. A press conference was held to announce the agreement, for which Fred Ohrenstein and I flew down and back from Albany in the state plane. I didn't feel that comfortable with the agreement, as the buildings were out of scale with the neighboring buildings on Riverside Drive.

I continued to criticize some of the buildings as they went up and also that Trump never contributed to the improvement of the Seventy-Second Street subway station, which was finally done by the MTA after some prodding from me and others. But the buildings went up, and all had Trump's name on them, though most removed it just recently because of demands by the tenants. Overall, the area is now called Riverside South. Trump doesn't own the buildings, as he sold the development rights to a Hong Kong group, similar to most of the properties that bear his name. He just gets a fee for use of his name and may have a very minor equity interest. So Riverside South buildings went up. They are not very attractive, but they haven't really hurt the skyline. This is New York City, where buildings get taller and taller, and to maintain scale and neighborhood size is mostly a lost battle. The park, called Riverside South, was built and is attractive and connects Riverside Park with the Hudson River Park.

In 1995, a city council colleague and I held a press conference accusing Trump of making misleading claims to get $335 million of federal mortgage insurance for his Riverside South project. Never one to let a criticism go unanswered, Trump shot back. In an item on page 6, the *New York Post*'s widely read gossip page, which Trump was in constant contact with, this item appeared: "Don't invite State Senator Franz Leichter and Donald Trump to the same groundbreaking." After mentioning my press conference, the item continued: "Trump faxed Leichter a hand scrawled note that read, 'Franz—I can't believe you would do this to get some cheap PR. Thanks for your loyalty.' Then yesterday we received a copy of a letter to Trump in which Leichter shot back, 'I would never try to compete with you for cheap publicity. And I acknowledge that you are New York's crown prince of publicity. My loyalties are with my constituents and not with a mega developer who is trying to connive the federal government.' A steamed Donald fumed, 'Leichter is a loser who badly represents the people and the district.'"

In 1997, I saw that $150,000 was given to the Senate Republican campaign by Marla Trump, then Donald's wife. Trump himself had made large contributions to the Republican Senate Committee but had maxed out. It was clear to me that this was not Marla's money but Donald's. I asked the State Election Commission to investigate and issue a press release, which some of the newspapers picked up. Trump accused me of sexism. No investigation was ever conducted.

In 2000, I was at a party also attended by Trump. At that time, there were stories that he was considering running for president, either as a Democrat or an independent. I approached him and said, "Donald, I hope you run for president." He looked pleased. I then added, "It will be good for laughs." He turned his back on me. Sadly, the laugh is on me, and the pain has been on the nation.

Printed in the United States
by Baker & Taylor Publisher Services